10

72679

INTERNET POLICIES AND ISSUES, VOLUME II

INTERNET POLICIES AND ISSUES, VOLUME II

B. G. KUTAIS (ED.)

Nova Science Publishers, Inc.
Huntington, NY

Senior Editors: Susan Boriotti and Donna Dennis
Office Manager: Annette Hellinger
Graphics: Wanda Serrano
Information Editor: Tatiana Shohov
Book Production: Cathy DeGregory, Kay Seymour and Jennifer Vogt
Circulation: Ave Maria Gonzalez, Ron Hedges and Andre Tillman

Library of Congress Cataloging-in-Publication Data
Available Upon Requiest

Copyright © 2001 by Nova Science Publishers, Inc.
        227 Main Street, Suite 100
        Huntington, New York 11743
        Tele. 631-424-6682   Fax 631-424-4666
        E Mail Novascil@aol.com

Printed in the United States of America

CONTENTS

Internet Policies and Issues
Volume 2

INTERNET: AN OVERVIEW OF SIX KEY POLICY ISSUES AFFECTING ITS USE AND GROWTH

*Marcia S. Smith, Jane Bortnick Griffith, Richard M. Nunno,
John D. Moteff and Lennard G. Kruger*

The continued growth of the Internet for personal, government, and business purposes may be affected by a number of issues debated by the 105th Congress but many of which remain unresolved. Among them are ensuring the privacy of information transmitted over the Internet or stored in computer databases, establishing "trustworthiness" by authenticating and verifying the origin and content of messages, protecting children from unsuitable material, safeguarding system security, protecting intellectual property, limiting unsolicited electronic mail, and issuing Internet domain names. This report provides short overviews of each of these issues from a technology policy perspective, referencing other CRS reports for more detail. Related legislation is identified for each issue, and a list of the bills by topic is provided at the end.

Summary of Legislation Passed by the 105th Congress

As this report demonstrates, the 105th Congress considered a wide variety of bills related to the Internet issues, but only a few finally passed both chambers and were sent to the President. Of the issues covered in this report, legislation was enacted concerning protecting children, identity theft, intellectual property, digital signatures, and Internet domain names. Further information on the legislation is included in later sections of this report. (Legislation concerning Internet taxes also passed. That topic per se is not included in this report. See: *Internet Tax Bills in the 105th Congress*, CRS Report 98-509 E, Aug. 21, 1998, 21 p., by Nonna Noto. However, the Act also included language relating to protecting children, so is discussed in that context).

Protecting Children: Child Online Protection Act, Children's Online Privacy Protection Act, and Child Protection and Sexual Predator Protection Act

In the FY1999 Omnibus Consolidated and Emergency Supplemental Appropriations Act (P.L. 105-277), Congress included several provisions related to protecting children on the Internet. Included is legislation making it a crime to send material that is "harmful to minors" to children and protecting the privacy of information provided by children under 13 over interactive computer services. Separately, Congress passed a law (P.L. 105-314) that, *inter alia*, strengthens penalties against sexual predators using the Internet.

The "harmful to minors" language is in the **Child Online Protection Act**, Title XIV of Division C of the Omnibus Appropriations Act. Similar language was also included in the Internet Tax Freedom Act (Title XI of Division C of the Omnibus Appropriations Act). The language originated in S. 1482 (Coats) and H.R. 3783 (Oxley). Called "CDA II" by some in reference to the Communications Decency Act that passed Congress in 1996 but was overturned by the Supreme Court, the bill restricts access to commercial material that is "harmful to minors" distributed on the World Wide Web to those 17 and older. The American Civil Liberties Union (ACLU) and others have filed suit against enforcement of the Act. The sponsors of the new law hope they have written it in a way that will pass judicial review.

The **Children's Online Privacy Protection Act**, also part of the Omnibus Appropriations Act (Title XIII of Division C), requires verifiable parental consent for the collection, use, or dissemination of personally identifiable information from children under 13. The language originated in S. 2326 (Bryan).

The Omnibus Appropriation Act also includes a Faircloth provision intended to make it easier for the FBI to gain access to Internet service provider records of suspected sexual predators (Section 102 of General Provisions—Justice Department). It also sets aside $2.4 million in the Customs Service appropriations account to double the staffing and resources for the child pornography cyber-smuggling initiative and provides $1 million in the Violent Crime Reduction Trust Fund for technology support for that initiative.

The **Protection of Children from Sexual Predators Act** (P.L. 105-314) is a broad bill addressing concerns about sexual predators. The language originated in H.R. 3494 (McCollum) and S. 2491 (Hatch). Among its provisions are increased penalties for anyone who uses a computer to persuade, entice, coerce, or facilitate the transport of a child to engage in prohibited sexual activity, a requirement that Internet service providers report to law enforcement if they become aware of child pornography activities, a requirement that federal prisoners using the Internet be supervised, and a requirement for a study by the National Academy of Sciences on how to reduce the availability to children of pornography on the Internet.

Identity Theft and Assumption Deterrence Act

Congress also passed the Identity Theft and Assumption Deterrence Act (P.L. 105-318). The language originated in H.R. 4151 (Shadegg) and S. 512 (Kyl) and sets penalties for persons who knowingly, and with the intent to commit unlawful activities, possess, transfer, or use one or more means of identification not legally issued for use to that person.

Intellectual Property: Digital Millenium Copyright Act

Congress passed legislation (P.L. 105-304) implementing the World Intellectual Property Organization (WIPO) treaties regarding protection of copyright on the Internet. The language originated in H.R. 2281(Coble) and S. 2037 (Hatch). The law also limits copyright infringement liability for online service providers that serve only as conduits of information. Provisions relating to database protection that were included by the House were not included in the enacted version.

Digital Signatures: Government Paperwork Elimination Act

Congress passed the Government Paperwork Elimination Act (Title XVII of Division C of the Omnibus Appropriations Act, P.L. 105-277) that directs the Office of Management and Budget to develop procedures for the use and acceptance of "electronic" signatures (of which digital signatures are one type) by executive branch agencies. The language originated in S. 2107 (Abraham).

Internet Domain Names: Next Generation Internet Research Act

The Next Generation Internet Research Act (P.L. 105-305) directs the National Academy of Sciences to conduct a study of the short and long-term effects on trademark rights of adding new generation top-level domains and related dispute resolution procedures. The language originated in H.R. 3332 and S. 1609.

Table 1. Related Legislation Passed by the 105th Congress

Title	Public Law and Bill Numbers
FY1999 Omnibus Consolidated and Emergency Supplemental Appropriations Act	P.L. 105-277 H.R. 4328
Division C, Title XI: Internet Tax Freedom Act	H.R. 1054/S. 442
Division C, Title XIII: Children's Online Privacy Protection Act	S. 2326
Division C, Title XIV: Child Online Protection Act	H.R. 3783/S. 1482
Division C, Title XVII: Government Paperwork Elimination Act	S. 2107
Protection of Children from Sexual Predators Act	P.L. 105-314 H.R. 3494/S. 2491
Identity Theft and Assumption Deterrence Act	P.L. 105-318 H.R. 4151/S. 512
Digital Millenium Copyright Act	P.L. 105-304 H.R. 2281/S. 2037
Next Generation Internet Research Act	P.L. 105-305 H.R. 3332/S. 1609

Cryptography: Encryption and Digital Signatures

Cryptography can be used to ensure the confidentiality of data and messages (encryption), as well as to authenticate the sender of a computer message and to verify that nothing in the message has been changed (digital signatures).

Encryption

Encryption and decryption are methods of applying the science of cryptography to ensure the privacy of data and communications. CRS Issue Brief 96039, *Encryption Technology: Congressional Issues*, discusses the topic in more detail.

Cryptography traditionally has been the province of those seeking to protect military secrets, and until the 1970s relied on "secret key" cryptography where the sender and the recipient both had to have the same key. Thus a trusted courier or some other method was required to get the key from the sender to the recipient. The advent of "public key cryptography" in 1976 made it possible for encryption to be used on a much broader scale. In this form of cryptography, each user has a pair of keys: a public key available to anyone with which a message can be encrypted, and a private key known only to that user with which messages are decrypted. The "key pair" is electronically generated by whatever encryption product is used. In a hypothetical example, if Bob wants to sent a private e-mail message to Carol and ensure that no one else can read it, he obtains Carol's public key from Carol herself or from a publicly available list. Using Carol's public key, Bob encrypts his message. When Carol receives the message, she uses her private key to decrypt it. To reply to Bob, Carol gets Bob's public key from Bob or from a publicly available list and uses it to encrypt her response. When Bob receives the message, he uses his private key to decrypt it.

Use of strong (difficult to break) encryption is considered vital to the growth in use of the Internet, particularly for electronic commerce, because businesses and consumers want to protect the privacy of information exchanged via computer networks. When a message is encrypted, it is referred to as "ciphertext." That message is called "plaintext" before it is encrypted and after it has been decrypted. The Clinton Administration wants to ensure that authorized law enforcement officials and government entities can access the plaintext of a message if undesirable activity is suspected (terrorism, drug trafficking, and child pornography are often cited as examples). If the message is encrypted, they either have to break the encryption by "brute force" (trying all possible combinations until they get the right one), or get access to the decryption key.

The Clinton Administration has supported the wide use of strong encryption as long as it has a feature called "key recovery" to allow authorized law enforcement agents to access the plaintext in a timely manner by getting access to the decryption key. This has raised privacy issues. Also, although there are no limits on what type of encryption is sold in or imported into the United States, the Administration has sought to influence what type of products are available domestically by limiting exports, knowing that companies do not want to make one product for domestic use and another for export. This has raised industry concerns about placing U.S.

computer hardware and software companies at a competitive disadvantage because they are subject to restraints on what they can export. The congressional debate today over encryption policy is focused on striking a "balance" among individual rights of privacy; the global competitiveness of U.S. companies making, using, or selling encryption products; promotion of secure electronic commerce; and law enforcement and national security needs to monitor undesirable behavior.

In December 1996, the Clinton Administration released temporary (two-year) export regulations designed to encourage computer hardware and software manufacturers to develop and implement key recovery technologies. Although there are other factors that affect the strength of an encryption product, the number of binary digits (bits) in the key has been used as the benchmark in this debate. The larger the number of bits, the more difficult it is to break the encryption. Under the interim regulations, companies were allowed to export 56 bit encryption products if they agreed to incorporate key recovery features into the product within the two years. If they already incorporated key recovery into the product, there was no limit on the bit length that could be exported (with some exceptions for banking.) Previously, only 40 bit encryption could be legally exported.

In September 1998, the Clinton Administration announced plans to allow the export of 56-bit encryption products without requiring provisions for key recovery, after a one-time review, to all users outside the seven "terrorist countries." The new policy will apply only to U.S. companies in the finance (which had already been granted in July), health care, insurance, and electronic commerce industries. Export of encryption products of any strength will be permitted to 42 designated countries if key recovery or access to plaintext is provided to a third party. The Administration will also support the FBI's proposal to establish a technical support center to help law enforcement in keeping abreast of encryption technologies. While industry groups approve of the new policy, they argue that 56-bit encryption has been broken and that stronger encryption is now necessary, and that the implementation of the new policy by federal agencies could possibly render it ineffective in increasing their ability to export encryption products. Privacy rights groups argue that the new policy will not increase the availability or use of 56-bit or stronger encryption by individual users of Internet communications.

There were seven bills in the 105th Congress addressing these encryption issues. Six of the seven bills (all except H.R.1964) addressed the export issue. In summary, H.R.695 (Goodlatte, as introduced), S.376 (Leahy), and S.377 (Burns), sought to relax export controls on encryption, although versions of H.R.695 as reported from various committees had substantially different provisions. S.909 (McCain) would have permitted easy export of 56 bit encryption without key recovery, and easy export of any strength encryption if it is based on a qualified system of key recovery. (S.909 further provided that the 56 bit limit could increase as recommended by an Encryption Export Advisory Board established by the Act unless the President determines it would harm national security. The bill also allowed the President to waive any provision of the bill, including the export limits, in the interest of national security, or domestic safety and security.) Modifications to S.909 announced by Senators McCain and Kerrey on March 4, 1998 included allowing U.S. companies to export products with optional recovery features to approved end users. S.2067 (Ashcroft) allowed the removal of controls for encryption products deemed to be generally available in the international market, and allowed the Department of Justice to create a National Electronic Technologies Center to assist law enforcement in gaining efficient access to plaintext of communications and electronic information. The primary section of H.R.1903 (Sensenbrenner) that dealt with export issues (section 7) was deleted before it passed the House, but the bill still called for export policy to be determined in light of the "public availability of comparable technology."

In the key recovery concept, a "key recovery agent" (or "key holder" in S. 376) would hold a copy of the decryption key. (Or the key could be split among two or more key recovery agents for added security.) Having access to such a "spare key" through a key recovery agent could be desirable for a user if a key is lost, stolen, or corrupted. Most parties to the encryption debate agree that market forces will drive the development of key recovery-based encryption products for stored computer data because businesses and individuals will want to be sure they can get copies of keys in an emergency. The questions involve the role of the government in "encouraging" the development of key recovery-based encryption, whether key recovery agents should be required to provide keys to duly authorized law enforcement officials, and the government's role in determining who can serve as key recovery agents. The Administration's 1996 interim regulations established criteria for key recovery agents that the Department of Commerce uses to support its decisions on whether or not to approve the export of key recovery encryption products. The Administration sought legislation to provide liability protection for such agents, as well as penalties if they make an unauthorized release of such information. S.376 and S.909 both addressed those issues. Under the Administration's new 1998 policy, key recovery business plans will not be required, and the regulatory requirements for key recovery agents will be reduced.

Another element needed for the widespread use of encryption is certificate authorities who would issue and manage electronic certificates (electronic records that identify a user within a secure information system) and verify that a particular individual is associated with a particular public key. This is especially important for the conduct of electronic commerce, for example, where buyers and sellers want to be assured of each other's identities. The combination of public key encryption and certificate authorities (some would add key recovery agents) is referred to as a "public key infrastructure" (PKI). There is debate over whether there should be a single, global PKI, or many different PKIs, but the establishment of one or more PKIs is expected to add the requisite element of "trust" to the Internet needed for its use to expand. H.R.1903 (Sensenbrenner) called for a National Research Council study of PKIs.

Originally, S.909 established mechanisms for the government to register key recovery agents and certificate authorities. While registration would have been voluntary, they would not have been fully covered by the bill's liability protections if they did not register. If a certificate authority registered with the government, it could only issue certificates to persons who had stored key recovery information with a government-registered key recovery agent or made other arrangements to assure lawful recovery of plaintext in a timely fashion. The linkage between certificate authorities and key recovery was controversial because some observers felt that the ability to issue certificates should be independent from the debate over key recovery. In March 1998, Senators McCain and Kerrey announced modifications to S. 909

including deletion of that linkage. H.R.1964 (Markey) and H.R.695 as reported from the House Commerce Committee prohibited conditioning the issuance of certificates on escrowing or sharing of encryption keys.

The Clinton Administration has not changed its policy that allows any type of encryption to be sold in or imported into the United States. However, on September 3, 1997 FBI Director Louis Freeh discussed domestic use restrictions at a hearing before the Senate Judiciary Committee's Subcommittee on Technology, Terrorism and Government Information. He expressed the point of view that only encryption products with key recovery be sold or imported for sale in the United States. Apparently the FBI also had drafted legislation along those lines (reportedly for a House committee) and the issue of domestic use restraints has become an integral part of the encryption debate. Publicly, the Administration maintains that it is not proposing domestic use restraints, but it did not prevent the FBI Director from promoting that course of action. Civil liberties groups in particular are opposed to domestic use controls. S.376 (Leahy), S.909 (McCain), and S.2067 (Ashcroft) all prohibited mandatory key recovery and provided that persons in any state (and U.S. persons in foreign countries per S.376 and S.2067) may use any type of encryption they choose except as otherwise provided by the Act. S.377 (Burns), H.R.695 (Goodlatte, as introduced), and H.R.1964 (Markey) said that federal and state governments may not restrict or regulate the sale of encryption products solely because they have encryption. The House Intelligence Committee's version of H.R. 695 included provisions supportive of the FBI's position. A similar amendment was defeated by the House Commerce Committee during its markup of the bill.

On March 4, 1998, Vice President Gore wrote to Senator Daschle restating the Administration's desire for a "balanced approach" to encryption policy and seeking a "good faith dialogue" to "produce cooperative solutions, rather than seeking to legislate domestic controls." The letter added that the discussions could also enable additional steps to relax export controls on encryption products. On April 15, Secretary of Commerce Daley made a speech wherein he said that although the Administration's policy was the right one, its implementation was a failure. He urged both industry and government to strive harder to reach consensus on the issue. At an April 24, 1998 meeting of the Congressional Internet Caucus, Undersecretary of Commerce William Reinsch commented that the Administration was not seeking a legislative solution to encryption issues in the 105th Congress.

The changes made to the Administration's encryption policy in September 1998 could have been related to an announcement made in July 1998 by a group of software companies of their plans to develop a product to capture data that could be given to law enforcement before it is encrypted and sent over the Internet. Privacy advocates argued, however, that although that proposal might generate more business for companies offering encryption products, it did not satisfy the demands of advocates of electronic privacy.

On October 7, five Representatives and four Senators signed a letter to the Vice President supporting the Administration's new policy, but stating that it was only the first step. The letter also indicated that they plan to introduce bills similar to H.R. 695 and S.2067 in the 106th Congress to foster the widespread use of the strongest encryption.

Digital Signatures

Another use of cryptography on the Internet is for authentication and verification. Digital signatures, which are unique to each individual and to each message, can be used in conjunction with certificate authorities to verify that the individuals on each end of a communication are who they claim to be and to authenticate that nothing in the message has been changed. Through the use of digital signatures, legally valid signatures can be produced for use in electronic commerce. Digital signatures typically encrypt only the identification information and not the content of a message. (Digital signatures are one type of electronic signature. In general, electronic signatures can refer to any electronically created identifier meant to authenticate a writing, but do not necessarily involve encryption.)

While neither law enforcement nor national security organizations oppose the use of digital signatures, many question whether a standard for digital signatures should be established to enhance electronic commerce. Of a total of 40 states that have enacted or are considering electronic signature laws, 10 have enacted digital signature or combination electronic/digital signature laws (Florida, Indiana, Minnesota, Mississippi, New Hampshire, New Mexico, Oregon, Utah, Virginia, and Washington). Another eight are considering them. These laws are summarized in *Survey of State Electronic & Digital Signature Legislative Initiatives* by Albert Gidari and John Morgan of Perkins Cole. The article is available on the Internet Law & Policy Forum's (ILPF's) Web site:[http:// www.ilpf.org/digdig/digrep.htm]. Links to the texts of the state laws are provided on another ILPF Web site, www.ilpf.org/digsig/digsig2.htm.

According to Gidari and Morgan, three models have developed at the state level: the "Utah" or "prescriptive" model with a specific public key infrastructure scheme including state-licensed certificate authorities; the "California" or "criteria-based" model that requires digital or electronic signatures to satisfy certain criteria of reliability and security; and the "Massachusetts" or "signature enabling" model that adopts no specific technological approach or criteria, but recognizes electronic signatures and documents in a manner parallel to traditional signatures. Some of the proposed state laws are general, applying to a wide range of government or private sector activities, while others are more narrowly cast. One controversial aspect of the debate over digital signatures is whether there should be a single federal law in place of the various state laws.

One bill regarding electronic signatures, the Government Paperwork Elimination Act (S. 2107), was enacted as part of the Omnibus Appropriations Act (P.L. 105-277). This measure directs the Office of Management and Budget (OMB) to establish procedures for executive branch agencies to accept electronic submissions using electronic signatures, and requires agencies to accept those electronic submissions except where found to be impractical or inappropriate. Specifically, within five years of enactment, executive branch agencies must provide for the option of electronic maintenance, submission, or disclosure of information as a substitute for paper. Within 18 months of enactment, OMB must develop procedures to permit private employers to electronically store and file with executive agencies forms pertaining to their employees. In addition, OMB, together with the National Telecommunications and Information Administration, is to conduct an ongoing study of the use of electronic signatures, including an analysis of its impact on paperwork reduction, electronic commerce, individual privacy, and the security and authenticity of electronic transactions, and report to Congress periodically on these issues. Electronic records generated from this law will have full legal effect, and information collected from an executive agency using electronic signature services may only be used or disclosed by those using the information for business or government practices. None of these provisions, however, will apply to the Department of Treasury or the Internal Revenue Service, if the provisions conflict with internal revenue laws or the Internal Revenue Service Restructuring and Reform Act of 1998 or the Internal Revenue Code of 1986.

Two other bills were introduced in the House and one in the Senate regarding digital signatures — H.R.2937 (Baker), H.R.2991 (Eshoo), and S.1594 (Bennett). Also, the House passed H.R.1903, the Computer Security Enhancement Act, on September 16, 1997, and the Senate Commerce Committee reported on the bill on October 13, 1998. H.R.1903 included a provision establishing a panel to develop policy, guidelines, and technical standards for digital signatures. The House Banking Committee held a hearing on the federal role in electronic authentication on July 9, 1997. The House Science Committee held a hearing on digital signatures on October 28, 1997. The Senate Banking Committee held a general hearing on the topic on October 28, 1997 and specifically on S.1594 on March 11, 1998. The Senate Commerce Committee held a hearing on S. 2107 on July 15, 1998.

Computer Security

Although unauthorized access to computer networks ("hacking") is by no means a new problem, growing use of the Internet increases the threat. Hacking or "cracking"(hacking with the intent to do harm) is a growing problem both for the government and the private sector. The extent of the problem is difficult to quantify because many institutions do not want the negative publicity associated with public acknowledgment of hacking attempts (whether successful or not). Also, many attempts to hack into a computer system may go undetected.

A 1996 report by the Senate Governmental Affairs Permanent Select Subcommittee on Investigations, together with a related series of hearings and a General Accounting Office report (GAO/AIMD-96-84) have provided some estimates. The GAO study referenced an assessment by the Defense Information Systems Agency that Department of Defense computers may have been attacked 250,000 times during 1995. The assessment added that the number may represent just a small fraction of the attempts because only an estimated 1 in 150 attacks are detected and reported. In the private sector, the subcommittee's report cited an estimate from one private security company that the private sector had lost $800 million in 1995 due to computer intrusions. Most losses have not been publicly acknowledged, however.

A 1998 survey by the Computer Security Institute (CSI) conducted in cooperation with the FBI reported that of the 520 responses from commercial, government, and academic security practitioners, 64% reported security breaches (an increase of 16% over its 1997 survey results). Breaches included theft of proprietary information, sabotage, insider abuse of Internet access, financial fraud, spoofing, denial of service, viruses, telecommunications fraud, wiretapping, eavesdropping, and laptop theft[1]. Based on respondents' estimates, total financial losses in 1998 amounted to $137 million. However, only 46% of those reporting losses were able to quantify them. Therefore, the financial losses may be much greater. Financial losses include not only direct costs (theft of funds, costs to repair databases) but also indirect costs such as system "down-time" and, if measurable, losses due to loss of confidence. Tables from the CSI report and a press release are available at [http://www.gosci.com/prelea11.htm].

Computer security administrators lament that not enough attention and resources are being paid to the security risks associated with networked systems. Even where the problems are recognized, fixes need to solve "Year 2000" problems (see CRS Issue Brief 97036) are taking precedent. Nevertheless, the market for computer security assessments and security products is growing. And, because of the demand for knowledgeable personnel, many former "hackers" are making legitimate money in the security business. Some security specialists insist that this is not without its risks.

Rules and regulations governing the security of federal computer systems are guided by the Computer Security Act of 1987 (P.L. 100-235) and OMB Circular A-130, Annex III. The Act requires each agency to submit to the Office of Management and Budget (OMB) a security plan. OMB chairs an interagency committee of Chief Information Officers (CIOs) in which a subcommittee is devoted to security issues. In addition, the Act authorizes the National Institute of Standards and Technology (NIST) to set standards for all civilian unclassified government systems. The National Security Agency (NSA) does the same for the federal government's classified computer systems. NIST and NSA have recently formed a partnership, along with a few other foreign countries, that is providing common criteria for certifying security products. This partnership facilitates an international market in security products.

Various federal agencies also have groups that will perform vulnerability analyses on federal systems, recommend fixes to problems identified, and to assist in integrating those fixes into systems. A variety of agencies have also set up computer emergency response teams (CERTs) that help system administrators deal with intrusions and the problems that might arise. The CERT at Carnegie Mellon University was established to provide such services to Internet users anywhere in the country and has recently signed a contract with the General Services Administration to provide similar services to government agencies that may not have their own capability.

Of growing concern is the risk hacking poses to America's basic infrastructures (e.g., transportation systems, electric utilities), which increasingly rely on networked

---

[1] Reports of unauthorized access to credit card numbers stored on computers also have attracted much interest. Not only is there the risk of direct financial loss from someone using a credit card without authorization of the card owner, but increasingly people are concerned about consumer identity theft that involves use of another's personally identifiable information such as credit card numbers. That issue is addressed below.

computer systems (see CRS Report 98-675, *Critical Infrastructures: A Primer*). The President's Commission on Critical Infrastructure Protection (PCCIP) issued a report in November 1997 regarding the "cyberthreat" to five of the nation's basic infrastructures — information and communications, banking and finance, energy (including electric power, oil, and gas), physical distribution, and vital human services. While not finding an immediate crisis, the PCCIP concluded that the nation's infrastructures are vulnerable and the consequences threatening to the security of the nation. The report, *Critical Foundations: Protecting America's Infrastructures*, led to a Presidential Decision Directive (PDD-63) that was released May 22, 1998.

PDD-63 sets as a national goal the ability to protect critical infrastructures from intentional attacks (both physical and cyber) by 2003. It sets up an organizational structure for achieving this goal. Nineteen critical infrastructures (including four for which the federal government has the primary responsibility) have been identified. A lead agency has been assigned to each infrastructure. The lead agency is to work with the appropriate private sector actors, and state and local governments in developing a national plan for their sector. Each plan is to include a vulnerability assessment, a remedial action plan, appropriate warning procedures, response strategies, reconstitution of services strategies, education and awareness program, research and development needs, intelligence enhancements, international cooperation, and any legislative and budgetary requirements.

A Critical Infrastructure Assurance Office is being set up in the Department of Commerce to help coordinate the development of these plans. A Critical Infrastructure Coordination Group, an interagency group, will address interdependencies between agencies and sectors. The Group is chaired by a National Coordinator for Security, Infrastructure Protection, and Counter-Terrorism, and will report to the President through the Principal's Committee of the National Security Council on progress in implementing the PDD and the development of the national plans. The National Coordinator will also be the Executive Director of a National Infrastructure Assurance Council which will act as a Presidential advisory panel and include private, and state and local representatives.

PDD-63 also authorizes the Federal Bureau of Investigation to be the executive agent for a National Infrastructure Protection Center (NIPC). According to PDD-63, the NIPC will be the operational focal point for coordinating federal response to "attacks." The NIPC will also be the federal point of contact for developing threat analyses, issuing warnings and sharing information regarding intrusions, hacking methods and fixes. The NIPC will draw upon expertise found throughout the federal government. The PDD encourages the private sector to set up a parallel center to interact with the NIPC. The Joint Economic Committee held a hearing on "Cybercrime, Transnational Crime and Intellectual Property Theft" on March 24, 1998 highlighting the FBI's role in fighting such crime.

The federal computer fraud and abuse statute, 18 U.S.C. 1030, addresses protection of federal and bank computers, and computers used in interstate and foreign commerce. CRS Report 97-1025, *Computer Fraud & Abuse: An Overview of 18 U.S.C. 1030 And Related Federal Criminal Laws*, provides more information on the statute. In general, it prohibits trespassing, threats, damage, espionage, and using computers for committing fraud.

In December 1997, acknowledging the growing problem of crime on the Internet, the United States, Britain, Canada, France, Germany, Italy, Japan and Russia agreed on steps to fight computer crimes: insure that a sufficient number of trained and equipped law enforcement personnel are allocated to fighting high-tech crime; establish high-tech crime contacts available on a 24-hour basis; develop faster ways to trace attacks coming through computer networks to allow for identification of the responsible hacker or criminal; where extradition of a criminal is not possible, devote the same commitment of time and resources to that prosecution that a victim nation would have devoted; preserve information on computer networks so computer criminals cannot alter or destroy electronic evidence; review legal systems to ensure they appropriately criminalize computer wrongdoing and facilitate investigation of high-tech crimes; and work with industry to devise new solutions to make it easier to detect, prevent and punish computer crimes.

Computer Privacy

Computer Fraud and Scams, Protection of Personal Information, and General Computer Privacy Issues

Computer networks offer a new mechanism for the commission of fraud and scams against unwitting consumers. Although the types of fraud and scams that have been identified on the Internet are not new, perpetrators have easy access to a wide audience via the Internet. The Senate Governmental Affairs Committee's Permanent Subcommittee on Investigations held a hearing on the topic on February 10, 1998. On July 14, 1998, the Federal Trade Commission (FTC) released a list of the 12 most common scams found in unsolicited commercial electronic mail (for a general discussion of unsolicited email, see below). The list is available on the World Wide Web at [http://www.ftc.gov./opa/9807/dozen.htm]. The Securities and Exchange Commission (SEC) established a new Office of Internet Enforcement to handle Internet fraud cases in July 1998. The SEC reported that since 1995 it had brought more than 30 cases involving Internet-related securities fraud and now was receiving 120 complaints daily about Internet-related potential securities violations. On October 28, 1998, the SEC filed 23 enforcement actions against 44 individuals and companies for using the Internet to commit stock fraud (the SEC's press release is available at [http://www.sec.gov/news/netfraud.htm]).

As noted above, 18 U.S.C. 1030 addresses computer fraud, and the United States and seven other countries agreed in December 1997 to coordinate their efforts at fighting computer crime, including fraud. On May 12, 1998, just prior to President Clinton's attendance at the G-8 meeting, the White House announced an International Crime Control Strategy (ICCS) to provide new authorities and resources to fight international crime including fraud involving credit cards and other access devices, and authorizing wiretapping for investigations of felony computer crime offenses.

Consumer identity theft, in which one individual assumes the identity of another using personal information such as credit card and Social Security numbers, is also seen as increasing due to the widespread use of computers for storing and transmitting information. Congress directed the Federal Reserve Board to study the issue of the availability to the public of sensitive identifying information, whether such information could be used to commit financial fraud, and the risk to insured depository institutions.   Its March 1997 report, *Report to the Congress Concerning the Availability of Consumer Identifying Information and Financial Fraud*, concluded that there are insufficient data to draw conclusions about losses from this particular subset of financial fraud.   Although the Board noted that anecdotal information suggested that type of fraud is increasing, it concluded that the losses are a small part of overall fraud losses and do not pose a significant threat to insured depository institutions.   A May 1998 General Accounting Office report, *Identity Fraud: Information on Prevalence, Cost, and Internet Impact is Limited* (GAO/GGD-98-100BR), also found that few statistics are available on identity fraud, but that many of the individuals it interviewed believe the Internet increases opportunities for identity theft and fraud.

Many bills were introduced in the Senate and House regarding protection of personally identifiable information generally, and especially Social Security numbers. Some of the legislation was targeted towards all consumers, while other bills focused primarily on preventing acquisition of a child's personally identifiable information without a parent's knowledge, or attempting to obtain information about parents from children. Four bills concerning protection of personal identifiable information were introduced in the Senate (S. 504, Feinstein; S. 512, Kyl; S. 600, Feinstein, and S. 2326, Bryan) and 12 in the House (H.R. 98, Vento; H.R. 1287, Franks; H.R. 1330, Kanjorski; H.R. 1331, Kennelly; H.R. 1367, Barrett; H.R. 1813, Kleczka; H.R. 1964, Markey; H.R. 1972, Franks; H.R. 2368, Tauzin; H.R. 3551, DeLauro; H.R. 3601, Shadegg; H.R. 4151, Shadegg; and H.R. 4667, Markey). CRS Report 97-833, *Information Privacy*, provides more information on the legal aspects of these issues.

Of all those bills, the only legislation that passed Congress concerns identify theft (S. 512/H.R. 4151) and requiring parental consent for the collection, use, and distribution of information about children under 13 (S. 2326).

The Senate passed S. 512 (Kyl) on July 30. The House passed H.R. 4151 (Shadegg) on October 7 after modifying it to more closely resemble S. 512. The Senate then passed H.R. 4151 on October 14. The bill was signed into law on October 30 (P.L. 105-318). The bill sets penalties for persons who knowingly, and with the intent to commit unlawful activities, possess, transfer, or use one or more means of identification not legally issued for use to that person. Vice President Gore hailed the passage of S. 512 in a July 31 press conference (see below). The House Judiciary Subcommittee on Courts and Intellectual Property held a general hearing on privacy in electronic communications on March 26, 1998.   That Committee's Subcommittee on Crime held a hearing on H.R. 1972 and related legislation on April 30, 1998.

Congress and the Administration devoted considerable attention to the overall issue of protecting privacy on the Internet. Despite the large number of bills that were introduced, the focus of both branches of government is to encourage industry to self-regulate rather than passing new laws. As noted, the only bill that passed concerns the collection, use, and dissemination of information about children (S. 2326, see below).

Voluntary self regulation is the focus of the Clinton Administration's approach to Internet privacy. In its July 1997 report, *A Framework for Global Electronic Commerce*, the Administration endorsed industry self regulation for protecting consumer Internet privacy, stressing that if industry did not self-regulate effectively, the government might have to step in, particularly regarding children's Internet privacy.

The Federal Trade Commission (FTC) held a public workshop in June 1996 that addressed general issues of online privacy. Another workshop, in June 1997, focused on the collection of information about consumers by companies that operate computerized databases of personal information, called "individual reference services" or "look-up services." Just prior to the workshop, several of those companies announced voluntary principles they would follow to protect consumer privacy. In December 1997, the FTC released a report on the workshop and the industry principles: *Individual Reference Services: A Report to Congress* [http://www/ftc/gov/opa/9712/inrefser.htm]. Among the principles are that individual reference services will not distribute to the general public non-public information such as Social Security numbers, birth dates, mother's maiden names, credit histories, financial histories, medical records, or any information about children. Look-up services may not allow the general public to run searches using a Social Security number as a search term or make available information gathered from marketing transactions. Also, consumers will be allowed to obtain access to the non-public information maintained about them and to "opt-out" of that non-public information. The FTC noted that the principles did not address all areas of concern and made a number of recommendations accordingly.

On July 16, 1997, the FTC issued a letter advising the online industry that it was a deceptive practice to collect personal information from children without fully disclosing to parents how the data would be used and that Web sites must obtain parental permission before releasing such data to third parties. In December 1997, the FTC conducted a survey of 126 children's Web sites to determine the extent to which information collection practices were being disclosed. It found 86% of the Web sites collected information from children but fewer than 30% posted a privacy policy statement and only 4% required parental notification. Another survey was conducted in June 1998 of a broader range of 1,400 Web sites intended for children or adults. In its subsequent report, *Privacy Online: A Report to Congress* [http://www.ftc.gov/reports/privacy3/index.htm], the FTC reported that of the 212 children's sites in this survey, 89% collected personal identifiable information but only 54% disclosed their information collection practices and fewer than 10% provided any form of parental control. The survey also included 674 commercial Web sites of which 92% collected personal information. Only 14% provided any notice of their information collection practices and only 2% provided a comprehensive privacy policy.

Frustrated at those results, the FTC announced on June 4, 1998 that it would seek legislation protecting children's privacy on the Internet by requiring parental permission before a Web site could request information about a child. Vice President Gore issued a statement supporting the FTC's actions. Earlier, on May 14, the Vice President had called for an "electronic bill of rights" to protect consumers' privacy. He encouraged Congress to pass medical records privacy legislation (see CRS Issue

Brief 98002), and announced the establishment of an "opt-out" Web site [http://www.consumer.gov] by the FTC to allow individuals to indicate they do not wish personal information passed on to others. At a June 23-24, 1998 "summit" on Internet privacy organized by the Department of Commerce at the direction of the White House, Secretary of Commerce Daley warned industry that the Administration would seek legislation to protect all online consumers if industry did not accelerate its privacy protection efforts in general.

The House Commerce Committee's Subcommittee on Telecommunications held a hearing on H.R. 2368, the Data Privacy Act (Tauzin), on July 21, 1998. The bill would have provided incentives to industry to develop and implement voluntary privacy guidelines. The hearing focused on efforts to encourage the private sector to self regulate in this area. At the hearing, FTC Chairman Pitofsky said the FTC would wait until the end of the year to propose such legislation for adults to give industry one last chance to self regulate. He outlined the framework for such potential legislation at the hearing. Industry representatives defended the pace of their efforts to develop "seals of approval"for Web sites that clearly explain their privacy policies to users and agree to work with organizations overseeing the seals (such as the Better Business Bureau or TRUSTe) to resolve consumer complaints. Representatives of the Center for Democracy and Technology and the Center for Media Education expressed concern that self-regulation was insufficient to protect privacy on the Web. The Direct Marketing Association witness emphasized that many privacy concerns are about "chat rooms" and electronic mail, not Web sites, and each type of Internet usage needs to be treated separately.

On July 31, 1998, Vice President Gore addressed a wide range of privacy issues, reiterating his call for Congress to pass legislation protecting medical records, hailing passage of S. 512 (discussed above) as a first step towards dealing with identity theft issues, and asking Congress to pass legislation requiring parental consent before information is collected about children under 13. The Vice President renewed the Administration's emphasis on industry self-regulation, but noted the test of success would be the degree of industry participation.

Congress did pass legislation requiring operators of Web sites to obtain verifiable parental consent before collecting, using, or disseminating information about children under 13, and allowing parents to "opt out" of dissemination of information already collected about that child. It was included as the Children's Online Privacy Protection Act (originally S. 2326, Bryan), which is Title XIII of Division C of the FY1999 Omnibus Consolidated and Emergency Supplemental Appropriations Act (P.L. 105-277). The Senate Commerce Committee held a hearing on S. 2326 on September 23. Medical records confidentiality legislation did not pass, however.

Many European countries believe that strong measures are needed to protect privacy in the processing of personal data. Over a period of many years, the European Union (EU) developed a policy referred to as the "European data directive" that requires member countries to pass laws prohibiting the transfer of personal data to countries that are not members of the EU ("third countries") unless the third countries ensure an "adequate level of protection" for personal data. The directive went into force on October 26, 1998. Since the United States does not have such legislation in force, the U.S. Department of Commerce is working with the EU to ensure that business between Europe and the United States is not disrupted. It is expected that the EU will accept some type of certification developed by the Commerce Department and industry that U.S. companies are satisfying the intent of the EU data directive (formally entitled "Directive 95/46/EC of the European Parliament and of the Council of 24 October 1995 on the Protection of Individuals With Regard to the Processing of Personal Data and on the Free Movement of Such Data"). For more information on the history and content of the EU data directive, see: *The European Union's Data Protection Directive: Selected Issues* by Gina Stevens, CRS American Law Division General Distribution Memorandum, June 5, 1998.

Protecting Children from Unsuitable Material and Sexual Predators

Concern is growing about what children are encountering over the World Wide Web, particularly in terms of indecent material or contacts with strangers who intend to do them harm. The private sector has responded by developing filtering and tracking software to allow parents either to prevent their children from visiting certain Web sites or to provide a record of what sites their children have visited.

Congress passed the Communications Decency Act (CDA) as part of the 1996 Telecommunications Act (P.L. 104-104). Among other things, CDA would have made it illegal to send indecent material to children via the Internet (see CRS Report 97-841, *Indecency: Restrictions on Broadcast Media, Cable Television, and the Internet*). In June 1997, the Supreme Court overturned the portions of the CDA dealing with indecency and the Internet. (Existing law permits criminal prosecutions for transmitting obscenity or child pornography over the Internet.) Congress now has passed a replacement law, the Child Online Protection Act (see below).

Prohibiting Access by Children to Material That is "Harmful to Minors". Congress passed the Child Online Protection Act as part of the Omnibus Appropriations Act (P.L. 105-277, Title XIV of Division C). The language is based on S. 1482 (Coats) and H.R. 3783 (Oxley). The new law prohibits commercial distribution of material over the Web to children under 17 that is "harmful to minors." Web site operators are required to ask for a means of age verification such as a credit card number before displaying such material. It replaces provisions of the 1996 Communications Decency Act that were overturned by the Supreme Court. (See CRS Report 98-670 A, *Obscenity, Child Pornography, and Indecency: Recent Developments and Pending Issues* and CRS Report 98-328 A, *Restrictions on Minor's Access to Material on the Internet.*) By limiting the language to commercial activities and using the court-tested "harmful to minors" language instead of "indecent" as was used in the 1996 Act, the sponsors hope to have drafted a law that will survive court challenges. The American Civil Liberties Union (ACLU) and others filed suit against the new law in the U.S. District Court for the Eastern District of Pennsylvania on October 22, the day after President Clinton signed the bill into law.

The Senate Commerce Committee had held a hearing on S. 1482 on February 10, 1998 and reported the bill on June 25 (S.Rept. 105-225). The language of the bill was adopted as a Coats amendment to the FY1999 Commerce, Justice, State appropriations bill (S. 2260) on July 21. The House Commerce Telecommunications Subcommittee held a hearing on H.R. 3783 and related issues on September 11. That bill was reported from the Commerce Committee (H.Rept. 105-775) on October 5 and passed the House on October 7. It then was incorporated into the Omnibus Appropriations Act (Title XIV of Division C). A modified version of the Coats language also was attached to the Internet Tax Freedom Act, S. 442, which became Title XI of Division C of the Omnibus Appropriations Act.

The Child Online Protection Act establishes a Commission on Online Child Protection to conduct a one-year study of technologies and methods to help reduce access by children to material on the Web that is harmful to minors. Separately, the House adopted a Jackson-Lee amendment to H.R. 3494 (discussed below) on June 11 that required the FBI to prepare a study within two years on the capabilities of current computer-based control technologies to control the electronic transmission of pornographic images and identify needed research to develop such technologies and any inherent, operational, or constitutional impediments to their use. Similar language was included in the final version of H.R. 3494 (P.L. 105-314) although the National Academy of Sciences, not the FBI, is designated to perform the study.

Filtering Software. Although Congress considered legislation to require schools and libraries to use filtering software to screen out objectionable Web sites, no legislation passed. However, Congress did include a provision in the Child Online Protection Act requiring online service providers to advise parents that such software is available.

Software to block access to Web sites or e-mail addresses has existed for many years (commercial products include Cyber Patrol, Cyber Sitter, Net Nanny, Net Shepard, and SurfWatch). Other products (such as Net Snitch) do not prohibit access to sites, but maintain a record that a parent can review to know what sites a child has visited. Some filtering products screen sites based on keywords, while others use ratings systems based on ratings either by the software vendor or the Web site itself. Both types of ratings are becoming more available as industry attempts to self-regulate to stave off governmental regulation. Existing filtering software products have received mixed reviews, however, because they cannot effectively screen out all objectionable sites on the ever-changing Web, or because they inadvertently screen out useful material. Three House bills were introduced to require Internet service providers to offer filtering software to parents: H.R. 774 (Lofgren); H.R. 1180 (McDade); and H.R. 1964 (Markey). The Senate adopted a Dodd amendment to the FY1999 Commerce, State, Judiciary appropriations bill (S. 2260) on July 23 that required Internet service providers to offer filtering software to customers. Similar language was included in the Child Online Protection Act (discussed above).

Some privacy groups object to filtering software because of the amount of useful information to which it denies access. A November 1997 report on filtering software was released by the Electronic Privacy Information Center (EPIC) entitled *Faulty Filters: How Content Filters Block Access to Kid-Friendly Information on the Internet* [http://www2.epic.org/reports/filter-report.html]. EPIC tested a filtering program called Net Shepard, searching the Web for sites it expected to be useful to and suitable for children. For example, EPIC searched for Web sites about the "American Red Cross" (entered into the search engine in quotes to ensure that only items with that exact set of words in that order would be returned) with and without

Net Shepard activated. EPIC reported that Net Shepard prevented access to 99.8% of the sites. From this and other similar examples, EPIC concluded that in the effort to protect children from a small amount of unsuitable material, they were being denied access to a large amount of suitable information. Many privacy advocates also feel that filtering is a form of censorship. Other critics object to the fact that a parent would not know specifically what sites or words a particular software product was blocking out.

A particular focus of the debate has become filtering systems for schools and libraries. Policies adopted by local communities reflect the spectrum of attitudes on this topic. Some are choosing to allow children to use computers at local libraries only with parental permission, some are using filtering software, and others are choosing no restrictions.

Senator McCain and Representative Franks introduced bills (S. 1619 and H.R. 3177) to require schools receiving federally-provided "E-rate" subsidies through the universal service fund to use filtering software to block out Internet sites that might contain material inappropriate for children. (For information on universal service and the E-rate, see CRS Issue Brief 98040, *Telecommunications Discounts for Schools and Libraries: the "E-Rate" Program and Controversies*). As proposed, the bills would have required libraries receiving E-rate funds to have one or more computers that use filtering software. The determination of what is inappropriate was left to the school, school board, library, or "other authority responsible for making the required certification." Supporters of the requirement for filtering systems argued that children must be protected from inappropriate material, particularly when their parents are not present to supervise them. Opponents argued that it is censorship, that the filtering software also prevents access to appropriate sites, and that such decisions should be left to the local community.

The Senate Commerce Committee reported S. 1619 on June 25 (S.Rept. 105-226). The Senate adopted that language as an amendment to a Coats amendment to the FY1999 Commerce, Justice, State appropriations bill (S. 2260) on July 21. (The Coats amendment concerned commercial distribution via the World Wide Web of material that is harmful to minors, discussed elsewhere). The House Appropriations Committee took a broader approach, adopting an Istook amendment to the FY1999 Labor-HHS appropriations bill (H.R. 4274) that required schools and libraries to install filtering software if they receive funds under any federal agency program or activity to acquire or operate any computer that is accessible to minors and has access to the Internet. Neither was included in the final version of those appropriations bills, both of which were incorporated into the Omnibus Appropriations Act.

Sexual Predators on the Internet. Congress also was concerned about sexual predators using the Internet to entice children. Because conversations can take place anonymously on the Internet, a child may not know that (s)he is talking with an adult. The adult may persuade the child to agree to a meeting, with tragic results. Congress passed H.R. 3494 (P.L. 105-314) to address those and other non computer-related issues related to protecting children from sexual predators.

Hearings were held by the House Judiciary Committee's Subcommittee on Crime on H.R. 3494, and related legislation on November 7, 1997 and April 30, 1998. H.R.

3494 passed the House on June 11 with a number of amendments added during committee markup on May 6 (H.Rept. 105-557) or on the floor, several of which are discussed elsewhere in this section. A Senate bill, S. 2491 (Hatch), was subsequently introduced with modifications to H.R. 3494. The Senate Judiciary Committee adopted its language as a substitute for H.R. 3494 during markup on September 17 and passed the substitute version on October 9. The House agreed to the Senate version on October 12. The bill, the Protection of Children from Sexual Predators Act, was signed into law on October 30 (P.L. 105-314). The Senate also had adopted a Moseley-Braun amendment on July 23 to the FY1999 Commerce, Justice, State appropriations bill (S. 2260) based on S. 1965 that contained some provisions similar to those in H.R. 3494.

Among its provisions as enacted, the law —

- prohibits using the mail or any facility or means of interstate or foreign commerce (a) to initiate the transmission of the name, address, telephone number, social security number, or electronic mail address of an individual under 16 with the intent to entice, encourage, offer, or solicit any person to engage in any sexual activity for which any person can be charged with a criminal offense, or (b) to persuade, induce, entice, or coerce any individual under 18 to engage in prostitution or any sexual activity for which any person can be charged with a criminal offense;

- makes it a crime to transfer obscene matter by mail or any facility or means of interstate or foreign commerce to anyone under 16;

- calls for the U.S. Sentencing Commission to recommend appropriate changes to existing Federal Sentencing Guidelines if a defendant used a computer with the intent to persuade, induce, entice, coerce, or facilitate the transport of a child to engage in any prohibited sexual activity;

- requires electronic communication or remote computing services that have knowledge of violations of child pornography laws to report it to law enforcement officials;

- prohibits federal prisoners from having unsupervised access to the Internet and recommends that states do the same with their prisoners; and

- requires a study of technologies to control the electronic transmission of pornography (discussed earlier).

Legislation also was considered, but did not pass, to prevent sexual predators as defined in section 170101(a)(3) of the Violent Crime Control and Law Enforcement Act of 1994 from obtaining Internet accounts that could allow them to contact children (S. 1356, Faircloth; H.R. 2791, Roukema). Another House bill, H.R. 2815 (Weller), would have made it a crime to target children for sexually explicit messages or contacts.

A Faircloth amendment to the FY1999 Commerce, Justice, State appropriations bill (S. 2260) was adopted on July 22 giving the FBI administrative subpoena authority in cases involving a federal violation related to sexual exploitation and abuse of children. The provision is intended to make it easier for the FBI to gain access to Internet service provider records of suspected sexual predators. It was included in the final version of the Omnibus Appropriations Bill (P.L. 105-277, section 122 of General Provisions—Justice Department).

Other Legislation Related to Protecting Children. As already discussed, P.L. 105-314 (H.R. 3494) contains a number of provisions related to the protection of children other than the sexual predator issue. Other House bills were also considered related to protecting children and in some cases provisions similar to the bills were ultimately included in H.R. 3494 or other legislation. H.R. 2173 (Franks) would have required Internet service providers to report to law enforcement officials instances of suspected child abuse they discover or that are brought to their attention by users. The House Judiciary Committee's Subcommittee on Crime held a hearing on H.R. 2173 and related legislation on April 30, 1998, and language similar to H.R. 2173 was included in the final version of H.R. 3494. H.R. 3729 (Pryce) was very similar to language included in the final version of H.R. 3494 prohibiting federal prisoners from having unsupervised access to the Internet. H.R. 3985 (Lampson) would have authorized $2 million per year for FY1999-2002 for the U.S. Customs Service's International Child Pornography Investigation and Coordination Center to deal with the increase in child pornography activities due to the Internet. While that specific language did not pass, the Omnibus Appropriations Act (P.L. 105-277) sets aside $2.4 million in the Customs Service appropriation to double the staffing and resources for the child pornography cyber-smuggling initiative and provides $1 million in the Violent Crime Reduction Trust Fund for technology support for that initiative.

In the Senate, S. 900 (Feingold) would have amended federal sentencing guidelines to enhance a sentence "if the defendant used a computer with the intent to persuade, induce, entice, or coerce a child ... to engage in any prohibited sexual activity." S. 900 was reported from the Senate Judiciary Committee on October 9, 1997 without written report. Similar language was included in the final version of H.R. 3494 (P.L. 105-314).

Part of the concern about unsuitable material on the Internet involves unsolicited advertising ("junk e-mail") that contains pornography or links to pornographic Web sites (see below).

Industry Response. The Internet community is anxious to avoid legislation. At a "Kids Online Summit" in December 1997, several major players in the Internet industry pledged to do what they could to make the Internet safer for children. America Online (AOL), one of the largest Internet service providers, for example, announced a new policy stating that "when child pornography is appropriately brought to our attention and we have control over it, we will remove it. Subject to constitutional safeguards and statutory privacy safeguards, we will cooperate fully with law enforcement officials investigating child pornography on the Internet." AOL, AT&T, and Microsoft promised to offer filtering software to parents and implement an outreach and educational campaign to increase its use. Those companies and others debuted a public awareness and educational campaign called "America Links Up: A Kids Online Teach-in" [http://www.americalinksup.org/] on September 15, 1998 during National Kids Online Week. It includes public service announcements, teach-ins around the country, information and guidance for parents, and a videotape. The campaign advises parents to "take the trip together" with their children so they know what sites are being visited.

Privacy of Personal Information in Government Databases

The growth in the use of the Internet for providing government services raises similar concerns about how to ensure the confidentiality of personal information. Use of computer and telecommunications technologies by government agencies for storing, accessing, and disseminating information offers the advantages of potentially reducing costs, while simultaneously improving customer service. For these reasons, agencies have placed considerable emphasis on developing online access to information and enhancing the ability of citizens to supply information electronically to the government to receive services or comply with rules and regulations. Both the Administration's National Performance Review (NPR) effort and its National Information Infrastructure (NII) initiative emphasized the use of information technology for improving efficiency of government operations, increasing citizen access to government information, and providing better service to individuals.

As these efforts move from the planning to the operational phases, agencies are faced with the need to provide adequate privacy protections for these systems and services. While the Internet offers considerable advantages in terms of the ease with which large numbers of people can interact with agency computer systems, it also lacks security. It is critical for the success of these new "electronic government" initiatives that the public has confidence that personal privacy is not jeopardized. Thus, agencies must develop adequate procedures and apply technological safeguards to ensure that confidentiality of agency records is not compromised.

An example is the development of an online Personal Earnings and Benefit Estimate Statement (PEBES) by the Social Security Administration (SSA). As summarized in its September 1997 report *Social Security: Privacy and Customer Service in the Electronic Age,* the SSA initiated an online PEBES service in March 1997, following earlier pilot testing and after considerable study and developmental work. The system allowed individuals to query the system for their PEBES data and receive instantaneous response over the Internet. People needed to supply five authenticating elements (name, social security number, date of birth, state of birth, and mother's maiden name) to gain access to the data. While these authentication procedures were consistent with what is required using SSA's 800-number and for written requests, there was a strong public response to potential privacy abuses.

The concerns centered on the fact that the authenticating data are readily available from a variety of sources and thus PEBES information could be obtained by those other than the individual whose records would be provided. In response to these concerns, SSA suspended operation of the online PEBES system and held six public forums around the country to solicit comments from experts and interested citizens. Based upon the input received from these forums and other sources, such as congressional hearings, SSA concluded that it would provide a modified version of online PEBES on the Internet with additional security and authentication safeguards. The now-operational modified system of online PEBES allows requests to be made via the Internet but responses are sent via mail. Since the law requires

SSA to provide, by 1999, PEBES statements each year to all workers 25 and older, SSA considers it a very high priority to establish an online PEBES system that will meet necessary security and privacy standards. It has announced plans to implement additional safeguards using a public key infrastructure in the future.

The SSA example is indicative of a major trend toward greater use of the Internet for these types of government functions. Congress passed the Government Paperwork Elimination Act (Title XVII of Division C of the Omnibus Appropriations Act, P.L. 105-277) that directs the Office of Management and Budget to develop procedures for the use and acceptance of "electronic" signatures (of which digital signatures are one type) by executive branch agencies. Legislation (H.R. 2991, Eshoo) that would have required agencies to create online versions of their forms and make them accessible to the public, did not pass. It was intended to enable citizens to fill out forms online, return them (along with payments, such as taxes owed), and verify the transactions using digital signature technology.

Major legislative changes to the welfare, immigration, and health care payments systems also necessitate the creation of large scale databases to monitor the status of applicants for programs. For example, the Personal Responsibility and Work Opportunity Reconciliation Act, P.L. 104-193 (welfare reform), establishes new federal databases for all new hires nationwide, quarterly wage reports of all working persons, unemployment insurance data, and lists of people who owe or are owed child support. The first component of this system, the National Directory of New Hires, requires every state to send data on new hires daily to the Department of Health and Human Services (HHS). The goal of this system is to track parents who are overdue on their child support payments, but some privacy advocates are concerned that it might be used for purposes beyond those identified in the statute, such as other government agencies using it to verify eligibility for benefits programs.

The Illegal Immigration Reform and Immigrant Responsibility Act (P.L. 104-208) required enhancements to the systems used to monitor immigration into the United States in an effort to thwart illegal immigration. The Health Insurance Portability and Accountability Act (P.L. 104-191) established requirements for the use of standard electronic transactions for activities such as the submissions of health insurance financial claims and transmission of payment and remittance advice. (See CRS Issue Brief 98002, *Medical Records Confidentiality*, for a discussion of those issues and related legislation: H.R. 52, H.R. 1815, H.R. 3900, S. 1368, and S. 1921). These developments, combined with efforts to move towards more electronic benefits delivery systems, reinforce the need for effective mechanisms to protect confidentiality and ensure system security in government computer operations.

Technical issues associated with implementation of these systems have caused delays in the systems becoming operational, but the privacy issues remain unchanged.

In a broad speech on Internet privacy issues on May 14, 1998, Vice President Gore announced the release of a memorandum for heads of executive department and agencies outlining steps agencies must take to ensure that the expanded use of information technologies does not erode privacy protections already provided in statute.

Intellectual Property

The era of global Internet connectivity presents significant challenges to effectively protecting the rights of copyright holders. Computers can make exact duplicates of originals and networks can provide access to literally millions of individuals. Some observers maintain that the growth of international computer networks will depend, in part, upon the willingness of individuals and businesses to make information available electronically. Absent adequate intellectual property protection, authors and publishers often are reluctant to provide Internet access to material of value. Some experts contend that technological solutions, such as encryption, digital signatures, digital watermarks, and other verification software, will address these concerns. Others suggest that the existing legal regime for intellectual property rights is inadequate for addressing the electronic distribution of material and must be replaced with different approaches to fostering creativity in the digital environment. Many maintain that existing legal authorities can and should be modified to account for the changing technological scene and recommend expanding the current legal framework to encompass the transmission of digital information.

The 105th Congress addressed three aspects of intellectual property rights in the digital era: implementation of two World Intellectual Property Organization (WIPO) treaties; copyright infringement liability protection for Online Service Providers (OSPs); and copyright protection of collections of information (databases). As the debate evolved, various bills merged with or were replaced by others. Ultimately, all three issues were combined in the House-passed version of H.R. 2281. In the Senate, WIPO implementation and OSP liability limitation were in S. 2037, which passed the Senate on May 14, while database protection issues were in S. 2291, which did not get out of committee. WIPO implementation and OSP liability limitation were signed into law (P.L. 105-304), while data protection issues were not included in that law and are expected to be debated again in the 106th Congress.

WIPO Implementation

The 105th Congress passed legislation (P.L. 105-304) to implement two new World Intellectual Property Organization (WIPO) treaties adopted in Geneva in December 1996 — the WIPO Performances and Phonograms Treaty and the WIPO Copyright Treaty. The law (originating as H.R. 2281 and S. 2037[2]) amends the Copyright Act to prohibit the circumvention of anti-copying technology and assure the integrity of copyright management information systems. Alternative bills (H.R. 3048, Boucher; and S. 1146, Ashcroft) were introduced that had somewhat different language concerning circumvention of anti-copying technologies and copyright management information systems, and including provisions related to use of copyrighted digital material by teachers and librarians. (See CRS Report 97-444, *World Intellectual Property Organization Copyright Treaty: An Overview.*) Librarians were particularly concerned that the circumvention language would mean that users had to pay each time they copied a small portion of a work on the Internet. As enacted, P.L. 105-304 delays implementation of that provision for two years,

---

[2] Two Senate bills, S. 1121 and S. 1146, were considered by the Senate Judiciary Committee. A new bill, S. 2037, was then reported from Committee on May 14, 1998.

during which time the Secretary of Commerce is to study its impact on fair use. The Secretary could waive the ban where fair use would be harmed.

Online Service Provider Liability Protection

P.L. 105-304 also addresses copyright infringement liability of Online Service Providers (OSPs)[3]. The debate focused on the legal liability of the OSPs in situations where they act strictly as conduits for material that infringes on copyright. While copyright holders generally asserted that existing copyright law is adequate to deal with the issue of OSP liability, others in the telecommunications industry and the academic and library communities advocated new legislation to specify the OSP exemption from liability. (See CRS Report 97-950, *Online Service Provider Copyright Liability: Analysis and Discussion of H.R. 2180 and S. 1146*.) As enacted, the law exempts OSPs from liability if they act only as conduits of information.

Database Protection

Legislation on the issue of database protection was also considered by the 105th Congress. It passed the House, but not the Senate. The Collections of Information Antipiracy Act (H.R. 2652, Coble), passed the House on May 19 and then was also attached to H.R. 2281 when it passed the House August 4. A Senate bill, S. 2291 (Grams), was introduced July 10, 1998. The House bill was the subject of hearings by the Subcommittee on Courts and Intellectual Property of House Judiciary on October 23, 1997 and February 12, 1998. The decision to attach the database protection bill (H.R. 2652) to the WIPO implementation/OSP liability protection bill (H.R. 2281) in the House was controversial. Critics who had concerns about the database provisions, including major scientific and library associations and the Clinton Administration, argued that the issue might prevent the rest of the bill from being enacted. The Clinton Administration had raised constitutional questions about Congress' authority to enact such legislation. The section was dropped from H.R. 2281 before it cleared Congress. The issues are likely to be debated again in the 106th Congress.

The issue is very controversial. Scientific groups and the library community have cautioned against establishing new protections for databases that might compromise fair use and access to data for scientific research. Among the issues they have raised are whether a need for a new intellectual property right has been adequately demonstrated, the definition of key terms such as "database" that might encompass a broader array of information than what would be necessary to protect competition in the information industry, and the importance of ensuring that information produced by government employees remains publicly available, free from copyright restrictions.

Database producers argue that the compilation of factual databases requires some form of protection beyond current law if companies are expected to make

---

[3] The OSP provisions of H.R. 2281 originated in H.R. 2180, that itself was superseded by H.R. 3209. They were merged into H.R. 2281 during markup by the House Judiciary Committee on April 1, 1998.

substantial investments in creating them. The ability to download and retransmit data over the Internet facilitates copying of information, making producers of factual, noncopyrightable, databases more vulnerable. They argue that the absence of some form of database-specific property rights has a chilling effect on the database industry that would result in fewer factual databases being compiled and thus could potentially reduce the availability of information to the public.

Unsolicited Commercial Electronic Mail ("Junk E-Mail" or "Spamming")

One aspect of increased use of the Internet for electronic mail (e-mail) has been the advent of unsolicited advertising, or "junk e-mail" (also called "spamming," "unsolicited commercial e-mail," or "unsolicited bulk e-mail"). The *Report to the Federal Trade Commission of the Ad-Hoc Working Group on Unsolicited Commercial Email* [http://www.cdt.org/spam] reviews the issues in this debate.

In 1991, Congress passed the Telephone Consumer Protection Act (P.L. 102-243) that prohibits, *inter alia*, unsolicited advertising via facsimile machines, or "junk fax" (see CRS Report 98-514, *Telemarketing Fraud: Congressional Efforts to Protect Consumers*). Many question whether there should be an analogous law for computers, or at least some method for letting a consumer know before opening an e-mail message whether or not it is unsolicited advertising and to direct the sender to cease transmission of such messages. At a June 17, 1998 hearing on spamming before the Senate Commerce Committee, America Online (AOL) stated that junk e-mail represents 5-30% of the 15 million Internet e-mail messages it handles each day.

Opponents of junk e-mail such as the Coalition Against Unsolicited Commercial Email (CAUCE) argue that not only is junk e-mail annoying, but its cost is borne by consumers, not marketers. Consumers are charged higher fees by Internet service providers that must invest resources to upgrade equipment to manage the high volume of e-mail, deal with customer complaints, and mount legal challenges to junk e-mailers. According to the May 4, 1998 issue of Internet Week, $2 of each customer's monthly bill is attributable to spam [http://www.techweb.com/se/directlink.cgi?INW19980504S0003]. Some want to prevent bulk e-mailers from sending messages to anyone with whom they do not have an established business relationship, treating junk e-mail the same way as junk fax. Proponents of unsolicited commercial e-mail argue that it is a valid method of advertising. The Direct Marketing Association (DMA), for example, argues that instead of banning unsolicited commercial e-mail, individuals should be given the opportunity to notify the sender of the message that they want to be removed from its mailing list — or "opt-out."

To date, the issue of restraining junk e-mail has been fought primarily over the Internet or in the courts. Some Internet service providers will return junk e-mail to its origin, and groups opposed to junk e-mail will send blasts of e-mail to a mass e-mail company, disrupting the company's computer systems. Filtering software also is available to screen out e-mail based on keywords or return addresses. Knowing this, mass e-mailers may avoid certain keywords or continually change addresses to foil the software, however. In the courts, Internet service providers with unhappy customers and businesses that believe their reputations have been tarnished by misrepresentations in junk e-mail have brought suit against mass e-mailers.

Although the House and Senate each passed legislation addressing the unsolicited commercial e-mail problem, no bill ultimately cleared the 105th Congress. The Senate had adopted a Murkowski-Torricelli amendment to S. 1618, the Anti-slamming[4] Amendments Act, that follows the "opt-out" philosophy and reflected provisions in S. 771 (Murkowski) and S. 875 (Torricelli). The language would have required senders of commercial e-mail to clearly identify in the subject line of the message that it was an advertisement, required Internet service providers to make software available to their subscribers to block such e-mail, and prohibited sending e-mail to anyone who had asked not to receive such mail. Similar language was included in the House version of the Anti-slamming bill, H.R. 3888, marked up by the House Commerce Telecommunications Subcommittee on August 6. Concerns were raised by several subcommittee members during the markup, however, that the language might infringe on First Amendment rights, and commented that they wanted more information before proceeding with the bill because of that and other issues. A very different version was adopted during full committee markup on September 24. As reported from the full committee (H.Rept. 105-801), the bill included only a sense of Congress statement that industry should self-regulate in this area. The bill passed the House on October 12, but differences between the House and Senate on this and other issues could not be resolved before Congress adjourned.

Four other House bills also addressed the issue. H.R. 1748 (Smith) would have amended the 1991 Telephone Consumer Protection Act to treat junk e-mail the same as junk fax. H.R. 2368 (Tauzin) encouraged industry to establish voluntary guidelines for transmission of junk e-mail. H.R. 4124 (Cook) and H.R. 4176 (Markey) reflected the opt-out approach.

As noted earlier, some unsolicited e-mail either contains indecent material or provides links to other sites where indecent material is available. Thus, controls over junk e-mail have also arisen in the context of protecting children from unsuitable material. In October 1997, AOL filed suit to prevent a company that sends unsolicited e-mails offering "cyberstrippers" from sending e-mail to AOL subscribers. The company, Over the Air Equipment, agreed on December 18, 1997 to drop its challenge to a preliminary injunction barring it from sending such advertisements to AOL subscribers (Reuters, December 18, 1997, 11:57 AET).

Internet Domain Names

During the 105th Congress, controversy surfaced over the disposition of the Internet domain name system (DNS). Internet domain names were created to provide users with a simple location name for computers on the Internet, rather than using the more complex, unique Internet Protocol (IP) number that designates their specific location. As the Internet has grown, the method for allocating and designating domain names has become increasingly controversial. The domain name issue is discussed in

---

[4] "Slamming" is the unauthorized change of someone's long distance telephone service provider. See CRS Issue Brief 98027.

more detail in CRS Report 97-868, *Internet Domain Names: Background and Policy Issues.*

The Internet originated with research funding provided by the Department of Defense Advanced Research Projects Agency (DARPA) to establish a military network. As its use expanded, a civilian segment evolved with support from the National Science Foundation (NSF) and other science agencies. While there are no formal statutory authorities or international agreements governing the management and operation of the Internet and the DNS, several entities play key roles in the DNS. The Internet Assigned Numbers Authority (IANA) makes technical decisions concerning root servers, determines qualifications for applicants to manage country code Top Level Domains (TLDs), assigns unique protocol parameters, and manages the IP address space, including delegating blocks of addresses to registries around the world to assign to users in their geographic area. IANA operates out of the University of Southern California's Information Sciences Institute and has been funded primarily by the Department of Defense.

Prior to 1993, the National Science Foundation (NSF) was responsible for registration of nonmilitary generic Top Level Domains (gTLDs) such as .com, .org, .net, and .edu. In 1993, the NSF entered into a 5-year cooperative agreement with Network Solutions, Inc. (NSI) to operate Internet domain name registration services. In 1995, the agreement was modified to allow NSI to charge registrants a $50 fee per year for the first two years, of which 70% went to NSI to cover its costs and 30% was deposited in the "Intellectual Infrastructure Fund" to be reinvested in the Internet. Since the imposition of fees in 1995, criticism arose over NSI's sole control over registration of the gTLDs. In addition, there was an increase in trademark disputes arising out of the enormous growth of registrations in the .com domain. With the cooperative agreement between NSI and NSF due to expire in 1998, the Administration, through the Department of Commerce (DOC), began exploring ways to transfer administration of the DNS to the private sector.

In the wake of much discussion among Internet stakeholders, and after extensive public comment on a previous proposal, the DOC, on June 5, 1998, issued a final statement of policy, *Management of Internet Names and Addresses* (also known as the "White Paper"). The White Paper states that the U.S. government is prepared to recognize and enter into agreement with "a new not-for-profit corporation formed by private sector Internet stakeholders to administer policy for the Internet name and address system." In deciding upon an entity with which to enter such an agreement, the U.S. government will assess whether the new system ensures stability, competition, private and bottom-up coordination, and fair representation of the Internet community as a whole.

In effect, the White Paper endorsed a process whereby the divergent interests of the Internet community would come together and decide how Internet names and addresses will be managed and administered. Accordingly, Internet constituencies from around the world (calling themselves "the International Forum on the White Paper"or IFWP) held a series of meetings during the summer of 1998 to discuss how the New Corporation (NewCo) might be constituted and structured. In September of 1998, IANA, in collaboration with NSI, released a proposed set of bylaws and articles of incorporation for a new entity called the Internet Corporation for Assigned

Names and Numbers (ICANN). The proposal was criticized by some Internet stakeholders, who claimed that ICANN does not adequately represent a consensus of the entire Internet community. Accordingly, other competing proposals for a NewCo were submitted to DOC. On October 20, 1998, the DOC tentatively approved the ICANN proposal. Pending the satisfactory resolution of several remaining concerns raised by the competing proposals — including accountability, transparent decision-making processes, and conflict of interest — the DOC will begin work on a transition agreement with ICANN. Meanwhile, nine members of ICANN's interim board have been chosen (four Americans, three Europeans, one from Japan, and one from Australia).

The White Paper also signaled DOC's intention to ramp down the government's Cooperative Agreement with NSI, with the objective of introducing competition into the domain name space while maintaining stability and ensuring an orderly transition. On October 6, 1998, DOC and NSI announced an extension of the Cooperative Agreement between the federal government and NSI through September 30, 2000. During this transition period, government obligations will be terminated as DNS responsibilities are transferred to the NewCo. Specifically, NSI has committed to a timetable for development of a Shared Registration System that will permit multiple registrars (including NSI) to provide registration services within the .com, .net., and .org gTLDs. By March 31, 1999, NSI will establish a test bed supporting actual registrations by five registrars who will be accredited by the NewCo. According to the agreement, the Shared Registration System will be deployed by June 1, 1999, and fully implemented and available to all accredited registrars by October 1, 1999. NSI will also continue to administer the root server system until receiving further instruction from the government.

During the 105th Congress, a number of DNS hearings were held by the House Committees on Science, on Commerce, and on the Judiciary. The hearings explored issues such as governance, trademark issues, how to foster competition in domain name registration services, and how the Administration will manage and oversee the transition to private sector ownership of the DNS. Most recently, the House Committees on Commerce and on Science held hearings on June 10 and October 7, 1998, respectively. On October 15, the Chairman of the House Committee on Commerce sent letters of inquiry to DOC and the White House reflecting concerns that the process that produced the ICANN proposal was insufficiently open and responsive to the interests of all Internet stakeholders.

One of the thorniest issues surrounding the DNS is the resolution of trademark disputes that arise in designating domain names. In the early years of the Internet, when the primary users were academic institutions and government agencies, little concern existed over trademarks and domain names. As the Internet grew, however, the fastest growing number of requests for domain names were in the .com domain because of the explosion of businesses offering products and services on the Internet. Since domain names have been available from NSI on a first-come, first-serve basis, some companies discovered that their name had already been registered. The situation was aggravated by some people registering domain names in the hope that they might be able to sell them to companies that place a high value on them and certain companies registering the names of all their product lines.

The increase in conflicts over property rights to certain trademarked names has resulted in several lawsuits. Under the current policy, NSI does not determine the legality of registrations, but when trademark ownership is demonstrated, has placed the use of a name on hold until the parties involved resolve the domain name dispute. The White Paper calls upon the World Intellectual Property Organization (WIPO) to convene an international process, including individuals from the private sector and government, to develop a set of recommendations for trademark/domain name dispute resolutions. WIPO is developing recommendations and is scheduled to present them to the NewCo in March 1999. Meanwhile, the Next Generation Internet Research Act of 1998 (P.L. 105-305) directs the National Academy of Sciences to conduct a study of the short and long-term effects on trademark rights of adding new generic top-level domains and related dispute resolution procedures.

Another DNS issue relates to the disposition of the Intellectual Infrastructure Fund, derived from domain name registration fees collected by NSI. The fund grew to $56 million before NSF and NSI discontinued collecting fees for the fund as of April 1, 1998. A number of suggestions were offered for use of the fund, including returning money to registrants, setting up a nonprofit entity to allocate funds, or using it for global administrative projects, such as Internet registries in developing countries. The VA/HUD/Independent Agencies FY1998 Appropriations Act (P.L. 105-65) directed NSF to credit up to $23 million of the funds to NSF's Research and Related Activities account for Next Generation Internet activities. A class action suit filed by six Internet users against NSF and NSI in October 1997 questioned the legal authority of NSF to allow NSI to charge for registering Internet addresses and requested $55 million in refunds. The suit also sought to prevent the government from spending the money as directed by Congress. On April 6, 1998, U.S. District Judge Thomas Hogan dismissed the charge that NSF lacked authority to permit NSI to collect fees, but let stand another charge challenging the portion of the fee collected for the infrastructure fund. However, the FY1998 Emergency Supplemental Appropriations Act (P.L. 105-174), enacted on May 1, 1998, contains language ratifying and legalizing the infrastructure fund. Accordingly, Judge Hogan reversed his decision, thereby allowing NSF to spend the $23 million from the fund through FY1999 on the Next Generation Internet program.

105th Congress Legislation

(*NOTE*: MANY BILLS WOULD FIT UNDER SEVERAL DIFFERENT CATEGORIES. THEY ARE CATEGORIZED HERE BASED ON EACH BILL'S MAJOR THRUST IN THE CONTEXT OF THE TOPICS DISCUSSED IN THIS REPORT. COMMITTEES TO WHICH THE BILLS WERE REFERRED ARE NOTED IN PARENTHESES. BILLS THAT WERE ENACTED ARE IN BOLD. SEE TEXT FOR DISPOSITION OF OTHER BILLS.)

Encryption and Digital Signatures

H.R. 695, Goodlatte, Safety and Freedom Through Encryption (JUDICIARY, INTERNATIONAL RELATIONS, NATIONAL SECURITY, INTELLIGENCE, COMMERCE)
H.R. 2937, Baker, Electronic Financial Services Efficiency Act (COMMERCE, GOVERNMENT REFORM AND OVERSIGHT, JUDICIARY, SCIENCE, BANKING AND FINANCIAL SERVICES)
H.R. 2991, Eshoo, Electronic Commerce Enhancement Act (GOVERNMENT REFORM AND OVERSIGHT, COMMERCE)

S. 376, Leahy,   Encrypted Communications Privacy Act (JUDICIARY)
S. 377, Burns, Promotion of Commerce On-Line in the Digital Era (COMMERCE, SCIENCE, AND TRANSPORTATION)
S. 909, McCain, Secure Public Networks Act (COMMERCE, SCIENCE, AND TRANSPORTATION)
S. 1594, Bennett, Digital Signature and Electronic Authentication Law (BANKING)
S. 2067, Ashcroft, Encryption Protects the Rights of Individuals from Violation and Abuse in Cyberspace (JUDICIARY)
P.L. 105-277 (Title XVII, Division C), S. 2107, Abraham, Government Paperwork Elimination Act (COMMERCE)

Computer Security (General)

H.R. 1903, Sensenbrenner, Computer Security Enhancement Act (SCIENCE)

Computer Privacy (General)

H.R. 98, Vento, Consumer Internet Privacy Protection (COMMERCE)
H.R. 1287, Bob Franks, Social Security On-line Privacy Protection (COMMERCE)
H.R. 1330, Kanjorski, American Family Privacy (GOVERNMENT REFORM AND OVERSIGHT)
H.R. 1331, Kennelly, Social Security Information Safeguards (WAYS AND MEANS)
H.R. 1367, Barrett, Federal Internet Privacy Protection (GOVERNMENT REFORM AND OVERSIGHT)
H.R. 1813, Kleczka, Personal Information Privacy (WAYS AND MEANS, BANKING AND FINANCIAL SERVICES, JUDICIARY)
H.R. 1964, Markey, Communications Privacy and Consumer Empowerment (COMMERCE)
H.R. 1972, Bob Franks, Children's Privacy Protection and Parental Empowerment (JUDICIARY)

H.R. 2368, Tauzin, Data Privacy Act (COMMERCE)

H.R. 3551, DeLauro, Identity Piracy Act (JUDICIARY, TRANSPORTATION AND INFRASTRUCTURE)

H.R. 3601, Shadegg, Identity Theft and Assumption Deterrence Act (JUDICIARY, TRANSPORTATION AND INFRASTRUCTURE)

P.L. 105-318, H.R. 4151, Shadegg, Identity Theft and Assumption Deterrence Act (JUDICIARY)

H.R. 4667, Markey, Electronic Privacy Bill of Rights (COMMERCE)

S. 504, Feinstein, Children's Privacy Protection and Parental Empowerment (JUDICIARY)

P.L. 105-318, S. 512, Kyl, Identify Theft and Assumption Deterrence Act (JUDICIARY)

S. 600, Feinstein, Personal Information Privacy (FINANCE)

P.L. 105-277 (Title XIII, Division C), S. 2326, Bryan, Children's Online Privacy Protection Act (COMMERCE)

Computer Privacy (Protecting Children from Pornography, Predators)

Filtering

HR 774, Lofgren, Internet Freedom and Child Protection (COMMERCE)

HR 1180, McDade, Family-Friendly Internet Access (COMMERCE)

H.R. 3177, Franks, Safe Schools Internet Act (COMMERCE)

S. 1619, McCain, Internet School Filtering Act (COMMERCE)

Other

H.R. 2173, Franks, Child Abuse Notification Act (JUDICIARY)

H.R. 2648, Bachus, Abolishing Child Pornography Act (JUDICIARY)

H.R. 2791, Roukema, Prohibition on Provision of Internet Service Accounts to Sexually Violent Predators (COMMERCE)

H.R. 2815, Weller, Protecting Children from Internet Predators (JUDICIARY)

P.L. 105-314, H.R. 3494, McCollum, Child Protection and Sexual Predator Punishment Act (JUDICIARY)

H.R. 3729, Pryce, Stop Trafficking of Pornography in Prisons (JUDICIARY)

P.L. 105-277 (Title XIV, Division C) H.R. 3783, Oxley, Child Online Protection Act (COMMERCE)

H.R. 3985, Lampson, Authorize Appropriations for International Child Pornography Investigation and Coordination Center of the Customs Service (WAYS AND MEANS)

S. 900, Feingold, Child Exploitation Sentencing Enhancement Act (JUDICIARY)

S. 1356, Faircloth, Prohibition on Provision of Internet Service Accounts to Sexually Violent Predators (COMMERCE, SCIENCE AND TRANSPORTATION)

P.L. 105-277 (Title XIV, Division C), S. 1482, Coats, Prohibition of Commercial Distribution on the World Wide Web of Material That is Harmful to Minors (COMMERCE)

S. 1965, Moseley-Braun, Internet Predator Prevention Act (JUDICIARY)

S. 1987, DeWine, Child Protection and Sexual Predator Punishment Act (JUDICIARY)

P.L. 105-314, S. 2491, Hatch, Protection of Children from Sexual Predators Act (JUDICIARY)

Computer Privacy (Medical Records Confidentiality)

H.R. 52, Condit, Fair Health Information Practices Act (COMMERCE, GOVERNMENT REFORM AND OVERSIGHT, JUDICIARY)

H.R. 1815, McDermott, Medical Privacy in the Age of Technologies Act (COMMERCE, GOVERNMENT REFORM AND OVERSIGHT)

H.R. 3900, Shays, Consumer Health and Research Technology Protection Act (COMMERCE, WAYS AND MEANS, GOVERNMENT REFORM AND OVERSIGHT)

S. 1368, Leahy, Medical Information Privacy and Security Act (LABOR AND HUMAN RESOURCES)

S. 1921, Jeffords, Health Care Personal Information Nondisclosure Act (LABOR AND HUMAN RESOURCES)

Intellectual Property

H.R. 2180, Coble, On-Line Copyright Liability Limitation Act (JUDICIARY)

P.L. 105-304, H.R. 2281, Coble, WIPO Copyright Treaties Implementation Act and On-Line Copyright Infringement Liability Limitation Act (JUDICIARY)

H.R. 2652, Coble, Collections of Information Antipiracy Act (JUDICIARY)

H.R. 3048, Boucher, Digital Era Copyright Enhancement Act (JUDICIARY)

H.R. 3209, Coble, On-Line Copyright Infringement Liability Limitation Act (JUDICIARY)

S. 1121, Hatch, WIPO Copyright and Performances and Phonograms Treaty Implementation Act of 1997 (JUDICIARY)

S. 1146, Ashcroft, Digital Copyright Clarification and Technology Education Act of 1997 (JUDICIARY)

P.L. 105-304, S. 2037, Hatch, Digital Millenium Copyright Act (JUDICIARY)

S. 2291, Grams, Collections of Information Antipiracy Act (JUDICIARY)

Unsolicited Commercial E-mail

H.R. 1748, Christopher Smith, Netizens Protection Act (COMMERCE)
H.R. 3888, Tauzin, Anti-Slamming Amendments (COMMERCE)
H.R. 4124, Cook, E-Mail User Protection Act (COMMERCE)
H.R. 4176, Markey, Digital Jamming Act, (COMMERCE)

S. 771, Murkowski, Unsolicited Commercial Electronic Mail Choice Act
    (COMMERCE, SCIENCE, AND TRANSPORTATION)
S. 875, Torricelli, Electronic Mailbox Protection Act (COMMERCE, SCIENCE, AND

    TRANSPORTATION)
S. 1618, McCain, Anti-Slamming Amendments (COMMERCE, SCIENCE, AND
    TRANSPORTATION)

Internet Domain Names

H.R. 3332, Sensenbrenner, Next Generation Internet Research Act (SCIENCE)

S. 1609, Frist, Next Generation Internet Research Act (COMMERCE, SCIENCE, AND
    TRANSPORTATION)
S. 1727, Leahy, to authorize the comprehensive independent study of the effects of
    trademark and intellectual property rights holders of adding new generic
    top-level domains and related dispute resolution procedures (JUDICIARY)

Related CRS Reports

Computer Fraud & Abuse: A Sketch of 18 U.S.C. 1030 And Related Federal Criminal Laws, by Charles Doyle. CRS Report 97-1024 A. 5 p. December 3, 1997.

Computer Fraud & Abuse: An Overview of 18 U.S.C. 1030 And Related Federal Criminal Laws, by Charles Doyle. CRS Report 97-1025 A. 85 p. November 28, 1997.

Critical Infrastructures: A Primer, by John Moteff. CRS Report 98-675 STM. 6 p. August 13, 1998.

"Digital Era Copyright Enhancement Act": Analysis of H.R. 3048, by Dorothy Schrader. CRS Report 98-520 A. 8 p. May 18, 1998.

Encryption and Banking, by M. Maureen Murphy. 12 p. CRS Report 97-835 A. September 15, 1997.

Encryption Export Controls, by Jeanne J. Grimmett. 6 p. CRS Report 97-837 A. September 12, 1997.

Encryption, Key Recovery & Law Enforcement: Selected Legal Issues and Legislative Proposals, by Charles Doyle. 41 p. CRS Report 97-845 A. September 12, 1997.

Encryption Technology and U.S. National Security, by Michael Vaden and Edward Bruner. 9 p. CRS Report 96-670 F. August 8, 1996.

Encryption Technology: Congressional Issues, by Richard Nunno. CRS Issue Brief 96039. 15 p. (Updated Regularly)

Indecency: Restrictions on Broadcast Media, Cable Television, and the Internet, by Henry Cohen. CRS Report 97-841 A. 14 p. September 12, 1997.

Information Privacy, by Gina Marie Stevens. CRS Report 97-833 A. 13 p. September 15, 1997.

Internet Domain Names: Background and Policy Issues, by Jane Bortnick Griffith. CRS Report 97-868 STM. 6 p. October 30, 1998.

Internet Gambling: A Sketch of Legislative Proposals, by Charles Doyle. CRS Report 980757 A. 17 p. September 14, 1998.

Internet: History, Infrastructure, and Selected Issues, by Rita Tehan. CRS Report 98-649 C. 21 p. July 28, 1998.

Internet Tax Bills in the 105ᵗʰ Congress, by Nonna Noto. CRS Report 98-509 E. 21 p. August 21, 1998.

Internet Technology, by Ivan Kaminow and Jane Bortnick Griffith. CRS Report 97-392 SPR. 6 p. December 24, 1997.

Medical Records Confidentiality, coordinated by Irene Stith-Coleman. CRS Issue Brief 98002. 15 p. (Updated Regularly)

Next Generation Internet, by Glenn J. McLoughlin. CRS Report 97-521 STM. 6 p. June 8, 1998.

Obscenity, Child Pornography, and Indecency: Recent Developments and Pending Issues, by Henry Cohen. CRS Report 98-670 A. 6 p. October 23, 1998.

Online Service Provider Copyright Liability: Analysis and Discussion of H.R. 2180 and S. 1146, by Dorothy Schrader. CRS Report 97-950 A. 15 p. April 14, 1998.

Protecting Privacy on the Internet: A Summary of Legislative Proposals, by Angela Choy, Marcia Smith, and Jane Bortnick Griffith. CRS Report 97-1061 STM. 6 p. December 19, 1997.

Restrictions on Minor's Access to Material on the Internet, by Henry Cohen. CRS Report 98-328 A. 6 p. July 16, 1998.

Telecommunications Discounts for Schools and Libraries: the "E-Rate" Program and Controversies, by Angele Gilroy. CRS Issue Brief 98040. 14 p. (Updated regularly).

Telemarketing Fraud: Congressional Efforts to Protect Consumers, by Bruce Mulock. CRS Report 98-514 E. 6 p. June 2, 1998.

World Intellectual Property Organization Copyright Treaty: An Overview, by Dorothy Schrader. CRS Report 97-444 A. 27 p. September 10, 1998.

WIPO Copyright Treaty Implementation Legislation: Recent Developments, by Dorothy Schrader. CRS Report 98-463. 17 p. September 24, 1998.

World Intellectual Property Organization Performance and Phonograms Treaty: An Overview, by Dorothy Schrader. CRS Report 97-523. 35 p. September 10, 1998.

Internet Policies and Issues
Volume 2

POINT AND CLICK: INTERNET SEARCHING TECHNIQUES

Rita Tehan

Challenges of Internet Searching

Finding information on the Internet can be challenging for even the most experienced searchers. Since the most popular means of accessing the Internet is through the World Wide Web (WWW), this report focuses on search strategies that locate Web information. Some search engines index gopher[1] and FTP (file transfer protocol)[2] sites as well as Web sites and Usenet newsgroups. When the most comprehensive search is needed, it might be necessary to search gopher and FTP sites using Archie and Veronica.[3]

If a searcher enters a simple query, such as "African elephant," into any of the top World Wide Web search engines, the resulting sets range from 503,644 hits in AltaVista, to 283,935 in Excite, 16,475 in HotBot, and 613,081 in InfoSeek. A quick review of the results shows some relevant hits near the top of each list, but retrieving so many items is counterproductive. Since there is no central catalog of Internet resources, a searcher must find other ways to retrieve more precise, relevant, and useful information. This report will suggest a number of strategies, tips, and techniques to use.

The tools that are available today are going to change, and there will be new and different ones a month or a week from now—or tomorrow. Ultimately you will find a handful of useful sites by trial and error. Bookmark[4] these and return to them for future reference. Internet sites may change their URL[5] addresses slightly, but usually only to move files from one directory to another. World Wide Web sites seldom disappear completely. If it is a valuable resource, the organization that created the

---

[1] See Glossary (p. 9) for definition.

[2] See Glossary (p. 9) for definition.

[3] Archie helps find files available at File Transfer Protocol (FTP) hosts. When searching for a particular term, Archie searches the database and displays the name of each FTP host that has that file or directory and the exact path to that directory. See *Archie Services*, a gateway to Archie servers on the Web at:[http://www.nexor.co.uk/archie.html/]

Veronica is an indexer that can query every gopher on the gopher system to search for a keyword or phrase in a menu title and give the address of all menus with those key words. gopher://munin.ub2.lu.se/11/resources/veronica

[4] See Glossary (p. 9) for definition.

[5] See Glossary (p. 9) for definition.

Web page has a stake in maintaining it. If the page moves, a responsible organization will provide a pointer URL to the new location.

Standards for Determining Information Quality

Almost anyone with an Internet connection can "publish" on the Web. Some criteria to consider when judging an Internet site's quality are:

Content. Is the site a provider of original content or merely a pointer site? What is the purpose of the site? Is it stated? Sites containing durable, timely, fresh, attributable information are more useful.

Comprehensiveness. What is the scope of the information? How deep and broad is the information coverage? If the site links to other resources, the links should be up-to-date and to appropriate resources.

Balance. Is the content accurate? (You may have to check other Internet or print resources.) Is it objective? If there are biases in the information, they should be noted at the site. The organization's motivation for placing the information on the Web should be clear (is it an advertisement? does it support a particular viewpoint?). An organization's Web page will provide information it wants to release and nothing more.

Currency. Is the site kept up-to-date? If it points to other sites, what percentage of the links work when you click on them? Dates of updates should be stated and correspond to the information listed in the resource.

Authority. Does the resource have a reputable organization or expert behind it? Who is the author? What is the author's authority? Does the author or institution have credibility in the field? Can the author be contacted for clarification or to be informed of new information? There is nothing wrong with amateur, club, or fan sites. In fact, they may deliver more passion and enthusiasm than professional sites. The researcher must remember, however, that many amateur sites have no standards for accuracy, no fact checkers, and no peer review board.

Where to Start

The first thing to decide is what type of resource is needed. One possibility is to obtain information from the World Wide Web; another would be to explore information posted to special interest e-mail lists or Usenet newsgroups. Some search engines concentrate on the Web, others focus on Usenet, and others, such as AltaVista and InfoSeek, let you search both. Many search engines scan for gopher and FTP sites as well.[6]

---

[6] For additional information on finding the best search tool for your needs, see: *How to* (continued...)

If you are looking for general information on a subject, start with subject guides, which are compiled and categorized by human indexers (discussed below). These are organized hierarchically, so you can move from broad topics to narrower ones. Once you find the correct terminology for your subject, you can use search engines to locate additional information. A rule of thumb for a comprehensive search would be to check three subject indexes and three search engines.

You will retrieve more information from a search engine than a subject index, because software robots[7] visit many more sites than human indexers. However, human indexers add structure and organization to their indexes.

Subject Guides

Subject guides typically present an organized hierarchy of categories for information browsing by subject. Under each category or sub-category, links to appropriate Web pages are listed. Some sites (for example, the Argus Clearinghouse) include subject guides that function as bibliographies for Internet resources and are authored by specialists.

The lack of a controlled vocabulary within and between different subject trees increases the difficulty of browsing them effectively. Some subject guides allow keyword searching, which is useful. Examples of well-organized and comprehensive subject guides are:

- Argus Clearinghouse (formerly the Subject-Oriented Clearinghouse Guide to Internet Resources): [http://www.clearinghouse.net/]
- Britannica Internet Guide: [http://www.ebig.com]
- Galaxy (formerly EINet Galaxy): [http://www.einet.net]
- Internet Public Library: [http://ipl.sils.umich.edu/ref/]
- Librarians' Index to the Internet: [http://sunsite.berkeley.edu/InternetIndex/]
- LookSmart: [http://www.looksmart.com/]
- World Wide Web Virtual Library: [http://www.w3.org/pub/DataSources/bySubject/Overview.html]
- [Yahoo: http://www.yahoo.com/]

---

[6](...continued)
Choose the Search Tools You Need from the University of California at Berkeley Library (updated January 15, 1998) at:
   http://www.lib.berkeley.edu/TeachingLib/Guides/Internet/ToolsTables.html

See also: *Tips on How to Search the Internet* from Sarnia Online at:
   http://www.sarnia.com/tech/class/searchtips.html

[7] See Glossary (p. 9) for definition.

Search Engines: Spiders, Crawlers, Robots

Search engines are automated software robots which typically begin at a known page and follow links from it to others, downloading pages and indexing them as they go.[8] Search engines vary according to the size of the index, the frequency of updating the index, the search options, the speed of returning a result, the relevancy of the results, and the overall ease of use. Unfortunately, no two search engines work the same way.[9]

To decide on which search engine to use, it helps to understand which parts of a Web page the search engines index. All search engines don't use the same syntax. For example, AltaVista, InfoSeek, and OpenText index every word of a Web page, while Lycos indexes the title, heading, and the most significant 200 words.

Search engines will also check to see if the keywords appear near the top of a Web page, such as in the headline or in the first few paragraphs of text. They assume that any page relevant to the topic will mention those words at the start. Many search engines ignore words of three or fewer letters, or will not search numbers (or a date).

These differences contribute to the different results returned by different search engines for the same query. Search engines are not in any way comprehensive maps of the Internet. The World Wide Web is simply too vast for even the most advanced search engine to cover adequately.

Frequency is the other major factor in how search engines determine relevancy. A search engine will analyze how often keywords appear in relation to other words in a Web page. Those with a higher frequency are often deemed more relevant that other Web pages.

Meta-search engines (MetaCrawler, SavvySearch, etc.) scan several search engines sequentially and eliminate duplicates, though not always reliably. The parallel (or meta-search) search engines are good for uncomplicated searches of very general concepts or very narrow searches of unique words or concepts, because you can't use advanced search techniques with them.

---

[8] For more information comparing the features of different search engines, spiders, robots, and crawlers, see "Search: Web Search Engines are Smarter and Stronger than Ever; We Test Six of the Best," by David Haskin, *Internet World*, December 1997, p. 79-92. See also *Top Keyword Resources of the Web*, March 19, 1997, from December Communications at: http://www.december.com/web/top/keyword.html

See also *A Higher Signal-to-Noise Ratio: Effective Use of Web Search Engines*, October 9, 1996 (last modified March 13, 1998), from the Wisconsin Educational Technology Conference, Green Bay, WI, at: http://www.dpi.state.wi.us/dpi/dlcl/lbstat/search2.html

[9] *Search Engine Watch*, from Mecklermedia, produces "Search Engine Facts and Fun," which gives information on how search engines work. Check the "Under the Hood of Search Engines" links at: http://searchenginewatch.com/facts/index.html

Examples of some of the most useful search engines are:[10]

- Altavista: [http://altavista.digital.com/]
- Excite: [http://www.excite.com/]
- Hotbot: [http://www.hotbot.com/]
- Infoseek: [http://www.infoseek.com/]
- Lycos: [http://www.lycos.com/]
- Metacrawler: [http://metacrawler.com/]
- Northern Light: [http://www.nlsearch.com/]
- Opentext: [http://www.opentext.com/]
- SavvySearch: [http://guaraldi.cs.colostate.edu:2000/]

There is no "best" search engine, and one search engine is not better than another at finding different types of documents (for example, government reports, or corporate press releases, or movie reviews). Search engines look for keywords, not concepts, so to find information on a particular topic, you need to create a precise search. That is why it is important to learn the advanced search syntax for a few different search engines, in order to refine and narrow a query when the number of items retrieved is too large.

Search Engine Features

- Most allow for phrase searching, usually by enclosing the phrase in quotation marks, for example, "aurora borealis."

- Most are case-insensitive, so you can enter a keyword in lower case, and the search engine will find both upper and lower case matches. Other search engines allow an exact match, which means you can retrieve words that are capitalized, such as "AIDS," or all lower case, such as "e.e. cummings."

- Most search for word variations. Some search engines support the asterisk (*) symbol (known as a wildcard) to find word variations. For example, if you enter "sing*," you will retrieve pages on singers, singing, and Sing Sing.

- Most allow for advanced searching. All of the top sites use Boolean search operators to help limit the set if a large number of results is retrieved. The most important of these is "AND." When you use "AND" in a search, for example, "travel AND Antarctica," the search engine will find Web pages where both those words appear. Another useful Boolean operator is "NOT" (or "AND NOT" in Alta Vista). For example, if the search is for "beetle NOT volkswagen," the search engine will find information on the insect and not the automobile. Some search engines allow you to use the Boolean operator

---

[10] Some sites with compilations of multiple search engines are:
All-in-One Search Page at: http://www.albany.net/allinone/
Scout Toolkit: Searching the Internet at:
    http://scout.cs.wisc.edu/scout/toolkit/searching/index.html
WebCrawler: Database of Web Robots, Overview at:
    http://info.webcrawler.com/mak/projects/robots/active/html/index.html

"NEAR." For example, "vaccine NEAR HIV." In this case, both words will be in the document and within a few words of each other.

Search Tips

- Read the help pages of the search engines you use regularly. These explain how to search, what is and is not covered by the database, and special syntax or retrieval rules. Take advantage of advanced searching features, such as narrowing the results by document title, date, or domain (i.e., .gov, .edu, .com, etc.)

- To increase the chance of precision searching, try to use unique or uncommon words or acronyms, especially when using a parallel search engine (such as Metacrawler or SavvySearch). If there is a synonym or less common word, this will reduce the number of items retrieved. Also remember to vary the spelling to account for differences in British or other spelling (for example, colour or labour.)

- Think of which organizations are interested in the subject and visit those Web sites to see if they provide position papers or link to material on it. For example, if you wanted to find information on handgun control issues, check the Web pages for the National Rifle Association and the Center to Prevent Handgun Violence.

- Use specialized search engines or indexes. These focus on collecting relevant sites for a particular subject. Some examples are:

  FindLaw—legal resources: http://www.findlaw.com
  Health Finder—health resources: http://www.healthfinder.gov
  Govbot—government information:
      http://www.business.gov/Search_Online.html

- If you do not find anything useful with one search engine, try another. There is surprisingly little overlap when using the same query in more than one Web search engine.

Some Common Problems

- *The search engine did not find a Web page you know is available.* No search engine—**none of them**—indexes everything on the Web. If the page is new, it is possible the Web robot has not found it yet. The search phrase or term is checked against an index of documents that the robot has scanned on a previous indexing run. While some robots search the Web continuously, others go out only once a week or every 2 or 3 weeks.[11] Some dynamic sites, by their very nature, are impossible to index correctly. News sites such as

---

[11] *Search Engine Tutorial for Web Designers*, from Northern Webs. The "Search Engine Summary" is a chart comparing database update times for seven major search engines. http://www.digital-cafe.com/~webmaster/set01.html#summary

CNN or the *New York Times* are updated daily. No search engine can find very recent material.

It's possible the desired document may be on a server that is not within a robot's scope. For example, files on a gopher or FTP server are missed by Web search tools that index only Web pages (only HTML files on Web servers).

Information can vanish for other reasons. Webmasters move pages or entire sites without notifying search engines. Pages are deleted when customers' accounts are terminated. The job of keeping search engine indexes up-to-date is unrelenting.

- *The Web robot found the document but was not permitted to access it.* If the page you want is on a server protected by a firewall,[12] access will be denied. Most search engines skip sites that demand a password or registration for entrance, even those like the *New York Times*, which offer passwords free of charge. Additionally, some Web servers install software specifically to prohibit Web robots from entering. Some search engines cannot index sites with frames or image maps.

- *The Web robot could not access the document, at least for the moment.* This problem is related to the vagaries of Internet traffic and connectivity. The Internet is most congested during the afternoon hours. If you see a message such as "no DNS entry found," this is an indication that the host server is busy or unavailble. Frequently, an immediate attempt to reconnect will be successful.

Usenet News Groups and E-mail Discussion Lists

Usenet is a discussion system distributed worldwide. It consists of a set of "newsgroups" with names that are classified hierarchically by subject. There are 15,000 newsgroups organized according to their specific areas of concentration. The groups are organized in a tree structure which has seven major categories: *Comp* (of interest to computer professionals and hobbyists, *Rec* (oriented towards hobbies and recreational activities, *Sci* (research or applications in the general sciences), *Soc* (discusses issues of different world cultures), *Talk* (debate oriented, general topics), *News* (concerned with the newsgroup network, maintenance, and software), and *Misc* (groups not easily classified into the other headings, or which incorporate themes from multiple categories). For example, fans of Stephen Sondheim could read articles posted to the *alt.music.sondheim* or the *rec.arts.theatre.musicals* newsgroups.

"Articles" or "messages" are "posted" to these newsgroups by people on computers with the appropriate software; these articles are then broadcast to other interconnected computer systems via a wide variety of networks. Some newsgroups

---

[12] See Glossary (p. 9) for definition.

are "moderated"; in these newsgroups, the articles are first sent to a moderator for approval before appearing in the newsgroup.[13]

Human expertise is very accessible on the Web. A researcher can find information from other people via Usenet newsgroups, listservs, or an e-mail link on a Web page.

The Web site *Reference.com* (http://www.reference.com/) allows you to find, browse, search, and participate in more than 150,000 newsgroups, mailing lists, and Web forums.

Before posting to a Usenet group, read its Frequently Asked Questions (FAQ) guide. Chances are good that your question will be answered there. The FAQ is often compiled by the experts who moderate a particular newsgroup. Two good sources of Usenet FAQs are the *FAQ Archive* at:
[http://www.cis.ohio-state.edu/hypertext/faq/usenet/FAQ-List.html] and *The FAQ Finder* at: [http://faqfinder.cs.uchicago.edu:8001/]

Another good practice is to read a few discussion threads before posting a question to a newsgroup. You will get a feeling for the group's style and attitudes and will reduce the chance of getting "flamed"[14] for posting an inappropriate query.

When you send a message to a Usenet group, your question may be sent out globally. People who take the time to answer are likely to feel strongly about the issue or have information that you need. Such direct personal communication is one of the Usenet's strengths. Some of its weaknesses, however, are that some Usenet groups are unmoderated, and there is no way to verify that a poster is who he/she claims to be, or that what they say is true.

If you see that a particular person frequently posts to a certain Usenet group or seems to be informative on a particular subject, you can search for the poster's name in *DejaNews* [http://www.dejanews.com/] to see what else he/she has written on that (or any other) topic.

An e-mail discussion list is a computerized mailing list in which a group of people are sent messages pertaining to a particular topic. The messages can be articles, comments, or whatever is appropriate to that topic. There are more than 70,000 electronic mailing lists on every imaginable topic.

E-mail lists have been used for more than a decade to distribute information efficiently to research and academic communities. Scholarly lists/newsgroups are still more common than scholarly Web sites. To find listservs on various topics, check the *Publicly Accessible Mailing Lists* at: [http://www.neosoft.com/internet/paml/] or *Liszt* at: [http://www.liszt.com].

---

[13] For more information on Usenet, see "What is Usenet" at the *FAQ Archive* at: http://www.cis.ohio-state.edu/hypertext/faq/usenet/usenet/what-is/part1/faq.html

[14] See Glossary (p. 9) for definition.

Gopher versus Web

The probability of finding something current, valuable, important, and unique on a gopher diminishes as the Web becomes more popular and gophers less so. Gophers are becoming less well-maintained. However, gophers cannot be ignored because a lot of static (but still useful) information is conveyed via gopher. Most search engines also index gophers. A catalog of many of the best Gopher sites by category is *Gopher Jewels* at: [http://galaxy.einet.net/GJ/]

Miscellaneous Sources

Additional information on Internet searching is available at the Library of Congress Home Page. See "Internet Search Tools" at:
[http://lcweb.loc.gov/global/search.html]

Internet News

The sites listed below provide annotated evaluations of new Internet resources within a few days of their availability. A user can also subscribe to them via e-mail, if desired. Most of the sites archive their previous issues, so it is not necessary to keep copies of postings.

- CNet Digital Dispatch: [http://www.cnet.com/]
- Edupage: [http://www.educom.edu/]
- Net Happenings: [http://scout.cs.wisc.edu/scout/net-hap]
- Netsurfer Digest: [http://www.netsurf.com/nsd/]
- Scout Report: [http://www.scout.cs.wisc.edu/scout/report/index.html]

Glossary

Bookmark — Using a World Wide Web browser, a bookmark is a saved link to a Web site. Like bookmarks for paper books, Web bookmarks are markers that permit you to quickly return to a Web page. Netscape and some other browsers use the term "bookmark." Microsoft's Internet Explorer uses the term "favorite."

Firewall — A dedicated gateway machine with special security precautions on it, used to service outside network connections and dial-in lines. The firewall protects a cluster of more loosely administered machines hidden behind it from individuals attempting to gain unauthorized access.

Flame — An electronic mail or Usenet news message intended to insult, provoke, or rebuke; the act of sending such a message.

FTP — The FTP command allows an Internet-connected computer to contact another computer, log-on anonymously, retrieve texts, graphics, audio, or computer program files, and transfer desired files back to itself.

Gopher — The gopher software program, developed at the University of Minnesota, organizes information into a series of menus. Using gopher is like browsing a table of contents: a user crawls through a set of "nested" menus to zero in on a specific subject.

Robot — A program that automatically explores the World Wide Web by retrieving a document and retrieving some or all the documents that are referenced in it. This is in contrast with normal Web browsers that are operated by a human and do not automatically follow links other than graphic images and redirections (pointers to new URLs).

Search engine — A remotely accessible program that lets you do keyword searches for information on the Internet. There are several types of search engines; the search may cover titles of documents, URLs, headers, or full text.

URL — Uniform Resource Locator is the unique Internet address which begins with "http://" This address is used to specify a WWW server and home page. For example, the House of Representatives URL is: [http://www.house.gov] and the Senate URL is: [http://www.senate.gov].

Internet Policies and Issues
Volume 2

NEXT GENERATION INTERNET

Glenn J. McLoughlin

Summary

The Next Generation Internet (NGI) proposal by the Clinton Administration would advance the current state of the Internet, advance university research capabilities, and assist federal agencies to achieve their missions. For the current fiscal year, FY1998, Congress provided less funding for NGI ($85 million) than the Clinton Administration requested ($100 million). This was because many congressional policymakers did not agree with the Administration that the Department of Energy should receive new funding to support its existing Internet and computing program. FY1999, the Administration has recommended $110 million for the NGI. On April 14, 1998, Vice President Gore announced that the Clinton Administration would work with industry to create an "Internet2" to enhance network connections. Two bills have been introduced, S. 1609 and H.R. 3332, to re-authorize NGI funding for FY1999 and FY2000. Both have been reported favorably out of their respective committees.

Background

Federal efforts to support computer and telecommunications applications and education have been strongly endorsed by the Clinton Administration since 1993. The Administration has sought to create a National Information Infrastructure (NII) through policies that will foster an environment conducive to the growth of technologies, networks, and applications.[1] In addition to the government, activities in academic and industry are intended to improve existing computational and communications technologies and applications for data transmission, storage, and retrieval.

In October 1996, President Clinton called for a renewed resolve to create the Next Generation Internet. His NGI proposal combines both policy and program prescriptions in three components. First, he recommended an additional $100 million per year for 5 years in federal investment for technological advances based on the U.S. university

---

[1] See: U.S. Library of Congress. Congressional Research Service. *The National Information Infrastructure: The Federal Role*, by Glenn J. McLoughlin. CRS Issue Brief 95051.

initiative ("Internet2"). This component includes three goals: connect at least 100 universities and national laboratories at speeds at least 100 times those that are currently available, and in the future connect additional institutions at speeds 1000 times greater than today; promote experimentation of the next generation of network technologies; and demonstrate new applications for national goals and missions.[2]

On January 28, 1998, President Clinton announced in his State of the Union address continued support for the NGI. On February 2, 1998, President Clinton included multi-agency funding for NGI as part of its FY1999 budget proposal. (See Table 1).

Table 1: Clinton Request for NGI in FY1999
Compared to FY1998 Appropriations
(in millions of dollars)

AGENCY	Clinton Request	FY1998 Approp.
DOD	40	42
DOE	25	-a
NASA	10	10
NSF	25	23
NIST	5	5
NLM/ NIH	5	5
TOTAL	110	85

ª The Clinton Administration request for the Department of Energy's (DOE's) participation in the NGI included $25 million for new funding and use of $10 million of existing (FY1997) agency funding. Congress approved only the use of existing DOE funding for the NGI, $10 million.

In February 1998, the National Coordinating Office that oversees the NGI released its second printing of the NGI Implementation Plan.[3] This document supplants the first draft NGI Implementation Plan released in June 1997. The February 1998 NGI

---

[2] President Clinton proposed two additional NII efforts in the original NGI proposal. He called for U.S. industry leaders to help raise money to match government-sponsored technology literacy programs at schools. This joint government-industry "challenge" would be intended to ensure that all schoolchildren have access to information and communication technologies. Also, the President called for the Federal Communications Commission (FCC) to approve a proposal making Internet connections free for all schools and libraries, as provided in P.L. 104-104, the Telecommunications Act of 1996.

[3] See: NGI Implementation Plan at http://www.ngi.gov/plan.html.

Implementation Plan is intended to supplement the NGI Initiative Concept Paper.[4] Both the NGI Implementation Plan and Initiative Concept Paper were released to answer questions raised by many about the NII.

The NII Implementation Plan highlights the link between the federal government's role in helping create the Internet and its explosive growth over the last several decades. The Internet has grown in size at nearly 100% per year since 1968, and traffic has been growing at a rate of 400% per year in recent years. By the year 2000, according to the NCO, more than 50% of the population will have access to the Internet. To facilitate increased growth and traffic, the NII is intended to develop the types of networks which are more powerful and versatile by supplementing and eventually superseding the current Internet structure.[5]

Table 2: Program Funding: FY1998 Appropriations for NGI
(in millions of dollars)

Program Title	DOD	NSF	NASA	NIST	NLM/ NIH	TOTAL
Experimental Research	20	5	2	3	-a	30
Next Generation Network Testbed	20	10	3	-a	-a	33
Revolutionary Applications	2	8	5	2	5	22
TOTAL	42	23	10	5	5	85

Source: National Economic Council, Office of the White House. Washington, DC. February 6, 1997.
    [a] The 105th Congress did not provide specific funding levels.

The Implementation Plan has three program goals. The first is **Experimental Research for Advanced Network Technologies**. Activities that will support this program goal include network growth engineering, end-to-end quality of service for networks, and network and communications security. The second program goal is **Next Generation Network Testbed**. If one views the Internet as a series of connected network strands comprising a fabric of connections, then this goal is intended to boost high-speed connectivity and performance. Two activities would be directed towards achieving this goal: a minimum improvement of 100x greater speed and capacity over current Internet connections for 100 participating institutions, and the creation of ten high-risk ultrahigh speed switching sites. The third goal is **Revolutionary Applications**. This is to combine

---

[4] The NGI Concept Paper was released in June 1997. As of February 1998, there has not been a second printing of the Concept Paper like there has been of the Implementation Plan. See: NGI Initiative Concept Paper at http://www.ccic.gov/ngi/concept-Jul97/introduction.html.

[5] NGI Initiative Implementation Plan at http://www.ccic.gov/ngi/implementation-Jul97/exec-summary.html.

the missions of federal agencies and the needs of universities, federal laboratories and industry with innovative applications. This could include the further development and use of digital libraries and telemedicine.[6]

The Concept Paper provides a broad outline for the development and applications of the NGI. The paper states that today's Internet "suffers from its own success" due to the large number of users and the heavy traffic of data sent across networks. The federal participation in the NGI is critical, according to the NGI Concept Paper, because "critical Federal missions require a next generation Internet for their success." The long-term and high-risk cost of this development makes it unlikely that the private sector will undertake all of the NGI. The paper stresses the importance of high-speed network computations and communications and its role in education, commerce, and medicine.

Internet 2

In the fall of 1995, just before the Administration announced its NGI proposal, over 200 universities committed to developing an expanded version of the Internet. This proposal would expand current Internet connections with greater data transmission capacity. It was called "Internet2." From 1996 through the beginning of 1998, university, industry and federal leaders and policymakers sought to develop the Internet2 through a variety of proposals. On April 14, 1998, Vice President Gore announced that several high technology companies, in concert with many of the universities already committed to Internet2, would provide $500 million for the Internet2. In addition, the Department of Defense would use $50 million over several years as part of the NGI to contribute to the Internet2.

105th Congress

First Session

On April 16, 1997, the House Committee on Science considered several authorization bills for FY1998. For four of the five agencies listed above, the committee voted to prohibit any funding for the NGI.[7] During this process, many policymakers expressed support for the idea of the NGI. However, they also had concerns about its lack of program details, why certain agencies are receiving more funding than others, and whether certain applications can be better left to the private sector.

On June 3, the Senate Committee on Commerce held a hearing on the future of the Internet and the relevance of the NGI proposal. Very strong concern was expressed by several Senators on the committee that the NGI proposal does not address the needs of residents in rural states. In particular, both Senators Stevens and Burns voiced displeasure that of the twenty members on the private sector advisory panel for the NGI, eleven are from California, and that rural states are under-represented. In addition, Senator Wyden

---

[6] Ibid.

[7] These bills were: H.R. 1273 (NSF), H.R. 1274 (NIST), H.R. 1275 (NASA), and H.R. 1277 (DOE). These four bills were approved by the House of Representatives by voice vote on April 24, 1997. The fifth bill, H.R. 1119 (DOD) was reported out of another committee.

echoed concerns raised earlier in the House of Representatives that the NGI lacks direction and coordination among federal agencies.[8]

On September 10, 1997, the House Committee on Science held hearings on the NGI. Committee chairman Sensenbrenner and other members of the committee expressed concern that Congress did not have enough details to adequately assess the specific program functions, goals, and administration of the NGI. Dr. John H. Gibbons, director of the Office of Science and Technology Policy, promised to address these concerns by providing additional program details. Dr. Gibbons also assured members of the committee that the July 1997 NGI draft more clearly and accurately describes the NGI as a research, rather than a technology deployment, initiative.[9]

On November 4, 1997, the Senate Committee on Commerce held hearings on the NGI. Several members of the committee expressed support for the NGI, but also raised concerns about connecting residents in rural states to the Internet, coordinating a broad federal interagency effort efficiently and effectively, and making sure that all, not just a select few, are served by the Internet. Witnesses testifying before the committee largely commended the federal effort to create the NGI, although cautioning that the government not try to micromanage the future course and direction of Internet growth.

Second Session

Congress has responded to these concerns by providing some, but not all, of the funding for the NGI for FY1998. For some agencies, such as DOE, there is a wide discrepancy between what the Clinton Administration requested, and what the 105th Congress approved for FY1998. Still, many policymakers have voiced stronger support for the NGI proposal. Several issues, such as redundancy with existing agency programs, the availability of rapidly developing commercial technologies, and concerns about the size and scope of the federal effort have been addressed by Administration officials.

On February 4, 1998, Senator Frist introduced The Next Generation Internet Research Act of 1998 (S. 1609). This bill is intended to amend the High Performance Computing Act of 1991 to authorize appropriations for NGI for FY1999 and FY2000. Other issues addressed in S. 1609 include updating and expanding the definition of "network" under federal statute and implementing better federal agency coordination of NGI policies and programs. A similar bill was introduced by Representative Sensenbrenner (H.R. 3332), also to re-authorize NGI funding for the next two fiscal years. Both bills have been reported favorably out of respective committees in the Senate and House of Representatives and await further action.

Another issue facing federal policymakers is the Clinton Administration's recommendation in its FY1999 budget request that the NGI be part of a larger federal Large Scale Networks (LSN) initiative. The LSN initiative would cost $850 million for the next fiscal year, and would replace the Computing, Information, and Communications R&D program currently supported by federal agencies. Some policymakers are

---

[8] U.S. Senate. Committee on Commerce. Hearing on the NGI. [Unpublished]. June 3, 1997.

[9] New Plan for Next Generation Internet: Is It Too Little Too Late? *Science & Technology in Congress.* October 1997: 1, 3.

questioning why the NGI should be a part of the LSN initiative, and why the LSN initiative has replaced the CIC R&D program.

Issues

Many in government, academia, and industry support the NGI. In 1995, the National Research Council published a report, *Evolving the High Performance Computing and Communications Initiative to Support the Nation's Infrastructure*. This report reflected public and private sector interest that federal support for high performance computing and communications be maintained. Included as part of the high performance computing and communications technologies are network connections, technologies, and applications. Similarly, this interest in advancing network capabilities was central to the "Internet II" initiative by U.S. universities in the fall of 1996. For many, the exponential growth of Internet use is sowing the seeds of yet slower network response times for users, greater security concerns in network use, and limiting computing processing at research facilities connected to the Internet (as transmitting and compiling data grows more cumbersome).

Even if there is general agreement that upgrading the Internet and related technologies is appropriate, many questions remain. One question many ask is: how much of the Next Generation Internet should be the government's responsibility, and how much should it be the private-sector or universities'? While it is unlikely that either the federal government could support the NGI all on its own, it also is clear that the private sector will unlikely bear its total cost, or that universities can go beyond "Internet II." Yet there is no agreement as to where disparate interests meet, and where the risk and cost can be shared. The NGI is intended to improve computing and communications capabilities for scientific research and support federal agencies in achieving their missions. But it is clear that, just as with the original Internet, others subsequently may benefit greatly from the NGI. Should the private sector and more universities contribute more significantly to the NGI than is in the current proposal?

Concerns also have been raised about how to manage the NGI as a large interagency federal program. Can federal coordination of NGI effectively administer multiple programs across several agencies, and avoid duplicating federal computer and network programs and activities? During the FY1998 budget consideration, congressional policymakers raised the issue of federal coordination and scope of NGI programs. Some would prefer that agencies receive incremental budget increases which reflect a more modest and decentralized approach to networking advances.

Finally, many are still concerned that participation in drafting the NGI Concept Paper and Implementation Plan has been too narrow. Members of Congress from rural states contend that their states have not had input into, nor will benefit from, the NGI. Representatives from the Clinton Administration have pledged to broaden participation in future NGI planning and implementation meetings. This may be a crucial issue which determines congressional support for the initiative. In a larger sense, it is also a crucial issue which will determine that the NGI does not contribute to 21st century "haves" and "have nots" in an advanced networked society.

Internet Policies and Issues
Volume 2

INTERNET TECHNOLOGY

Ivan P. Kaminow and Jane Bortnick Griffith

Summary

The Internet is often described as a "network of networks" because it is not a single physical entity but, in reality, hundreds of thousands of interconnecting networks (hence the term Internet). This global connectivity is the result of the initial network design by Internet pioneers that created a simple, common standard for linking computers over telecommunications networks. The Internet continues to grow at a fast pace and new hardware and software provide enhanced capacity and new services. The most popular Internet applications today are electronic mail and the World Wide Web. Rapid growth and the prospect for further expansion of the Internet have raised many issues for policymakers. Knowledge of the underlying technology provides a basis for analyzing public policy issues related to the Internet.

Introduction

The Internet links millions of host computers around the world. Each host may be linked to smaller local networks, such as office networks, that typically link several computers, or to individual computers that connect over conventional phone lines. As a result,

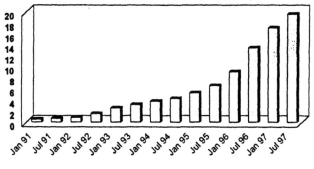

Growth of Internet Hosts (in millions)

millions of computer users worldwide are capable of exchanging many kinds of information easily. The Internet continues to grow at an enormous pace as indicated in the accompanying figure.

Making the Connection: The Telephone

With the growing popularity of the Internet, computer and consumer electronics manufacturers, cable operators, and other service providers are competing to provide Internet access in a variety of ways at lower costs. The competition follows naturally from the convergence of the underlying technologies. Computer data, and increasingly voice and video signals are processed, stored, and transported digitally.[1] The next generation of television equipment, called Advanced Television (ATV), will be digital instead of analog. Hence, any digital network, appropriately designed, will be able to deliver many electronic information services.

The Internet originated with research funding provided by the Department of Defense Advanced Research Projects Agency (DARPA).[2] Its initial goals were to create a military network connecting critical computers and providing remote computer access to military commanders, which could survive enemy attack. As its use expanded, a civilian segment evolved under the National Science Foundation (NSF) and other science agencies. For many years, experimental networks linked research computers in university, industrial, and government labs. They provided a means for sharing resources, exchanging computer files, and exchanging messages electronically. When the Internet began to thrive, the government decided to leave commercial development to U.S. industry, turning over support of the U.S. Internet backbone to the private sector in April 1995. NSF and several other science agencies continue to fund advanced networking for the research and education communities.

The key technical idea that enabled the Internet to grow so successfully was *open architecture networking*. This allowed network service providers much greater flexibility to design their systems independently as long as they could link through a high-level interconnection protocol. That was a significant departure from the traditional circuit-switching approach used by the telephone network.[3]

Telephone and Internet Technology

Most people see the Internet in terms of how they use it for applications, such as sending electronic mail (*email*) or retrieving information from a World Wide Web site. These are described more fully below. The computer interface is designed to be "transparent," so that the user does not "see" the intervening physical network. Because the telephone network and the Internet are closely related, but have significant distinctions, analysis of legislative issues concerning appropriate government roles and regulatory frameworks requires a modest understanding of the underlying technical infrastructure.

---

[1] Digital signals convert information into binary digits or bits, which are ones or zeros used to represent different kinds of data. See Congressional Research Service, *Telecommunication Signal Transmission: Digital vs Analog.* by Richard M. Nunno, Report 96-401, 7 May 1996.

[2] For an overview of the history, growth, and costs of the Internet, see Congressional Research Service, *Welcome to Cyberia: An Internet Overview.* by Rita Tehan, Report 96-242.

[3] Leiner, Cerf, Clark, Kahn, Kleinrock, Lynch, Postel, Roberts, and Wolff, *A Brief History of the Internet,* Available online at: http://www.isoc.org/internet-history. For another useful history of the Internet see also: John Adams, "Geek Gods," *Washingtonian*, November 1996, p. 66.

Connection: The Telephone

A good illustration of underlying telephone technology is provided by following a long distance call connection. The dial tone indicates a connection to a local central telephone office. The dialed ten-digit number is forwarded through a switch in the central office to a regional office, which sets up a path dedicated to the call through switches configured to handle the traffic across the country. The path is determined by automatically updated "routing tables," which take account of nationwide traffic patterns and possible equipment outages to select the optimum path. The switches in the local central office and the regional office are owned by a Local Exchange Carrier (LEC), such as Bell Atlantic, serving the originating area code. The next switch in the sequence may be owned by an Interexchange Carrier (IXC), such as AT&T, selected by the paying party. The IXC switches continue across the country to the area code of the destination. The final switches are the regional and local switches of the destination LEC, such as Mountain Bell. After the telephone rings and is answered, the circuit from the calling telephone, through all the switches, to the called telephone is assigned to that two-way conversation for the duration of the call — even if there are long silences.

The sound pressure of the speaker's voice is converted by the telephone instrument into an electrical current that is an exact replica, or analog, of the sound. At the first switch, the analog signal is converted to a digital code that represents the same information by a stream of regularly spaced *bits* (binary digits), which are electrical pulses that may be present (as "ones") or absent (as "zeros"). Because of their simplicity, digital signals can be manipulated much more readily than analog signals to eliminate extraneous noise and distortions. In addition, many calls can be combined by intermingling their bits to provide more efficient transmission on a high-speed cable. In summary: (1) telephone circuits are switched over networks owned by several independent, regulated companies that have cooperative agreements for exchanging traffic, maintaining quality, and billing calls; (2) the circuits are dedicated to the call and not shared (i.e., they are circuit-switched); (3) the charge (but not the cost) is proportional to the time and distance of the call (i.e., metered or usage-based charging); and (4) except for the first and last segments (of about one mile each), signals are digital.

Making the Connection: The Internet

An Internet connection operates differently from a telephone connection. Generally, the connection can take one of two configurations. In an organization — a business, a university, a government agency — individual workstations often are connected through a local area network (LAN) to a host computer that serves the organization. As a user composes an email message, for example, the keystrokes are stored digitally in his workstation. When the message is transmitted, the mail is transferred to the host computer. The host can distribute email and other services to clients on the LAN, or route it to an Internet gateway computer.

For the user at home, a cheaper solution is to dial up an Internet Service Provider (ISP) by telephone when access is desired. A modem, which converts the digital signals to analog signals and vice versa, installed in the home computer provides a telephone connection from the computer through the telephone central office to one of a bank of modems at the ISP. Currently, most commonly installed modems operate at 28.8

Electronic Mail

Electronic mail is the application that initially popularized the Internet. It allows a user to type an address or a group of addresses, compose a message, and send it to another user, a group of users, or a computer that can respond with textual information. The destination may be in the next office or residence, on the same campus, or on the other side of the Earth. Each user is assigned an address by the administrator of the host network serving that office, or by the Internet Service Provider (ISP) providing access from home.

Email Addresses

The addresses consist of a user name and a domain name. Examples include: *user@mail.house.gov* for the House e-mail server; *user@aol.com* for a user connected to America Online as Internet Service Provider; or *user@lab1.ntt.com.jp* for a user at lab1 in NTT in Japan. The portion to the right of @ (the "at" symbol) is the domain name, which gets wider in scope as one moves to the right. The "top level domains" (TLDs) *.com, .org, .edu, .gov, .mil*, and *.net* represent company, organizational, educational, governmental, military, and networking enterprises, respectively, and *.jp* or *.us* represent country domains. The actual addresses (called IP addresses) are numerical and are translated by a domain name server from the name addresses, such as those above. Recently proposals have been made to expand the number of TLDs. For a more extensive discussion of domain names see: CRS Report 97-868.

World Wide Web

The key application that has produced the recent dramatic increase in Internet traffic is the World Wide Web (WWW). It is based on the traditional academic concept of providing the reader with further references in a text. In the Web application, instead of footnotes or references, certain author-designated words or phrases are highlighted as *hypertext*. Companies can offer a wide array of distributed information and can advertise products in this manner. A simple click on the hypertext brings the associated file to the screen. If multiple series of links from a home page to subsequent references and back to the home page are mapped out, the map resembles a web; hence the term "world-wide web."

The real explosion of Web usage began when user-friendly software or *browsers* became available that offered attractive color graphics for retrieving Web pages. To access the Web, the user types in an address that is similar to an email address. However, the addresses generally are prefaced with "http://", where *http* refers to the *hypertext transfer protocol* (or software convention), while the *hypertext markup language* (*html*) provides the linking capability built into the Web software on servers and browsers. Web addresses are designated as Universal Resource Locators (URLs).

Internet Policies and Issues
Volume 2

THE COPYRIGHT DOCTRINE OF FAIR USE AND THE INTERNET: CASELAW

Douglas Reid Weimer

ABSTRACT

This report examines the evolving copyright doctrine of fair use within the context of copyrighted works published or placed on the Internet. American courts have been examining the various property rights of copyright owners concurrently with the unauthorized use of these copyrighted materials by Web site operators, Internet consumers, access providers, and other interested parties. This report analyzes the early fair use copyright cases concerning Internet use, as well as the most recent judicial interpretations.

Domestic case law has been developing which examines the copyright doctrine of fair use within the context of copyrighted works placed on the Internet without the permission of the copyright owner. Various efforts are being undertaken by the courts, Congress, and the industry to divide enforcement responsibilities and protection rights among the various interested parties: the copyright owners, the access providers, Web site operators, and Internet consumers.[1]

Generally speaking, American courts have considered the placement or publication of copyrighted materials on the Internet to be another form of expression or communication. Hence, the courts have applied a fair use legal analysis in Internet cases similar to that applied with respect to more traditional forms of communication. The report examines the statutory background and development of the fair use doctrine in copyright law and its application to works placed on the Internet.

Background

The copyright owner possesses various exclusive ownership rights in the work.[2] However, the fair use doctrine permits, under certain circumstances, the unauthorized use of copyrighted works. The doctrine, which has its origins in common law, was first codified in the Copyright Act of 1976.[3] The statute provides four criteria for the determination of whether the unauthorized use of a work is a "fair" use, or whether it is an infringing use.[4] These are: 1) the amount and character of the use; 2) the nature of the copryighted work; 3) the amount copied in relation to the whole copyrighted work; and 4) the effect of the copying on the potential market for the

---

[1] This report is limited to an examination of the domestic issues concerning the copyright doctrine of fair use within the context of the Internet. International copyright law and the Internet may present various currently unresolved concerns and legal issues.

[2] 17 U.S.C. § 106. These ownership rights include the rights to do and to authorize: 1) *reproduction* of the work; 2) preparation of *derivative works*; 3) *distribution* of copies of the work to the public by sale or other transfer; 4) with literary, musical, dramatic, and choreographic works and other works, *performance* of the work publicly; 5) with literary, musical, dramatic, and other works, the *display* of the copyrighted work publicly; and 6) in the case of sound recordings, public performance of digital audio transmissions.

[3] 17 U.S.C. § 107.

[4] If a use is infringing, the copyright owner may bring an action for infringement against the unauthorized user of the copyrighted work. 17 U.S.C. § 411.

copyrighted work.[5] Courts have examined the factual circumstances surrounding each case and have applied these criteria on a case-by-case basis.[6]

The Internet is a cooperative network of networks.[7] It links millions of users nationally and internationally, including individuals, schools, libraries, and corporations. There is no single individual or organization that owns, oversees, or controls the Internet. For many users, the costs of accessing the Internet are paid by their organizations, such as universities, national laboratories, corporations, and governments.[8] Other individuals pay subscription fees to Internet service providers, like American Online or CompuServe, which provide links to the Internet.[9] The World Wide Web is the Internet's most popular application. The growing number of Web sites and bulletin boards[10] provides great distribution capabilities for all types of material. Since computers can reproduce virtually perfect copies of copyrighted works, including text, audio, and video, the Internet provides the potential for distributing and redistributing replicas of copyrighted material to large numbers of Internet users. The technological achievements of the Internet have greatly increased the possibilities for copyright infringement.[11]

Internet users who view information and download that information are copying. If the material that is being copied is copyrighted, the possibility of infringement may rest upon an application of the fair use doctrine to the circumstances surrounding the unauthorized use of the material.[12] By viewing materials on the Internet, there is a fixation of materials on a computer's Random Access Memory (RAM). This fixation in the RAM may support an infringement claim based upon the copyright owner's

---

[5] 17 U.S.C. § 107.

[6] See, CRS Rept. No. 95-888, *Copyright and Fair Use After Acuff-Rose and Texaco;* CRS Rept. No. 93-396, *Copyright Law: Recent Case law Developments in The "Single Receiving" Exemption;* CRS Rept. No. 93-515, *Photocopying of Scientific Journal Articles: American Geophysical Union v. Texaco, Inc.*

[7] See CRS Rept. No. 98-649, *Spinning the Web: The History and Infrastructure of the Internet.*

[8] *Id.* at 13-14.

[9] *Id.* at 14. The extensive usage of the Web has generated various legal issues other than the fair use of copyrighted works. Among these issues are: trademarks, privacy, fraud, security, copyright first sale doctrine, trade secrets, and First Amendment issues.

[10] An electronic bulletin board is a means of exchanging information with distant areas through a computer and modem. The electronic bulletin board is comprised of an electronic storage medium (computer memories or hard disks), which is attached to telephone lines through modem devices which are controlled by a computer.

[11] Christopher Wolf, *'Net Users Could Face IP Liability,* NAT'L Law J. C34, C35 (May 20, 1996)(cited to afterward as "Wolf").

[12] Circumstances may exist where a user pays a subscription fee for the use of particular information on the Internet. The service provider may specifically address the issues of copying/downloading in the access agreements with the users. However, many Internet sites do not impose a user fee or contain copyright information concerning the material on the site.

exclusive rights of reproduction.[13] However, if the copyright owner places his/her work on the Internet, it could be inferred that the owner would expect other Internet users to read and download the copyrighted work. Legal complications arise when persons other than the copyright owner publish the copyrighted works on the Internet.

Case Law and the Internet

American courts have been seeking equitable resolutions to copyright infringement actions over the unauthorized use of copyrighted works on the Internet. Court decisions applying the fair use principles to Internet use provide some legal guidance; however, case law precedent is still developing and certain issues remain unresolved. Still, the most recent cases have continued the traditional application of the fair use principles to Internet use of copyrighted materials.

An early case that dealt with the fair use principles and online services involved an electronic bulletin board which was open to the public.[14] The scheme involved the electronic exchange of copyrighted Sega video games through the bulletin board. The bulletin board operators asserted a fair use defense which was based upon the argument that the operators themselves did not download or retain copies of any Sega video games. The court applied the four fair use factors to this situation and rejected the defendants' fair use defense. The court determined that the *use* was for a commercial purpose–to download the copyrighted games, so as to avoid their purchase from the copyright owner. Considering the *nature* of the copyrighted work, the court observed that the work involved creativity, fiction, and fantasy. Since the entire work was copied, the third factor–the *amount* of the work used, favored the plaintiff's claim. In considering the fourth factor, the *effect of copying on the potential market*, the court concluded that the unauthorized copying of the copyrighted works would adversely impact the potential market, as few persons would purchase the copyrighted works if they were available through the bulletin board. Hence, the court concluded that all four factors favored the plaintiff and that the defendants' unauthorized use of the copyrighted works was an infringing use. Another subsequent decision which dealt with the fair use doctrine and Internet use involved the same parties and a similar factual situation.[15] The court applied the four fair use factors to the facts at hand.[16] After balancing all of the factors, the court reached the same conclusion as in the earlier decision, finding that the fair use doctrine did not apply.[17]

Several online cases have involved the unauthorized use of certain written works of L. Ron Hubbard, founder of Scientology. The simplified factual situation concerning these cases follows. In unrelated litigation, the Religious Technology Center (RTC) attempted to seal an affidavit concerning church ideology. Lerma–a

---

[13] *See* Wolfe, *supra*, note 11.

[14] *Sega Enterprises, Ltd. v. MAPHIA*, 857 F.Supp. 679 (N.D.Cal. 1994).

[15] *Sega Enterprises, Ltd. v. MAPHIA*, 948 F.Supp. 923 (N.D.Cal. 1996).

[16] *Id.* at 934-935.

[17] *Id.* at 936.

former follower of Hubbard–obtained the affidavit and published it on the Internet through his Internet access provider–Digital Gateway Systems (DGS). The RTC brought an infringement action against Lerma, DGS, The Washington Post, and others. Another series of cases involved the RTC bringing an action for copyright infringement against a former minister–Erlich–for posting on an Internet bulletin board certain materials containing Hubbard's published and unpublished works. The RTC also named as defendants the bulletin board operator–Klemesrud and the Internet access provider–Netcom. These cases are summarized below.

In *Religious Technology Center v. Lerma,*[18] the court dealt primarily with RTC's infringement action against the Post, certain reporters, and Lerma. This case did not deal chiefly with the Internet or online aspects of fair use. The action was based primarily upon the unauthorized dissemination of information owned by the RTC and did not address the substantive copyright issues.[19]

In another case involving the RTC's infringement action, the same defendants moved for summary judgment and the district court concluded that the fair use doctrine was applicable to the Post and its reporters.[20] In reaching this conclusion, the court examined the four fair use factors and applied them in a traditional copyright analysis. The court concluded that the purpose and character of the use of the material was for news gathering and this favored the defendants. In evaluating the nature of the work, the court deemed it to be informational rather than creative, and that a broader fair use approach was appropriate. The court determined that the amount of the work used in relation to its entirety was not significant. Finally, the court found that the unauthorized use did not adversely impact the market value of the material. The court concluded that the unauthorized use of the copyrighted material by the Post and by its reporters was a fair use.

In an unpublished opinion, the court subsequently examined the copyright infringement claim against Lerma.[21] Lerma first argued that the disputed works were not copyrightable. The court rejected this argument. He next raised the fair use defense for his unauthorized use of the copyrighted works. After examining each of the four fair use factors, the court concluded that Lerma's use could not be construed as a fair use. Finally, Lerma argued that the RTC misused the copyright. The court concluded that the RTC had not misused its copyright and that Lerma's unauthorized use of the material was an infringing use. The RTC was awarded $2,500 in statutory damages.

In another series of cases, the RTC brought actions against Erlich (the former minister), the bulletin board operator, and the Internet access provider. In two separate opinions, the district court for the Northern District of California addressed

---

[18] 908 F.Supp. 1353 (E.D.Va. 1995).

[19] *Id.* at 1355-1358

[20] *Religious Technology Center v. Lerma*, 908 F.Supp. 1361 (E.D.Va. 1995).

[21] *Religious Technology Center v. Arnaldo Pagliarina Lerma*, 1996 U.S. Dist. LEXIS 15454 (E.D.Va. Oct. 4, 1996).

various copyright issues, including fair use.[22] Erlich did not dispute that he copied the works. He advanced a fair use defense.[23] The court granted in part the plaintiff's motion for a preliminary injunction against Erlich and concluded that his use of the RTC's materials was unlikely to qualify as fair use. In evaluating Erlich's purpose and character of the use, the court determined that it was for criticism or comment and was thus for noncommercial use. Therefore, the fair use factor was held to be slightly in Erlich's favor.[24] In looking at the nature of the copyrighted work, the court considered that some of the works were published while others were unpublished. The court determined that the unauthorized use of the unpublished works favored the plaintiffs. In assessing the third factor, the court favored the plaintiffs. As for the potential market for the work, the court concluded that Erlich's use would not have an adverse effect on the market. The court engaged in an "equitable balancing" of the factors and found that Erlich could not assert a fair use defense for his copying.[25]

In *Religious Technology Center v. Netcom On-Line Commu.,*[26] another action involving the RTC and Erlich's access provider and the bulletin board, the court granted in part and denied in part the defendants' motion for summary judgment and judgment on the pleadings, and denied the plaintiffs' motion for a preliminary injunction. The district court applied the fair use analysis to the action of the Internet access provider, Netcom. The court determined that the access provider was not liable for direct infringement; rather, the court examined it as a case of contributory infringement on the part of Netcom and determined that the plaintiffs raised a genuine issue of fact concerning Netcom's contributory infringement.[27] Although Netcom was a commercial enterprise, the court found that its use of copyrighted work was of a different nature than the plaintiffs' use. In looking at the nature of the copyrighted works, the court determined that Netcom's use of the works was merely to facilitate their posting to the bulletin board--an entirely different use from the use of plaintiffs-- and therefore favored Netcom. Regarding the amount of the copyrighted work copied, the court determined that Netcom copied no more of the plaintiffs' work than was necessary to function; thus, this factor did not favor the plaintiffs. The court concluded that the postings on the Internet by Netcom raised a genuine factual issue as to whether the market for plaintiff's works was diminished. Because the court was not able to make a determination concerning the fourth fair use factor–the market harm–the court decided that the fair use defense was *not* available to Netcom on motion for summary judgment.[28] In conclusion, the court determined that there were issues of fact to be determined in the case and that a fair use defense was not available for Netcom on summary judgment.

---

[22] The court examined other issues, such as trade secret and tort claims, which are not discussed in this report.

[23] *Id. at 1242-1250.*

[24] *Id.* at 1244.

[25] *Id.* at 1249-1250.

[26] 907 F.Supp. 1361 (N.D.Ca. 1995).

[27] *Id.* at 1373-1375.

[28] *Id.* at 1381. Apparently, the bulletin board provider did not assert a fair use defense; therefore, the court did not utilize the fair use analysis.

In late 1997, the U.S. District Court for the Northern District of Illinois ruled that an Internet service provider was not liable for direct copyright infringement, despite the fact that materials were directly copied on a web site that the service provider maintained for a subscriber.[29]   However, the Internet subscriber was found to have infringed certain copyrighted "clip art" images by using them on the Internet. The court concluded that the subscriber's use of the clip art was primarily for commercial uses, for promoting his organization, and for generating revenue. Hence, the fair use defense was not available for the defendant and the unauthorized use of the "clip art" on the Internet was found to be an infringing use. In 1998, the same court–the U.S. District Court for the Northern District of Illinois--reached a finding of infringement in a similar case involving the use of "shareware," copyrighted software which is loaned to potential purchasers under certain conditions.[30] The court went through an extensive fair use analysis within the context of shareware.[31]

In another case concerning fair use and the Internet, still images taken from a copyrighted videotape of a celebrity couple engaging in sexual activity were placed on the Internet without the couple's permission. Applying the fair use doctrine to a rather complex factual situation, the U.S. District Court for the Central District of California held that the unauthorized placement on the Internet of still images from a copyrighted videotape was not a fair use.[32] The court considered each fair use factor within the context of the factual situation.[33]

The U.S. District Court for the Eastern District of Texas examined a unique case where the plaintiff's copyrighted works–model legal codes--had been adopted as municipal laws by various communities.[34]   The defendant then posted these copyrighted works on the Internet and was sued for infringement. The court applied the fair use analysis to the factual situation at hand and determined that the fair use defense was not applicable in this situation.[35]   Hence, the posting of certain copyrighted model codes, even when they had been adopted as municipal laws or ordinances, did not lose their copyright protection, and could not be posted on the Internet without the permission of the copyright owner.

In *Kelly v. Arriba Soft Corp.*,[36] the court examined the fair use doctrine within the context of a "visual search engine" on the Internet. The defendant's visual search engine allows a user to obtain a list of related Web content following a search inquiry. The visual search engine produces a list of reduced "thumbnail" pictures related to the

---

[29] *Marobie-FL v. National Assn of Fire Equip. Dist.*, 983 F.Supp. 1167 (N.D. Ill. 1997).

[30] *Storm Impact v. Software of the Month Club*, 13 F.Supp. 2d 782 (N.D. Ill. 1998).

[31] *Id.* at 787-790.

[32] *Michaels v. Internet Entertainment Group, Inc.*, 5 F.Supp. 2d 823 (D.C. Cal. 1998).

[33] *Id.* at 834-836. The final disposition of this case was reached at *Michaels v. Internet Entertainment Group*, 1998 U.S. Dist. LEXIS 20786 (1998).

[34] *Veeck v. Southern Bldg. Code Congress Intern.*, 49 F.Supp. 885 (E.D. Tex. 1999).

[35] *Id.* at 891.

[36] 77 F.Supp. 1116 (C.D. Cal. 1999).

inquiry.[37] The plaintiff argued that the use of the "thumbnail" copyrighted pictures obtained through the visual search was an infringement of his copyright interest. The court undertook an extensive fair use evaluation of the circumstances surrounding the visual search engine and the unauthorized use of the copyrighted photographs.[38] The court weighed all of the fair use factors together and determined that the defendant's use of the copyrighted photographs as part of their visual search engine was a fair use of the plaintiff's images.[39]

The posting of copyrighted news articles on the Internet has been the subject of recent litigation.[40] The defendant posted copyrighted articles from newspapers on an Internet "bulletin board" website so that visitors to the site could comment and criticize the articles. Applying the fair use factors to the instant case, the court determined that the defendant's posting of full length, copyrighted articles on the Internet was not a fair use of the copyrighted material. The court noted that the website operator could have avoided infringement if summaries of the articles had been posted or if hyperlinks to the articles on the newspapers' own websites had been provided.

The practice of "streaming"--the visual transmission of copyrighted television programming--on the Internet was the subject of a recent action. The defendant was transmitting portions of the plaintiffs' copyrighted programming on the Internet. The plaintiff sought and received a temporary restraining order.[41] The U.S. District Court for the Western District of Pennsylvania did not examine the fair use doctrine or any other copyright defenses in its opinion.

In recent litigation, several motion picture studios brought an action to prevent the defendants from providing a computer program on their Web sites that allowed users to decrypt and copy the plaintiffs' copyrighted motion pictures from digital versatile disks.[42] Although the defendants argued that their activities were within the fair use exception, the court rejected this defense and granted the plaintiffs' motion for a preliminary injunction.

Conclusion

These cases have illustrated the judicial process--the "equitable balancing"--that courts undertake in their evaluation of fair use claims. It appears that the courts are using the same analysis and criteria for Internet litigation as they have with other intellectual property determinations. The courts have examined in detail the factual situation surrounding the litigation and they have applied each of the fair use criteria

---

[37] *Id.* at 1117.

[38] *Id.* at 1118-1121.

[39] *Id.* at 1121.

[40] *Los Angeles Times v. Free Republic*, (C.D. Cal., No. CV 98-7840-MMM-AJWX, 11/8/99).

[41] *Twentieth Century Fox Film Corporation v. ICRAVETV*, (2000 U.S. Dist. Lexis 1013).

[42] *Universal City Studios, Inc. v. Shawn C. Reimerdes*, 82 F.Supp. 2d 211 (S.D.N.Y. 2000).

to the case-by-case circumstances. The courts then evaluate or weigh the statutory criteria and determine whether, on balance, the evidence favors a finding of fair use of the copyrighted material or not.

While these cases provide judicial precedent, the use of copyrighted materials on the Internet is not entirely resolved. Factual circumstances may change the judicial outcome in various situations. In addition, various areas of fair use litigation and the Internet may still be developing. Among these subject areas are: possible liability for Internet server and bulletin board providers; whether online use is legally distinguishable from the use of the printed form; unintended or unintentional use of copyrighted materials; use of materials by schools and libraries; and other issues.

ELECTRONIC COMMERCE: AN INTRODUCTION

Glenn J. McLoughlin

Summary

Electronic commercial transactions over the Internet, or "e-commerce," have grown so fast over the last five years that many experts continue to underestimate its growth and development. Whether retail business-to-customer or business-to-business transactions, e-commerce shows no signs of slowing down. In turn, policymakers both in the United States and abroad are likely to face increasingly complex issues of security, privacy, taxation, infrastructure development and other issues in 2000 and beyond. This report will be updated periodically.

The Internet and E-Commerce[1]

The convergence of computer and telecommunications technologies has revolutionized how we get, store, retrieve, and share information. Many contend that this convergence has created the Information Economy, driven by the Internet, and fueled a surge in U.S. productivity and economic growth. Commercial transactions on the Internet, whether retail business-to-customer or business-to-business, are commonly called electronic commerce, or "e-commerce."

In 1995, it was estimated that between 1 and 2 million people in the United States used the Internet for some form of commercial transaction. By the next year, Internet traffic, including e-commerce, was doubling every 100 days. By mid-1997, the U.S. Department of Commerce reported that just over 4 million people were using e-commerce; by the end of 1997, that figure had grown to over 10 million users. The rate of e-commerce growth continues so rapidly that projections often are outdated as fast as they are published. One 1998 industry estimate projected that U.S. retail transactions would reach $7 billion by 2000 — a figure now widely accepted as having been reached in *the year the report came out*. Still, reliable industry sources report huge jumps in e-commerce

---

[1] For statistics and other data on e-commerce, sources include: [http://www.idc.com]; [http://www.abcnews.go.com]; [http://www.forrester.com], and [http://www.cs.cmu.edu]. It is important to note that some measurements of e-commerce, particularly that data reported in the media, have not been verified.

transactions, particularly during fourth quarter holiday shopping. The Census Bureau of the Department of Commerce, which began tracking national e-commerce sales in 1999, estimates that in the first quarter of 2000, total retail e-commerce sales reached $5.3 billion, an increase of 1.2% from fourth quarter 1999. Some analysts contend that financial transactions–such as electronic banking and online stock trading–are also fueling a large part of retail e-commerce growth.[2]

One of the fastest growing sectors of e-commerce is business-to-business transactions. The Forrester Group, a private sector consulting firm, estimates that by 2003, that sector of the U.S. economy will reach $1.5 trillion, up from $131 billion in 1999. In the United States, business-to-business transactions between small and medium sized businesses and their suppliers is rapidly growing, as many of these firms begin to use Internet connections for supply chain management, after-sales support, and payments.

Internationally, there are issues regarding Internet use and e-commerce growth. While the western industrialized nations dominate Internet development and use, by the year 2003 more than half of the material posted on the Internet will be in a language other than English. This has large ramifications for e-commerce and ease of transactions, security, and privacy issues. Policymakers, industry leaders, academicians, and others are concerned that this development will not correlate with equal access to the Internet for many in developing nations — therefore creating a global "digital divide." The United States and Canada represent the largest percentage of Internet users, at 56.6%. Europe follows with 23.4%. At the end of 1999, of approximately 180 million Internet users worldwide, only 3.1% are in Latin America, 0.5% are in the Middle East, and 0.6% are in Africa. The Asian Pacific region has 15.8% of all Internet users; but its rate of growth of Internet use is nearly twice as fast as the United States and Canada.

U.S. Perspectives

The Clinton Administration: Policies and Principles.[3] The Clinton Administration's approach to e-commerce was laid out in a 1994 speech by Vice President Gore. In that speech in Buenos Aires, the Vice President announced that the United States would pursue the development of a global network of networks that he called the Global Information Infrastructure, or GII. He stated that the United States would encourage private investment, promote competition, provide open access, create flexible regulatory environments, and ensure universal service so that the Internet would truly become a global network. According to Vice President Gore, the GII could act as a key for economic growth and increase global trade among nations.

In a subsequent series of reports, the Clinton Administration amplified and expanded upon these principles. In June 1997, the Clinton Administration released a report, "A Framework for Global Electronic Commerce." Building upon the GII, the Administration advocated a wide range of policy prescriptions. These included calling on the World Trade Organization (WTO) to declare the Internet to be a tax-free environment for delivering

---

[2] Many e-commerce services firms have yet to turn a profit.

[3] For more on the Clinton Administration policies, programs, and related reports, see: [http://www.whitehouse.gov].

both goods and services; recommending that no new tax policies should be imposed on Internet commerce; stating that nations develop a "uniform commercial code" for electronic commerce; requesting that intellectual property protection — patents, trademarks, and copyrights — be consistent and enforceable; that nations adhere to international agreements to protect the security and privacy of Internet commercial transactions; that governments and businesses cooperate to more fully develop and expand the Internet infrastructure; and that businesses self-regulate e-commerce content.

The Clinton Administration followed this report with the first annual report of the U.S. Government Working Group on Electronic Commerce in December 1998. This report highlighted the domestic and international e-commerce policies and achievements of the Clinton Administration, including summaries of President Clinton's Electronic Commerce Strategy and the major international agreements flowing from this strategy. Among the achievements listed were U.S. agreements with the Netherlands, Japan, France, Ireland, and Korea to remove barriers to e-commerce; and U.S. participation in agreements under the WTO, the European Union (EU), the Asian-Pacific Economic Council, and the Trans-Atlantic Business Dialogue, all of which provide broad policy guidelines to encourage continued e-commerce growth.

The Clinton Administration's "The Emerging Digital Economy" (April 1998) and "The Emerging Digital Economy II" (June 1999) provide overarching views on domestic and global e-commerce. These reports provide data on the explosive growth of e-commerce, its role in global trade and national Gross Domestic Product (GDP), and contributions that computer and telecommunications technology convergence is making to productivity gains in the United States and worldwide. On June 5, 2000 the third report, "Digital Economy 2000,"was released. Among the report highlights are the effects that information technologies have had on raising national productivity, lowering inflation, and creating high wage jobs.

Role of Congress. Since the mid-1990s, Congress also has taken an active interest in the e-commerce issue. Among many issues, Congress has considered legislation to establish federal encryption and electronic signature policies, and in 1998, Congress enacted legislation creating a 3-year moratorium on e-commerce taxation.

Encryption. Encryption is the encoding of electronic messages to transfer important information and data, in which "keys" are needed to unlock or decode the message. Encryption is an important element of e-commerce security, with the issue of who holds the keys at the core of the debate. The 105th Congress considered seven bills addressing national encryption/computer security policy; none was enacted. In the 106th Congress, two bills are being considered, with several congressional committees having significant differences regarding over the legislation. Also, the Clinton Administration has had differences with both congressional policymakers and representatives of U.S. industry over its encryption policy. Initially, the Administration favored a policy in which the federal government would hold keys for all major commercial transactions. However, industry and congressional critics contended that citizens' privacy rights could easily be violated. Currently, the Administration favors a policy in which a "spare key" would be held by a third party "key recovery agent," and not directly held by the federal government. Still, many critics are uncomfortable with the federal role in having direct access to the "spare key." (See CRS Issue Brief IB96039, *Encryption Technology: Congressional Issues*, by Richard M. Nunno, for more on this issue).

Export Control. In addition, U.S. export control policy makes it easy to export products with key recovery, and difficult to export those products without key recovery. The Clinton Administration's position is that export control is a way in which the federal government can ensure that unfriendly forces do not have encrypted communications or data transmission that the United States cannot recover. Some in U.S. industry contend that this policy is only restricting U.S. trade in electronic goods and services while foreign firms are freer to engage in this trade. In part due to this industry opposition, and because the 106th Congress has not fully supported the Clinton Administration's position on this issue, the Administration announced on January 14, 2000 new export regulations. The proposed rule changes would allow retail encryption commodities and software of any key length to be exported to most countries without a license, with certain qualifications. (See CRS Report RL30273, *Encryption Export Controls,* by Jeanne Grimmett, for more on U.S. encryption export control policy).

Electronic Signatures. Electronic signatures are a means of verifying the identity of a user of a computer system to control access to, or to authorize, a transaction. The main congressional interests in electronic signatures focus on enabling electronic signatures to carry legal weight in place of written signatures, removing the inconsistencies among state policies that some fear may retard the growth of e-commerce, and establishing federal government requirements for use of electronic signatures when filing information electronically. Neither federal law enforcement nor national security agencies oppose these objectives, and most U.S. businesses would like a national electronic signatures standard to further enhance e-commerce. In June 2000 the conference report for S. 761, the Electronic Signatures in Global and National Commerce Act, was approved by both the House and Senate. S.761, among its many provisions, establishes principles for U.S. negotiators to follow in setting global electronic signatures policies. It now awaits the President's signature (For more, see CRS Report RS20344, *Electronic Signatures: Technology Development and Legislative Issues,* by Richard M. Nunno).

Taxation.[4] Congress passed the Internet Tax Freedom Act on October 21, 1998, as Titles XI and XII of the Omnibus Consolidated and Emergency Supplemental Appropriations Act of 1999 (P.L. 105-277, 112 Stat 2681). Among its provisions, the Act imposes a 3-year moratorium on the ability of state and local governments to levy certain taxes on the Internet; it prohibits taxes on Internet access, unless such a tax was generally imposed and actually enforced prior to October 1, 1998; it creates an Advisory Commission on Electronic Commerce (ACEC), which may make recommendations to Congress on e-commerce taxation in the United States and abroad; and it opposes regulatory, tariff, and tax barriers to international e-commerce and asks the President to pursue international agreements to ban them. (See CRS Report RL30412, *Internet Taxation: Bills in the 106th Congress,* by Nonna A. Noto, for more on this issue).

The ACEC made its policy recommendations, after much debate and some divisiveness, to Congress on April 3, 2000. The ACEC called for, among its recommendations, extending the domestic Internet tax moratorium for five more years, through 2006; prohibiting the taxation of digitized goods over the Internet, regardless of national source; and a continued moratorium on any international tariffs on electronic

---

[4] The proposed domestic e-commerce tax is different from trade tariffs or duties to related e-commerce transactions.

transmissions over the Internet. On May 18, 2000 the House of Representatives passed H.R. 3709, the Internet Nondiscrimination Act, which extends the domestic tax moratorium for five additional years beyond October 1, 2001. This legislation has been referred to the Senate.

Beyond U.S. Policies: the WTO and the EU

While much of the debate on the government's role in e-commerce has focused on domestic issues in the United States, two important players — the WTO and the EU — will likely have an important impact on global e-commerce policy development.

The WTO. The success of the General Agreement on Tariffs and Trade (GATT) in reducing and eliminating many trade barriers led to an increased focus on other issues, such as reducing trade barriers in global service industries and high technology goods, by the WTO (its successor since January 1, 1995). (For more on the WTO, see CRS Report 98-928, *The World Trade Organization: Background and Issues,* by Lenore Sek).

The first WTO Ministerial conference was held in Singapore on December 9-13, 1996. Among the issues considered by the WTO participants was an agreement to reduce trade barriers for information technology goods and services. This issue was considered vital to the development of telecommunications infrastructure–including the Internet–among developing nations. A majority of participants signed an agreement to reduce these barriers. At the second WTO Ministerial conference, held in Geneva on May 18 and 20, 1998, an agreement was reached by the participating trade ministers to direct the WTO General Council to develop a work program on electronic commerce and to report on the progress of the work program, with recommendations, at the next conference. The ministers also agreed that countries continue the practice of not imposing tariffs on electronic transmissions. The third WTO Ministerial meeting in Seattle, December 7 -10, 1999, was marked both by strife in the streets of Seattle and disruption of the conference proceedings. While the General Council reported favorably on maintaining the international e-commerce tax moratorium, no final decision was reached at the conclusion of the Seattle Ministerial. (See CRS Report RS20319, *Telecommunications Services Trade and the WTO Agreement,* by Bernard A. Gelb, and CRS Report RS20387, *The World Trade Organization (WTO) Seattle Ministerial Conference,* by Lenore Sek).

The EU. The EU is very active in e-commerce issues. In some areas there is agreement with U.S. policies, and in some areas there are still tensions. While the EU as an entity represents a sizable portion of global Internet connections, users are concentrated in countries like the United Kingdom and Germany. In France, Italy, and Spain, the rate of Internet connection is reported at less than five percent of the total population. Thus, while EU policies can provide a broad regional context for e-commerce, across national boundaries, Internet use and e-commerce potential varies widely. The United Kingdom, Ireland, and France have advocated a common set of standards that, they contend, would provide a baseline of government regulation for e-commerce. These countries have opposed a more specific and perhaps restrictive approach across the EU. Germany, Austria, and the Netherlands have advocated extending domestic commercial legislation to e-commerce. Critics contend that this latter approach would ensnare e-commerce in a knot of differing national laws and regulations; supporters state that e-commerce policy should not be set by EU bureaucrats in Brussels.

To address this issue, the EU has approached e-commerce with what one observer has called a "light regulatory touch." On December 7, 1999, the European Commission announced an EU Directive that includes language that governs electronic contracts, the information an e-commerce trader must give to a customer, what advertising e-mails must say about the sender, and limits on the liabilities of intermediaries for unlawful content. The EU also has supported the temporary moratorium on new e-commerce taxes, and supports making the moratorium permanent. But the EU has taken a different approach than U.S. policy for treating electronic transactions under international tariff regimes. The EU favors treating electronic transmissions (including those that deliver electronic goods such as software) as services. This position would allow EU countries more flexibility in imposing trade restrictions, and would allow treating electronic transmissions — including e-commerce — as services, making them subject to EU value-added duties.

The EU also has taken a different approach to data protection and privacy, key components for strengthening e-commerce security and maintaining consumer confidence. The EU's Data Protection Directive went into effect in October 1998. This Directive prohibits the transfer of data in and out of the EU, unless the outside country provides sufficient privacy safeguards. The U.S. position has been to permit industry self-regulation of data protection and privacy safeguards. On May 31, 2000 U.S. and EU negotiators agreed to a "safe harbor" policy, in which U.S. organizations would voluntarily agree to adhere to EU principles of privacy protection. This issue may be revisited; many critics find this to be an unacceptable long-term solution, with ramifications that may possibly compromise U.S. corporate and citizens' privacy rights.

In the area of security, the EU has opposed restrictions on trade in encryption technology, contending that restrictions limit the security of the Internet and erodes European consumer and retailer confidence. As stated above, the Administration's January 2000 rule changes would allow retail encryption commodities and software of any key length to be exported to most countries without a license, but with certain qualifications. Some contend that these policy changes have adversely affected U.S. e-commerce interests globally, while others welcome the changes. U.S.-EU negotiations on encryption policy likely will focus on ways to find common ground on this issue..

Issues

The 106th Congress may address a series of complex questions on e-commerce. They include: how viable is the continuation of the Internet tax moratorium, and can a consensus be reached on an e-commerce tax policy? What are the appropriate roles of government and industry in U.S. policies on encryption, digital signatures, and data storage and protection for e-commerce? What is the best mechanism for achieving standard and consistent e-commerce policies between the United States and other nations? Will the United States, by virtue of its large proportion of Internet use and e-commerce development, try to dominate global e-commerce policy? Internet use erases national boundaries, and the growth of e-commerce on the Internet and the complexity of these issues may mean that domestic and global e-commerce policies become increasingly intertwined.

Internet Policies and Issues
Volume 2

INTERNET AND E-COMMERCE STATISTICS: WHAT THEY MEAN AND WHERE TO FIND THEM ON THE WEB

Rita Tehan

Abstract

It is important to understand how Internet and electronic commerce statistics are compiled, how they are used, and their limitations. Advertisers, who are spending a lot of money, are very interested in knowing how many eyes, and whose, are viewing their ads. Federal and state governments need demographic information also, to assist them in distributing resources and financial information. This report discusses the inherent complexities of estimating Internet and e-commerce growth, describes various types of Internet statistics, discusses how to evaluate them, and provides Web addresses for locating them.

This report also provides information on the size of the Internet (number of hosts, Web sites, and online users), demographic information about users (race, gender, location, etc.) and information about e-commerce. It briefly discusses the digital divide (i.e., the discrepancy between the information rich and the information poor).

Finally, the report lists selected Web sites which contain useful demographic and statistical information about the Internet and e-commerce. This report will be updated periodically.

Difficulties in Measuring the Internet

Statistics indicating Internet usage are imprecise. It is difficult to measure the scale of the Internet (or the World Wide Web), calculate the number and types of users (age, sex, race, gender, location, etc.), or forecast future growth. In addressing these topics, it is important to understand how the statistics are compiled, how they are used, and their limitations.

Estimates for the number of people using the Internet differ greatly. The difficulty in measuring Internet usage is partly due to the fact that analysts use different survey methods and different definitions of "Internet access." For example, some companies begin counting Net surfers at age 2, while others begin at 16 or 18. Some researchers include users who have been on the Web only within the past month, while others include people who have never used the Internet.[1]

The Internet presents a unique problem for surveying. At the heart of the issue is the methodology used to collect responses from individual users. Since there is no central registry of all Internet users, completing a census or attempting to contact every user of the Internet is neither practical nor financially feasible. Therefore, Internet surveys attempt to answer questions about all users by selecting a subset to participate in the survey. This process is called sampling. The following discussion of survey methodologies is excerpted from the Georgia Institute of Technology's *GVU's World Wide Web User Survey Background Information* Web page.[2]

There are two types of sampling, random and non-probabilistic. Random sampling creates a sample using a random process for selecting members from the entire population. Since each person has an equal chance of being selected for the sample, results obtained from measuring the sample can be generalized to the entire population. Non-probabilistic sampling is not a pure random selection process, and can introduce bias into the sampling selection process because, for example, there is a desire for convenience or expediency. With non-probabilistic sampling, it is difficult

---

[1] Lake, David. Spotlight: how big is the U.S. Net population? *The Standard*, November 29, 1999. [http://www.thestandard.com/metrics/display/0,2149,1071,00.html].

[2] GVU's WWW User Survey Background Information. Graphics, Visualization & Usability Center, Georgia Institute of Technology.
[http://www.cc.gatech.edu/gvu/user_surveys/background.html].

to guarantee that certain portions of the population were not excluded from the sample, since elements do not have an equal chance of being selected.

Since Internet users are spread out all over the world, it becomes quite difficult to select users from the entire population at random. To simplify the problem, most surveys of the Internet focus on a particular region of users, which is typically the United States, though surveys of European, Asian, and Oceanic users have also been conducted. Still, the question becomes how to contact users and get them to participate. The traditional methodology is to use random digit dialing (RDD). While this ensures that the phone numbers and thus users are selected at random, it potentially suffers from other problems as well, namely, self-selection.

Self-selection occurs when the entities in the sample are given a choice to participate. If a set of members in the sample decides not to participate, it reduces the ability of the results to be generalized to the entire population. This decrease in the confidence of the survey occurs since the group that decided not to participate may differ in some manner from the group that participated. It is important to note that self-selection occurs in nearly all surveys of people. Thus, conventional means of surveying Internet usage are subject to error.

Most of the statistics gathered during the early days of the Internet only concerned the number of hosts connected to the Internet or the amount of traffic flowing over the backbones. Such statistics were usually collected by large universities or government agencies on behalf of the research and scientific community, who were the largest users of the Internet at the time. This changed in 1991 when the National Science Foundation lifted its restrictions on the commercial use of the Internet. More businesses began to realize the commercial opportunities of the Internet, and the demand for an accurate accounting of the Internet's population increased.

Complexities of Measuring E-Commerce

A new activity emerged to fill the need to gather e-commerce statistics: gathering and selling strategic and statistical information about the Internet. Internet organizations, such as the Internet Society and the International Telecommunications Union, began to compile information on the size and growth of the Internet. Traditional research and polling firms such as Nielsen and Gallup also entered the field, along with new types of companies, such as Forrester Research, Gartner Group, Jupiter Communications, International Data Corporation (IDC), and Zona Research, which provide estimates of the impact of the Internet on consumers and business.

Web traffic measurement may seem tedious, but with the number of dollars at stake, it is very important to businesses. Advertisers, who are spending a lot of money, are very interested in knowing how many eyes, and whose, are viewing their ads. Federal and state governments need demographic information also, to assist them in distributing resources and financial assistance.

Another factor must be considered in evaluating Internet statistics. More and more businesses have decided that the Internet is the key to success and are aware of their acute need for e-commerce guidance. With increasing frequency, yet another e-commerce research firm declares that it has all the answers for e-commerce strategies and schemes. "No one knows how much real insight online consulting firms provide, but what would-be Internet player can afford not to subscribe? Planning for the future is hard in a mature industry; it's nearly impossible in one still teething."[3]

Forrester Research in Cambridge, MA, and Jupiter Communications in New York City are two of the largest Internet research firms. They are so-called syndicated research firms, which means that they publish a wide range of reports with high subscription fees to a small, targeted audience of corporate executives. For approximately $20,000 a company can buy a subscription for one of eight subjects from Jupiter Communications. Then every month for a year, it receives a 32-page report filled with analysis and advice, survey data, and industry forecasts, on the impact of e-commerce.

"Stepping boldly into the answer vacuum, the companies [Forrester and Jupiter] have transformed themselves into prediction factories, supplying the world with a steady stream of airy, context-free, yet reassuringly precise projections ..."[4] These firms don't simply pull forecasts out of thin air; they strive to guess methodically: the analysts interview advertisers and executives at top Web sites, review annual reports, adjust overly-optimistic figures, assemble historical research comparing ad spending with consumer research, and estimate spending for online advertising. Forrester's chief Internet advertising analyst says, "The interesting thing about projections is that they come out looking very exact. But really, it's just your opinion expressed numerically."[5]

One observer says the models used by Forrester or Jupiter "have little resemblance to statistical techniques, like regression analysis or time-series analysis, used by traditional market researchers or industrial forecasters to determine next year's worldwide consumption of, say, gasoline or Coca-Cola. That, of course, is because enterprises that forecast the consumption of resources or consumer items can draw on decades of historical data."[6] Using such techniques would not now work for Forrester or Jupiter because the Internet e-commerce environment has existed for only 3 to 4 years for most businesses.

There is much debate over which Web measurement company's methods are more accurate. The research firms disagree about sampling methods and panel

---

[3] Roth, Daniel. My, what big Internet numbers you have! *Fortune*, March 15, 1999. p. 114-20.

[4] Frederick, Jim. $6 billion on online holiday sales by the end of this month! $24 billion in Internet ads by 2003! 2.3 trillion E-biz predictions by 2010! *New York Times Magazine*, December 19, 1999. p. 70-73.

[5] Roth, p. 120.

[6] Frederick, p. 70.

selection, since differing methods of identifying and soliciting the survey participants result in different ratings.

Yet, in the business of assessing the Internet's future, there seems to be little accountability for incorrect forecasts. Many industry executives "admit that they view the companies and the media froth they generate as necessary evils ...."[7] Businesses need the Internet research consultants' estimates to write business plans and attract investors, but at this time, the estimates are not based on historically valid measurement models.

Another controversy centers around how to measure Web use in the workplace, which is estimated to account for 35% to 45% of Internet use. Companies are notoriously reluctant to place Web measurement software on their workers' computers.[8] Privacy and the protection of proprietary business information would most likely have to be resolved before this could become a common measurement tool.

E-Commerce Growth Statistics

With all the caveats discussed above, below is a sampling of estimates of the size and growth of e-commerce. (For a selected list of Web sites for e-commerce statistics, see the *Selected Web Addresses for Internet and E-Commerce Statistics*, on pages 10-11.) Recent e-commerce statistics include:

- online retail sales estimated at $66 billion for 1999[9]

- 96.7% of online consumers plan to buy online again[10]

- 1999 online holiday sales hit $7 billion (customers who shopped between November 1 and December 31, 1999)[11]

- 13% of Americans used the Internet to buy holiday gifts, and online purchases averaged $314 each[12]

---

[7] Ibid., p. 73.

[8] O'Leary, Mike. Web measurers wrestle with methodologies, each other. *Online*, May/June 1999. p. 106.

[9] ActivMedia Research LLC, January 12, 2000. [http://www.activmediaresearch.com].

[10] Customer satisfaction is high after the holidays. PC Data and Goldman Sachs. *e-Marketer*, January 14, 2000. [http://www.pcdataonline.com].

[11] Online holiday sales hit $7 billion, consumer satisfaction rising. Jupiter Communications press release, January 13, 2000.
[http://www.jup.com/company/pressrelease.jsp?doc=pr000113].

[12] Langer, Gary. Internet shopping booming. ABC News.com, January 3, 2000.
[http://abcnews.go.com/sections/politics/DailyNews/poll000103.html].

- retail spending from America Online's (AOL) members totaled $2.5 billion for the period between Thanksgiving and Christmas, double that of 1998. This figure contributes to a 1999 total of $10 billion for AOL members online purchasing. Roughly two-thirds of AOL's members (13.2 million of 20 million) shopped for the holidays.[13]

In March 2000, the U.S. Department of Commerce will release total e-commerce sales figures for the fourth quarter of 1999. The first e-commerce sales report will provide a simple tally of Internet retail sales, based on a survey of roughly 2,000 Web merchants. One analyst concludes, "That is a far cry from the monthly retail reports released by the Census Bureau, which break down sales totals of traditional retailers by categories like shoes, liquor, and furniture."[14] Census Bureau officials hope to achieve a similar level of detail with e-commerce reports, but they must overcome obstacles which have slowed the effort.

First is the issue of how to categorize retailers who appear, disappear, or change their products with dizzying regularity. For instance, Lee Price, chief economist for the Economics and Statistics Administration, said, "It's not just a question of taxonomy. It's one of evolving taxonomy. Amazon used to just sell books. Now they sell a much more varied selection. You have to figure out how to capture that."[15] Also, businesses are still developing interactions between bricks and mortar establishments and their e-commerce equivalents (for example, Wal-Mart's physical stores compete with its Internet presence).

Second, projecting data from 2,000 respondents so it represents the entire universe of e-commerce spending also presents analytical dilemmas. For example, analysts must weigh the data from those who did not respond, just as they weigh the results of those who responded. The Commerce Department cannot compel companies to respond. Finally, there is the hurdle of actually collecting the data. Some electronic retailers do not want to be bothered, and others want assurances that the information they send will be safe and protected.

Industry analysts and executives are hopeful that Commerce Department figures will provide more reliable information than is now available. This will be important for seeing long-term trends, but they will not provide immediate data on Internet sales. According to Jack Staff, chief economist with Zona Research, "It'll take at least three years for the government data to be highly usable. But there's a whole segment of the Internet industry that's devoted to the numbers, and it'll be fundamentally changed once better numbers come along. And that's as it should be."[16]

---

[13] AOL's holiday report. eMarketer, January 4, 2000. [http://www.emarketer.com].

[14] Tedeschi, Bob. Government figures will shed little light on holiday online sales. New York Times Cybertimes, January 10, 2000.
         [http://www.nytimes.com/library/tech/00/01/cyber/commerce/10commerce.html].

[15] Ibid.

[16] Ibid.

Estimated Size of the Internet

The Internet connects more than 56 million host computers in 247 countries.[17] The Internet is now growing at a rate of about 40% to 50% annually (for machines physically connected to the Internet), according to data from the Internet Domain Survey, the longest-running survey of Internet hosts. Such exponential growth has led to the expansion of the Internet from 562 connected host computers in 1983 to 56.2 million such computers in July 1999.[18] At any time from 1983 through 1996, half of the Internet's historical growth had occurred in the preceding 12 to 14 months.[19] In 1997, the editor of *Wired* magazine argued that "the Internet is actually being underhyped. Of all the people [who will be online] in 10 years, only a tenth are online today."[20]

Another way to think about growth in Internet access is to compare it to other technologies from the past. It took 38 years for the telephone to penetrate 30% of U.S. households. Television took 17 years to become that available. Personal computers took 13 years. Once the Internet became popular because of the World Wide Web, it took less than 7 years to reach a 30% penetration level.[21]

Although the number of people using the Internet can only be estimated, the number of host computers can be counted fairly accurately. A host is a computer server hooked to the Internet. The growth of Internet hosts is shown below:

YEAR	NUMBER OF INTERNET HOSTS
1969	4 hosts
04/1971	23 hosts
08/1981	213 hosts
08/1983	562 hosts
12/1987	28,174 hosts
07/1988	33,000 hosts
07/1989	130,000 hosts
10/1990	313,000 hosts

---

[17] International E-mail Accessibility Based on International Standard ISO 3166 Codes. This document is a guide to country codes, showing which countries have access to the Internet or general e-mail services. Released June 1, 1999, at: [http://www.nsrc.org/codes/].

[18] Number of Internet Hosts. Network Wizards, January 1999 at: [http://www.nw.com/zone/host-count-history].

[19] *Standard & Poor's Industry Surveys.* Computers: consumer services and the Internet, September 30, 1999. p. 6.

[20] Kelly, Kevin. New Rules for a New Economy. *Wired,* September 1997. [http://www.wired.com/wired/5.09/newrules_pr.html].

[21] *State of the Internet: USIC's Report on Use & Threats in 1999.* U.S. Internet Council, April 1999 at: [http://www.usic.org/usic_state_of_net99.htm].

07/1991	535,000 hosts
07/1992	992,000 hosts
07/1993	1,776,000 hosts
07/1994	2,217,000 hosts
07/1995	6,642,000 hosts
01/1996	9,472,000 hosts
01/1997	17,753,266 hosts
01/1998	29,670,000 hosts
01/1999	43,230,000 hosts
06/1999	56,218,000 hosts[22]

Packet traffic, a measure of the amount of data flowing over the network, continues to increase exponentially. Traffic and capacity of the Internet grew at rates of about 100% per year in the early 1990s. There was then a brief period of explosive growth in 1995 and 1996. During those two years, traffic grew by a factor of about 100, which is about 1,000% a year. In 1997, traffic growth slowed to about 100% per year.[23] UUNet, an Internet access provider, estimates that Internet traffic is doubling every 100 days.[24]

Number of Web Sites and Web Pages

In January 2000, Inktomi Corp., a developer of Internet infrastructure software, announced that it and the NEC Research Institute, Inc., completed a study that verifies that the Web has grown to more than one billion unique pages.[25] A number of facts have emerged from the study:

Number of documents in Inktomi database: over 1 billion
Number of servers discovered: 6,409,521
Number of mirrors (identical Web sites) in servers discovered: 1,457,946
Number of sites (total servers minus mirrors): 4,951,247
Number of good sites (reachable over 10-day period): 4,217,324
Number of bad sites (unreachable): 733,923

---

[22] Internet statistics are compiled by Mark Lottor of Network Wizards. The Internet Domain Survey attempts to discover every host on the Internet by doing a complete search of the Domain Name System (DNS). It is sponsored by the Internet Software Consortium technical operations which are subcontracted to Network Wizards. Survey results are available from Network Wizards at: [http://www.isc.org/ds/WWW-9907/report.html].

[23] *The Size and Growth Rate of the Internet.* First Monday, October 5, 1998, at: [http://www.firstmonday.dk/issues/issue3_10/coffman/index.html].

[24] U.S. Department of Commerce. Secretariat for Electronic Commerce. *Framework for Global Electronic Commerce, Chapter Two: Building Out the Internet*, updated April 16, 1998, at: [http://www.ecommerce.gov/chapter2.htm].

[25] Reka Albert, Hawoong Jeong, and Albert-Laszlo Barabasi. Diameter of the World Wide Web. *Nature*, September 9, 1999. p. 130-1.

Top level domains	Percentage
.com	54.68%
.net	7.82%
.org	4.35%
.gov	1.15%
.mil	0.17%

Percentage of documents in English: 86.55%
Percentage of documents in French: 2.36%

A statistical survey has measured the Web's "diameter," finding that there's an average of 19 clicks separating random Internet sites. Three Notre Dame physicists found that although the average Web page has seven links to other pages, "there is a very, very high number of Web pages that have a huge number of connections"—far higher than they anticipated based on traditional mathematical models. The researchers studied the Net's topology and found that the Web's growth dynamics and its topology—that is, the way it is put together—follows what is known in physics as a power law. "A power-law distribution means that the Web doesn't follow the usual mathematical models of random networks, but instead exhibits the type of physical order found in, say, magnetic fields, galaxies, and plant growth."[26] Thus, the Web seems to have taken on an organic life of its own.

The scientists studied the distribution of links on a variety of sites and found that there was a consistent relationship between size and connectedness. That relationship can be used to determine the average shortest path between two points in a network, that is, the "diameter." Thus, if there are 800 million documents on the Web, there is an average "distance" of 19 links between two randomly selected sites. If you picked any two random Web pages, they might be linked directly to each other, or it might take hundreds of intermediate clicks to get from one page to the other. But by going through that exercise thousands of times and tallying all those clicks, the findings indicate the average would be roughly 19.

Researchers at the Online Computer Library Center (OCLC) are conducting a study to describe the structure, size, usage, and content of the Web. In September 1999, the Web Characterization Project published the results of a study which determined that there were 3.6 million Web sites on the World Wide Web. In addition, the largest 25,000 sites account for approximately 50% of content on the Web. Out of the 3.6 million total sites, 2.2. million offer publicly accessible content with about 300 million Web pages. This represents a considerable increase from 1997, when there were 800,000 sites. Approximately 400 million pages are restricted, requiring either fees or authorization. The report further notes that about 2% of the public sites, or 42,000, contain sexually explicit material. The mean average Web site contains 129 pages, which is a 13% jump over 1998's estimate of 114 pages.[27]

---

[26] Ibid., p. 130.

[27] OCLC Research Project Measures Scope of the Web. OCLC press release, September 8, 1999. [http://www.oclc.org/oclc/press/19990908a.htm].

Demographics

Various research and consulting firms have estimated the number of U.S. users to be 31.3 million, 83 million, and 92 million in 1999.[28] There are other estimates of 102 million in North America to 179 million worldwide.[29] These figures do not include military computers, which for security reasons are invisible to other users. Many hosts support multiple users, and hosts in some organizations support hundreds or thousands of users.

Two surveys in December 1999 reported increases in the number of Internet users in the United States. According to a Harris Poll, the number has soared from 9% of adults in 1995 to 56% in 1999. The number of U.S. Internet users has increased 600% in the past 4 years. Harris also found that 81% of computer users access the Internet from home, the office, school, or a library, compared to 18% in 1995.[30] Zona Research, in a survey conducted in the third quarter of 1999, estimated that 90 million U.S. adults are Internet users, compared with 85.3 million adults who are not. It is the first time that Zona's Worldwide Internet Tracking Study has shown more Internet users than non-users.[31]

According to the Computer Industry Almanac, Inc., the United States has an overwhelming lead in Internet users with over 50% of an estimated total 150 million Internet users worldwide at the end of 1998; but, the United States is only ranked fifth in Internet users per capita. The Nordic countries (Finland, Iceland, Norway, and Sweden) are the leaders with 29% or more of the population being regular Internet users.[32]

Digital Divide

More Americans than ever have access to telephones, computers, and the Internet. At the same time, however, according to the U.S. Department of Commerce's recent report, *Falling through the Net: Defining the Digital Divide*,

---

[28] 31.3 million—Infobeads, June 1999; 83 million —Cyberatlas, April 1999; 92 million —CommerceNet, June 1999. *Reports for the US.* Headcount.com
[http://www.headcount.com/count/morereports.htm?choice=country&choicev=The+US].

[29] Headcount.com summarizes market research reports which estimate the size of the Internet worldwide [at the home page, choose the "region count" or "country count" buttons] at: [http://www.headcount.com/], and Nua Internet Surveys links to estimates of Internet users at: [http://www.nua.ie/surveys/how_many_online/index.html].

[30] Online Population Reaches 56% of Americans. *AIM's Research Update Service*, January 5, 2000 [online newsletter].

[31] Johnston, Margret. *Most Americans are online.* PC World Online, December 22, 1999. [http://www.pcworld.com/shared/printable_articles/0,1440,14494,00.html].

[32] Computer Industry Almanac, Inc., press release, July 6, 1999, at:
[http://www.c-i-a.com/199907ciaiu.htm].

there is still a significant "digital divide" separating American information "haves" and "have nots."[33] Indeed, in many instances, the digital divide has widened in the last year. As the Commerce Department report (issued by its National Telecommunications and Information Administration) states, there is a persistent discrepancy between the information rich (who frequently include whites, Asians/Pacific Islanders, those with higher incomes, those more educated, and dual-parent households) and the information poor (many of whom are younger, with lower incomes and education levels, certain minorities, and those in rural areas or central cities).

Households with annual incomes of $75,000 and above are more than 20 times as likely to have Internet access as households at the lowest income levels. Households that identified themselves as being black or Hispanic are only 40% as likely as white households to be online. The differences cannot be explained by income alone. More than a third of white families earning between $15,000 and $35,000 per year owned computers, but only one in five black families at the same income level did.

Regardless of income, Americans living in rural areas are, in general, lagging behind in Internet access, according to the Commerce Department's *Falling Through the Net* report. Indeed, at the lowest income levels, those in urban areas are more than twice as likely to have Internet access than those earning the same income in rural areas. Community access centers, such as schools, libraries, and other public locations, play an important role. The 1998 data demonstrate that community access centers are particularly well used by those groups who lack access at home or at work. These same groups (which often include those with lower incomes and education levels, certain minorities, and the unemployed) are also using the Internet at higher rates to search for jobs or take courses.

President Clinton proposed federal subsidies to narrow the digital divide and help millions of low-income families go online. The FY2001 budget proposal calls for spending:

- $2 billion over 10 years in tax incentives to encourage private sector donation of computers, sponsorship of community technology centers, and technology training for workers.

- $150 million to help train all new teachers entering the workforce to use technology effectively.

- $100 million to create 1,000 Community Technology Centers in low-income urban and rural neighborhoods.

- $50 million for a public/private partnership to expand home access to computers and the Internet for low-income families.

---

[33] U.S. National Telecommunications and Information Administration. *Falling through the Net: Defining the Digital Divide,* July 8, 1999, at:
[http://www.ntia.doc.gov/ntiahome/fttn99/contents.html].

- $45 million to promote innovative applications of information and communications technology for under-served communities.

- $25 million to accelerate private sector deployment of broadband networks in under-served urban and rural communities.

- $10 million to prepare Native Americans for careers in information technology and other technical fields.[34]

In addition, the Commerce Department's Techology Opportunities Program is offering $12.5 million in grants to fund projects that will help close the digital divide. The funds will be made available to local governments and non-profit organizations that develop projects that provide opportunities for technologically underserved communities to use the Internet in homes, education, and business. The program, under its previous name, Telecommunications and Information Infrastructure Assistance Program, has made $135 million in matching grants since 1994.[35]

Selected Web Addresses for Internet and E-Commerce Statistics

The sites listed below are generally stable and timely in providing Internet and e-commerce statistics:

E-Commerce (General)

- U.S. Government Electronic Commerce Policy [http://www.ecommerce.gov/]

- *Emerging Digital Economy II* (report from the U.S. Department of Commerce, June 1999)   [http://www.ecommerce.gov/ede/report.html]

- Center for Research in Electronic Commerce (University of Texas, Austin) [http://cism.bus.utexas.edu/]

- University of California E-conomy Project   [http://e-conomy.berkeley.edu/]

---

[34] The Clinton-Gore Administration: From Digital Divide to Digital Opportunity, White House press release, February 2, 2000.
[http://www.pub.whitehouse.gov/uri-res/I2R?urn:pdi://oma.eop.gov.us/2000/2/2/4.text.1]
Another summary is available at the Digital Divide Network at:
                    [http://www.digitaldividenetwork.org/clinton_budget.adp].

[35] For more information, see the U.S. Department of Commerce, Technology Opportunities Program Overview Web page at:
                    [http://www.ntia.doc.gov/otiahome/tiiap/index.html].

E-Commerce (Statistics)

- eMarketer   [http://www.emarketer.com/estats/]
- The Internet Economy Indicators
                            [http://www.internetindicators.com/facts.html]

Demographics

- Headcount (Internet usage around the world) [http://www.headcount.com/]

- Nua Internet Surveys—*How Many Online*
                    [http://www.nua.ie/surveys/how_many_online/index.html]

- Nua Internet Surveys (general demographic information)
                                              [http://www.nua.ie/surveys/]

- Internet Domain Survey (Network Wizards)
                                        [http://www.nw.com/zone/WWW/]

Digital Divide

- Digital Divide (*Education Week*)
                        [http://www.edweek.org/context/topics/digital.htm]

- Digital Divide Network   [http://www.digitaldividenetwork.org/]
  Click on Grants & Funding for information on government, corporate, and
  private funding.

Internet Policies and Issues
Volume 2

INTERNET SERVICE AND ACCESS CHARGES

Angele A. Gilroy

Summary

On May 10, 2000, the House Commerce Committee approved a bill (H.R. 1291) by voice vote, which prohibits the Federal Communications Commission (FCC) from levying access charges on providers of Internet data services. Although the FCC has had a long-standing policy exempting Internet service providers (ISPs) from paying such charges, concerns have been voiced that the FCC may at some point in time reverse this policy. H.R. 1291 seeks to codify the policy by barring the FCC from requiring ISPs to make universal service contributions based on per-minute use of Internet access services. The measure also clarifies that it does not preclude the FCC from imposing access charges on providers of Internet telephone services.

What Are Access Charges?

In 1982 the FCC established a new framework to compensate local telephone companies for the costs they incur for the origination and termination of interstate telephone calls.[1] Under this framework, part of the local telephone company's fixed costs (e.g., telephone wires, poles, switches) are recovered through fees placed on those who access the network. These charges are called access charges. Presently interstate (long distance) telephone carriers are among those who rely on the local telephone network to access their customers and therefore are assessed access charges. In most cases, when a subscriber makes a long distance telephone call in addition to using the long distance network, two local telephone networks are involved – the local telephone company network of the consumer who originates the call, and the local telephone company of the receiving party to complete the call. The long distance company is required to pay for this access. Part of this interstate carrier access charge is recovered based on a per-minute of use structure.[2]

---

[1] The FCC implemented this order in 1984 but has continued to address various aspects of the access charge issue in subsequent rulemakings. See: FCC Access Charge Reform Homepage at [http://www.fcc.gov/isp.html].

[2] For further information on the FCC's interstate access charge system see: Consumer Information *The FCC's Interstate Access Charge System.* Available at the FCC web site

The ISP Exemption

Although there are many categories of users who are subject to access charges of varying types, the FCC has upheld a long standing policy exempting Internet service providers (ISP's) from paying such charges. Under this special exemption, the FCC treats ISPs as local telephone customers, or "end users", thereby exempting them from interstate access charges paid by the interstate carriers. Although the FCC has continually confirmed that there are no plans to remove this exemption, and that the FCC will not impose long distance charges for dialing up the Internet, rumors to the contrary continue to exist. Concerns have also been expressed that even though this Commission and past Commissions have chosen to grant an exemption, at some point in time, the FCC may choose to rescind this policy and levy such charges. The fear is that if ISPs are subject to interstate access charges, theses charges would be passed along to consumers, leading to the charging of a per-minute of use pricing structure for use of the Internet.[3]

H.R. 1291

The House Commerce Committee passed H.R. 1291, as amended in the nature of a substitute, by voice vote on May 10, 2000. H.R. 1291, the "Internet Access Charge Prohibition Act of 2000", amends Section 254 of the Communications Act of 1934 (47 U.S.C.254) to prohibit the FCC from imposing on any provider of Internet access service any universal service support contribution "... that is based on a measure of the time that telecommunications services are used in the provision of such Internet access service" (i.e., minutes of use). [4] The measure also clarifies that it does not preclude the FCC from imposing access charges on providers of Internet telephone services.[5]

Supporters of the measure claim that the bill codifies existing FCC long term policies exempting ISP's from per-minute access charges, ending constant rumors regarding the imposition of per minute usage charges for traditional Internet usage. This measure, they claim, will help to ensure that the Internet remains free from regulations that could result in Internet per-minute usage fees.

---

[2] (...continued)
[http://www.fcc.gov/Bureaus/Common_Carrier/Factsheets/access2.html]

[3] Federal Communications Commission Fact Sheet. *No Consumer Per-Minute Charges to Access ISPs.* FCC web site: [http://www.fcc.gov/Bureaus/Common_Carrier/Factsheets/nominute.html]. *Answers From FCC Commissioner William Kennard Concerning Reciprocal Compensation and Dial-Up Internet Traffic.*
[http://www.fcc.gov/Bureaus/Common_Carrier/Factsheets/faq_recp.html].

[4] H.R. 4202, the "Internet Services Promotion Act of 2000", contains a similar provision. Section 2(a)(1), prohibits the FCC from imposing on any provider of Internet access service "... any contribution for the support of universal service, or any access charge... that is based on a measure of the time that telecommunications services are used in the provision of such Internet access service.". This measure is pending in the House Subcommittee on Telecommunications and the Subcommittee on Commercial and Administrative Law.

[5] Internet telephony refers to the use of the Internet to send and receive voice messages.

Others have questioned the need for a bill at this time. They point to the FCC's long standing policy exempting ISPs from interstate access charges. Furthermore, they state, there is no attempt on behalf of the FCC, other regulators, or Congress to impose such a charge. Although they admit that rumors and misinformation continue to circulate regarding this issue, they question the need to address it at this juncture.

Concern was also expressed over the provision which permits, but does not require, the FCC to impose access charges on Internet telephony. Opponents to that provision fear that the potential for the FCC to levy per-minute charges on this service could discourage investment in and development of this nascent service. Supporters of this provision, however, stated that it would be unfair to exempt providers of Internet telephone service from paying charges that traditional long distance providers are required to pay. Furthermore they state the debate over what type of charges, flat rate or usage sensitive, if any, should be levied on Internet telephony needs further examination before any decisions can be made.[6]

Internet Policies and Issues
Volume 2

CHINA'S INTERNET INDUSTRY

Thomas Lum

Internet Usage in China

Internet usage in China is expected to grow rapidly over the next decade, providing greater business opportunities and access to information. The Chinese government has attempted develop the Internet while regulating its operation and content. While it has been unable to completely control regional Internet development plans, private business ventures, and individual activities online, the Internet's political effects have so far been minimal. As China addresses its World Trade Organization agreements to open its telecommunications sector and Internet industry to foreign investment and trade, U.S. companies will likely find both opportunities and obstacles.

Rapid Growth

During the past four years, the number of Internet users in China has doubled annually; industry analysts expect this growth to continue. Some experts estimate that the number of Internet users in China will reach 15-20 million by the end of 2000, ranking fifth in the world. By 2005, China may have the second-largest Internet population, though it will still trail far behind the United States.[1] Chinese users are predominately urban, male (over two-thirds), university-educated, and young (see **Figure 1**). The regions with the greatest Internet activity are the cities of Beijing and Shanghai and the province of Guangdong. The largest occupational user groups are students (19.3%), computer technicians (14.9%), engineers (9.9%), foreign enterprise employees (8.9%), Post and Telecommunications Ministry (now Information Industry Ministry) engineers (7.4%), and government staff (6.9%). Most Chinese get online at home (50%), at the office (37%),[2] or at an Internet café (11%). The average monthly income of home Internet users is more than twice that of those without home access. Favored activities are using e-mail, gathering information, downloading software, and chatting online.[3]

The totals of domain addresses and Web sites have also been growing rapidly, at about 20% per quarter. In 1999, there were 48,695 domain addresses and 15,153

---

[1] Stephen J. Anderson, "China's Widening Web," *The China Business Review*, March-April 2000; "China to Have World's Second Largest Net-population in 2005," *Muzi Daily News*, May 1, 2000 [http://www.dailynews.muzi.com]. By year-end 2000, the top five countries in Internet users are projected as follows (in millions): U.S. (135.7), Japan (26.9), Germany (19.1), the UK (17.9); China (15.8).

[2] Foreign companies in China are an important source of Internet access.

[3] China Internet Network Information Center [http://www.cnnic.net.cn].

Web sites. An industry analyst predicts that by 2003, China will surpass South Korea to rank first in Asia for the number of domain names registered annually.[4]

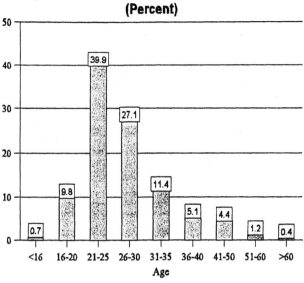

Figure 1. China Internet User Profile by Age (Percent)

Source: China Internet Network Information Center

Computer Ownership

About 32 million Chinese own personal computers. Less than 2% of Chinese households own a computer compared to over 50% of U.S. households. Nonetheless, China's demand for computers is expected to be the second highest in the world after the United States' by the end of 2000. Major American suppliers in China – including IBM, Hewlett-Packard, Compaq, and Dell – have captured approximately 25% of the personal computer market through exports and local production. Legend, a domestic personal computer manufacturer which is owned jointly by the Chinese Academy of Sciences and private investors, is the largest single vendor with 25% of the market.[5]

Mobile Telephones

Because personal computers are still beyond the financial reach of most Chinese, mobile telephones are expected to be the primary means of Internet activity over the

---

[4] Stephen J. Anderson, "China's Widening Web," *The China Business Review*, March-April 2000; Paul Mooney, "Master of His Domain," *ChinaOnline*, May 30, 2000.

[5] Peggy Lim and Ivan Trinh, "Personal Computers and Peripherals," United States Department of State, 1999; Stephen Anderson and S. Cao, and Z. Huang, "Computer Internet Service," United States Department of State, 1999.

next decade. In 1999, China had approximately 40 million cellular phone subscribers.[6] One expert predicts that in two years, the Internet may become available to 60 million Chinese via their cell phones. According to one estimate, by 2004, 250 million cell phones in China will be equipped with wireless application protocol (WAP) or Internet access capability.[7] China's mobile telephone market is dominated by foreign brands. Motorola, Nokia, and Ericsson hold 31.9%, 29.4%, and 21.4% of the market, respectively.[8]

The Chinese Internet Industry

China's Internet services market – Internet service providers (ISPs) and Internet content providers (ICPs)[9] – is characterized by dynamic private entrepreneurship and government involvement and regulation. Central and local governments have demonstrated conflicting attitudes toward private Internet companies. They have attempted to maintain or develop their own Internet services while both supporting and controlling the private sector. U.S. companies have broken little ground in providing Internet services. In September 1999, America Online (AOL) and a local partner launched Internet service in Hong Kong with an eye toward mainland China. AOL has engaged in preliminary discussions with PRC officials on setting up a Chinese Internet service or teaming up with a local service provider, but it is holding off due to regulatory and market uncertainties.[10] In June 2000, Sinobull.com,[11] an e-finance or online securities trading company, announced an agreement with China Telecom to provide financial services through sinohome.com [http://www.sinohome.com], the Web portal of Chinanet, China Telecom's ISP.

Internet Service Providers

China's ISP market is dominated by state-owned telecommunications companies administered by the Ministry of Information Industry (MII). China Telecom was the original national telephone monopoly and continues to dominate land line services. In 1999, MII broke up China Telecom and created China Unicom to specialize in

---

[6] "White House Fact Sheet on the U.S.-China WTO Accession Deal," *U.S. Newswire*, March 1, 2000.

[7] Jonathan S. Landreth, "'Don't Be Dewy-Eyed,' Author Schell Warns," *Sina.com News*, 5/23/00 [http://www.Sina.com.cn]; Inside China Today [http://www.insidechina.com], "Mobile Phones the Future of the Internet in China," 4/17/00, *Agence France Presse*.

[8] "Motorola, Nokia, Ericsson, Siemens Top China's Cellphone Sector, Survey Says," *ChinaOnline*, July 31, 2000.

[9] Internet service providers such as America Online sell access links to the World Wide Web; Internet content providers offer search engines, vertical channels, news, e-mail, and other services. In the United States, the many Internet service providers also offer content services; in China, the two functions remain distinct.

[10] "'You've Got Mail' May Be Heard in China Soon," *ChinaOnline*, July 21, 2000.

[11] Sinobull.com [http://www.sinobull.com.cn] is a subsidiary of The Hartcourt Companies, Inc.

pager services, China Mobile to serve the cellular phone market, and China Star to provide satellite communications. Other major telecommunications competitors offering Internet services include Jitong Communications, also operated by MII, and Netcom Corporation,[12] which offers high bandwidth services. Both China Telecom and China Unicom are owned partially by private investors: China Telecom raised $4.2 billion in 1997 when it went public on the New York Stock Exchange (NYSE); China Unicom garnered nearly $5 billion in a June 2000 NYSE initial public offering.[13]

In 1999, China Telecom's ISP, Chinanet [http://www.chinanet.cn.net], and its local subsidiaries dominated China's ISP market, controlling 83% of Internet connections. Nearly all of China's privately-owned ISP's have struggled to make profits. Eighty percent of their costs involve leasing telephone lines from China Telecom.[14] Furthermore, because the major ISPs are administered by MII, they reportedly often enjoy preferential treatment by the regulatory agency. Observers predict that 70% of the country's Internet companies will go bankrupt or merge with others by the end of 2000.[15] Those with venture-capital, government affiliations, or specialized services have better chances of success.

In July 2000, MII began considering relaxing regulations on small, private ISP's in order to create a more competitive environment in anticipation of China's membership in the WTO. However, some industry experts expect China Telecom to remain dominant and MII to continue to resist market liberalization in order to maintain its controls over Chinese Web access and content.[16] In July 2000, China Telecom offered special low rates to several state media organizations, including Xinhua News Agency, *People's Daily*, and China Central Television, who operate Web sites.

Controls over Internet Content

The Chinese government attempts to control the Internet in three ways:

(1) The state constrains Internet activity through granting or withholding permits and licenses, government contracts, and other privileges. For example, many users are required to register with the local police when they purchase Internet service. Internet content providers (ICPs) must obtain approval from government agencies to connect to ISPs, disseminate news, and list on foreign stock exchanges.

---

[12] Netcom is a joint stock company owned by five central government divisions and Shanghai municipality.

[13] Anderson, "China's Widening Web."

[14] By contrast, connector fees constitute only 5-6% of American ISP costs. Wei Liming, "Are You Online?"*Beijing Review*, November 30-December 6, 1998, pp. 8-10.

[15] "70% of China Internet Firms Face Bankruptcy, Merger," *Muzi Daily News*, May 4, 2000 [http://www.dailynews.muzi.com]; "MII Report Card: China's ISPs Demonstrate Weaknesses but Are Progressing," *ChinaOnline*, July 13, 2000.

[16] "After WTO, China Will Partially Open Telecom Sector to Foreign Investment," *ChinaOnline*, July 26, 2000.

(2) The Internet is directly censored. For example, Chinese police and state telecommunications authorities sporadically monitor and intermittently block e-mail communication and domestic and foreign Web sites that contain views that are highly critical of the government. Twenty provinces and municipalities have reportedly established Internet police forces. Censors at Government-run chat rooms delete provocative messages. Obstructed foreign Web sites have included the *Washington Post* and *New York Times*. However, both central and local governments lack the capacity to screen all e-mailings and close all objectionable sites all the time.

(3) The Chinese Communist Party Propaganda Department, the State Council Information Office, the Ministry of Public Security, and other agencies set general guidelines for Internet and other mass media content. For example, the state prohibits both official and non-official news sites from quoting foreign news sources or reporting without Communist Party approval. The Chinese government forbids Internet users, ISPs, and ICPs to directly broach sensitive political topics or to access or provide links to Web sites that contain banned content.[17] The State Secrecy Bureau forbids any communication or information involving "state secrets."[18]

Reported examples of punishable Internet activity have included having a personal Web site that is *indirectly* linked to a pornographic Web address, selling Chinese e-mail addresses to a dissident group located in the United States, and posting "subversive" news or views on such issues as the Tiananmen Square crackdown and the Falun Gong movement. Sanctions for illegal Internet activity have included temporarily shutting down Web sites, fines, and prison sentences of one to ten years. There are reportedly two Chinese "cyberdissidents" currently serving jail terms.[19] In February 2000, hundreds of Internet cafés in Beijing and Shanghai were closed for operating without an official license, not paying taxes, or disseminating provocative political or pornographic material.[20] In August 2000, Chinese police closed a dissident Web site, "New Culture Forum," but could not find its sponsors.

Most Chinese e-mail writers, Web site creators, and private Internet content providers such as Sina.com engage in self-censorship in order to avoid trouble with the government. ChinaOnline [http://www.chinaonline.com], an American Web site that provides information on China's business environment and high tech industry, avoids controversial political issues regarding human rights, Tibet, and Taiwan. Many Chinese Internet portals utilize software to weed out politically sensitive language in their chat rooms. Moreover, high user fees and telephone charges and slow Internet access speeds discourage many Chinese from surfing the Web for relatively

---

[17] Lester J. Gesteland, "Internet Censored Further in China," *ChinaOnline*, January 26, 2000; Gary Chen, "China Internet: Government Tightens Controls, Clamps Down On News," *ChinaOnline*, May 18, 2000.

[18] "State secrets" can mean any information that has not been officially released. "Passing state secrets" is punishable by death, though sentences are usually commuted to prison terms of 10-15 years.

[19] Huang Qi posted information over the Internet about the Tiananmen Square crackdown; Qi Yanchen posted articles critical of the PRC government.

[20] In 1999, Beijing and Shanghai reportedly had 1000 and 900 Internet cafés, respectively.

superfluous, including political, purposes.[21] In order to better deal with regulatory and content issues and break into the saturated ICP market, Yahoo! negotiated a joint venture with Founder Electronics,[22] a Chinese software company, to produce a Chinese Web portal.

The Chinese government is also exploiting the Internet for its own purposes. Agencies and news media of the Communist Party and state are developing their own Web sites to compete with private ones and to disseminate propaganda. The Internet is being used to connect regional government units. Police and security forces are developing software to monitor Internet communication .

"Plugging a Sieve". Many government officials acknowledge that the state lacks sufficient resources and capabilities to monitor the entire Internet.[23] Despite government controls and self-censorship, the Internet has provided many Chinese with a rapid and largely unmonitored means of communication through e-mail, relatively open forums of expression via chat rooms, and unprecedented exposure to foreign news and ideas by way of the World Wide Web. For example, both the banned China Democracy Party and Falun Gong movement relied on e-mail and their own Web sites to cultivate members.[24] Internet cafés, which sell terminal access for an hourly fee, provide anonymity for individuals who express controversial ideas in chat rooms; the Taiwanese presidential election and a corruption scandal in Xiamen city have been popular recent topics.[25] Authors often criticize political leaders by using nicknames which escape monitoring personnel and software.

Many foreign-language Web sites, even those with political content, evade censors. Hong Kong Web sites are a popular source of foreign news. Chinese gays, lacking open spaces to meet, have reportedly used the Internet to make contacts in China and abroad.

Since the majority of China's most popular ICP's are privately-owned, content is driven not only by concerns about censors but also about readership. In order to attract readers, Chinese Internet portals provide current and sometimes controversial news and links about the economy, society, and alternative lifestyles. They occasionally push the boundaries of acceptable political coverage. For example,

---

[21] Slow access speeds are caused by low bandwidth, slow modems of Internet servers, and insufficient telephone trunk lines that link China to the outside world.

[22] Founder Group is owned by Beijing University and private investors in China and Hong Kong.

[23] Scott Savin, "China's Internet Shakedown," *Asian Wall Street Journal*, February 2, 2000, p. 10.

[24] When the government cracked down on these movements, it also closed their Web sites.

[25] Elisabeth Rosenthal, "Web Sites Bloom in China, and Are Weeded," *New York Times*, December 23, 1999; Lorien Holland and Trish Saywell, "Plugging a Sieve," *Far Eastern Economic Review*, February 10, 2000, p. 20; John Pomfret, "Chinese Web Opens Portals to New Way of Life," *Washington Post*, February 13, 2000, p. A1.

Sohu.com was the first Web site to carry the text of Taiwan President Chen Shui-bian's inauguration speech.[26]

Some Chinese dissidents have reportedly found ways to avoid detection and bypass government filters. They have spread political news by sending mass e-mailings to random e-mail addresses while changing their own Internet addresses frequently. Underground Internet magazines have been written in China, sent overseas, and then e-mailed back to China.[27] Some Internet users connect to special Web sites that can access banned URL's. Chinese Web surfers can also evade government controls by setting up accounts with foreign Internet service providers. Hackers have disrupted official Web sites and disabled the devices that block Internet addresses.[28]

The Internet's Possible Effects on Chinese Politics

The Internet has given a small but rapidly growing number of Chinese economic opportunities and a potent communication and information tool. Analysts suggest several factors that may influence how Chinese use the Internet politically: the government's efforts to regulate content; MII's regulatory powers over Internet services; the economic and political influence of the new technological elite; and the political atmosphere in general.

As with economic reforms, the PRC government both welcomes its contributions to China's modernization and guards against its adverse effects on political control. Some of the government's efforts at regulating the Internet are new and only partially successful; they involve employing personnel, software, and servers that monitor Internet traffic. Other means of controlling the Internet have long been used to effectively regulate other forms of social activity. These methods include granting compliant individuals and companies government approval or material rewards and severely punishing those who violate state laws or prohibitions.

China's "new economy" entrepreneurs are reportedly eroding the state's sphere of influence and gaining a voice in policy-making, but they lack real political power. They possess the capability of attracting relatively large amounts of foreign capital and the potential capability of disseminating information on a vast scale. Some observers note that Premier Zhu Rongji and many other reformers in the Communist Party leadership acknowledge and support the desires of Chinese Internet and e-commerce visionaries to create a stable legal foundation for the Internet industry, encourage foreign investment, break down China Telecom's monopoly of the ISP

---

[26] "Sohu's Struggle," *Far Eastern Economic Review*, June 8, 2000, p. 62.

[27] Maggie Farley, "'Cyberdissident' in China on Trial for Subversion," *Los Angeles Times*, December 5, 1998, p. A1.

[28] Maggie Farley, "Dissidents Hack Holes in China's New Wall," *Los Angeles Times*, January 4, 1999, p. A1; Julie Schmit and Paul Wiseman, "Surfing the Dragon: Web Surfers Find Cracks in Wall of Official China," *USA Today*, March 15, 2000, p. 01B.

sector, and restrain government censorship of content.[29] IT executives have formed industry organizations such as I & I (Internet & Industry) and arranged regular meetings such as the Internet Content Providers' Management Summit to share information, coordinate activities, and present their positions to MII and the State Council Information Office. In July 2000, private and state-owned Web enterprises established the National Internet Society which plans to hold symposiums and offer advice to Internet start-up companies.

However, the Internet industry also faces government opposition and ignorance and lacks its own political connections and agenda. Many MII officials, Communist Party conservatives, and heads of "old economy" state-owned industries fear losing political and economic influence to the IT industry and have attempted to control its growth. Internet industry leaders have complained that even many scientifically-trained government officials lack sufficient understanding of high tech issues.[30] Some analysts suggest that because of their youth and independence, most Internet industry entrepreneurs remain largely outside the political process. Many of them have expressed a disinterest in politics.[31] Some of China's most disaffected groups, such as unemployed workers, have made little use of the Internet to advance their causes.

U.S. Interests

Congressional Legislation

In the May 2000 House debates on H.R. 4444 granting China permanent normal trade relations (PNTR) status, many proponents of the bill argued that the PRC's accession to the WTO would bolster American values and business interests in China.[32] They cited studies claiming that China ranks among the fastest growing markets in the world for personal computers, computer software, and telecommunications products and services. Clinton administration officials and many Members of Congress argued that American investment in China's high technology sector would generate profits for American businesses, spur research and development, and help maintain U.S. global leadership in information technology (IT). Furthermore, proponents contended, it would promote freedom and human rights in China by facilitating the access and exchange of information and undermining the PRC government's controls in these areas.[33] Opponents, on the other hand, retorted that

---

[29] Scott Savitt, "China's Internet Shakedown," *Asian Wall Street Journal*, p. 10.

[30] Interview with Chinese information industry analyst, July 2000; Gary Chen, "China Internet: Government Tightens Controls, Clamps Down on News," *ChinaOnline*.

[31] "Wired China – The Flies Swarm In," *The Economist*, July 22, 2000, pp. 24-6.

[32] Some of the most powerful backers of PNTR status for China were leading technology associations, such as the American Electronics Association. See Testimony of the U.S. High-Tech Industry on China, Senate Finance Committee, February 23, 2000, and *Congressional Record*, May 24, 2000.

[33] *M2Presswire*, March 2, 2000.

the Communist Party's political controls not only remained undeterred by the Internet but also were enhanced by it.[34]

On March 11, 1999, H.Con.Res. 28, which urges the U.S. government to pass a United Nations resolution criticizing China for its human rights abuses, passed the House. The bill condemns China for, among other human rights violations, putting businessman Lin Hai on trial because he allegedly provided e-mail addresses to a pro-democracy Internet magazine based in the United States.[35] On May 24, 2000, H.R. 4444 passed the House. Title VII of the bill authorizes appropriations for international broadcasting operations, including Voice of America and Radio Free Asia broadcasting and Radio Free Asia's Internet services to China.

WTO Provisions

According to China's WTO agreements, the PRC (People's Republic of China) is to allow foreign investment in all telecommunications services for the first time, eliminate tariffs on IT products, and grant foreign companies trading and distribution rights. The PRC government has promised, for example, to open value-added telecommunications services (including Internet, paging, and facsimile) to 50% foreign ownership within two years of China's accession to the WTO. The government has agreed to allow up to 49% foreign equity in mobile telephone services within three years. It has assented to reduce its tariffs on electronics (including computers, semiconductors, and Internet-related equipment) from 13.3% to 0 by 2005. The PRC has promised to abide by the WTO Basic Telecommunications Agreement (BTA) and WTO Information Technology Agreement (ITA), by which WTO members open their telecommunications and IT markets to other members.

U.S. companies have established a strong presence in computer and cellular telephone manufacturing and sales, software development, and telecommunications infrastructure in China. However, the PRC has been more protective of its fledgling Internet industry; the government has generally welcomed American capital and expertise but has been wary about foreign management or control. Analysts suggest that even after China accedes to the WTO, foreign investors in telecommunications, especially Internet services, may be caught in a tug-of-war between conservative and liberal Chinese interpretations of WTO regulations. On the one hand, Minister of Information Industry Wu Jichuan has reportedly opposed foreign investment in the Chinese Internet industry. On the other hand, economic reformers, such as Premier Zhu Rongji, and many provincial and municipal government officials have been more supportive of foreign investment and increased competition in Internet goods and services.

---

[34] Ellen Bork, "The Red Internet," *Washington Post*, June 21, 2000.

[35] Lin was released in March 2000 after serving 18 months in prison.

U.S. Private Sector Involvement

Although Chinese Internet services have remained relatively closed to foreign involvement, American companies have already made considerable progress in other areas. U.S. high tech exports to the PRC increased over 500 percent between 1990 and 1998.[36] American telecommunications and information technology firms have invested heavily in products and systems that support Internet use in China. For example, Motorola has committed $1.5 billion in direct investment and operates the largest wholly foreign-owned subsidiary in the PRC.[37] China Telecom has hired AT&T to help expand China's telephone lines and capabilities. In May 2000, AT&T entered into a joint-venture with Shanghai Telecom, a subsidiary of China Telecom, and private investors to launch Internet Protocol (IP) based broadband network services in Shanghai.[38] Many American IT companies have set up research and design centers in China that utilize local talent. Motorola plans to open a micro chip design center in the city of Suzhou. Hewlett-Packard has set up an "electronic services technology center" in Beijing. Microsoft is investing $80 million in a software research facility in Beijing – one of only two international research facilities operated by Microsoft – and providing additional funds for Beijing University's new Law Center.[39] Lucent Technologies plans to inject $15 million into a research and development center in Shanghai, its largest R&D center in Asia.

American high tech, financial, and venture capital enterprises have injected an estimated $200 million into China's Internet industry.[40] Many of China's most influential "dotcom"companies combine Chinese and American human and financial resources. Many indigenous Chinese Internet entrepreneurs were educated in the United States. For example, Sohu.com [http://www.Sohu.com.cn] is one of the leading Chinese Web portals with over 2.3 million registered users. Charles Zhang, Sohu's founder, is a Chinese national who earned his doctorate at M.I.T. His financial backers include former M.I.T. associates, Intel, and Dow Jones and well as Japanese and Chinese companies. Sina.com [http://www.sina.com], one of China's most popular Web sites, was created in 1998 via a merger between a Bejiing high tech firm (Stone Group) and a Silicon Valley Internet company. Sina.com developed its reputation for providing breaking news with its continuous coverage of the U.S.

---

[36] U.S. exports of office machines and automatic data processing machines (computers) in 1999 totaled $843 million. See CRS Report RL30557, "China's International Trade: Data and Trends," by Dick K. Nanto and Thomas Lum.

[37] Testimony of Christopher B. Galvin, Chairman and CEO, Motorola, before the Senate Finance Committee, February 23, 2000.

[38] Bien Perez, "AT&T to make Inroads: Landmark Broadband Joint Venture in Shanghai Points to the Future for Foreign Companies," *South China Morning Post*, May 30, 2000, p. 1.

[39] Jingjuan Hou, "Hewlett-Packard Offers E-Service Support," *China Daily*, May 21, 2000; Bill Gates, "Yes, More Trade With China," *Washington Post*, May 23, 2000.

[40] John Pomfret, op. cit.

accidental bombing of the Chinese embassy in Belgrade in May 1999.[41] In July 2000, Sina.com began trading on the NASDAQ stock exchange.[42] The Dow Jones Company is a major shareholder.

Etang.com [http://www.etang.com] is a new Chinese Internet portal targeting the more individualistic and affluent younger (18-35) generation. Haisong Tang, Etang's Shanghainese founder, is a Harvard graduate who returned to China with other Harvard-educated Chinese and $45 million in venture capital from the United States.[43] Alibaba.com [http://www.alibaba.com], a new e-commerce site, has garnered a global customer base of 140,000 registered members from 188 countries, including 90,000 from China. Its customer base is reportedly growing at a rate of 2,000 new members per day. The company recently lured John Wu from Yahoo! to be its chief technology officer and raised $20 million from Japan's Softbank and $5 million from Goldman Sachs.[44]

It is difficult to make predictions about either American participation in the Chinese Internet industry following China's likely accession to the WTO or the Internet's effects upon Chinese politics. The Chinese government remains ambivalent toward foreign investment and management in some areas, such as the ISP and ICP markets. The industry's laws and regulations are in flux. Nonetheless, U.S. companies have made significant inroads in related sectors, such as computers, cell phones, and telecommunications infrastructure. Furthermore, the level of U.S. venture capital in China's Internet services sector indicates strong American interest and commitment. However, even as American and Chinese IT companies overcome economic hurdles, they will likely face resistance from the PRC government if they are perceived to interfere with the government's efforts at maintaining social and political control.

---

[41] Since embassy bombing, the Chinese government has restricted news reporting over the Web.

[42] "Biographic Profile: Zhang Chaoyang, Founder, CEO and President of Sohu.com," *ChinaOnline*; "Biographic Profile: Wang Zhidong: CEO and President of Sina.com," *ChinaOnline*.

[43] Paul Mooney, "Etang.com Targets Chinese Yuppies," *ChinaOnline*, March 2, 2000.

[44] Ching-Ching Ni, "Yahoo Executive, Searching for New Challenge, Signs on With Chinese Firm," *Los Angeles Times*, May 15, 2000.

Internet Policies and Issues
Volume 2

PRESCRIPTION DRUG SALES OVER THE INTERNET

Christopher J. Sroka

ABSTRACT

This report provides an overview of prescription drug sales over the Internet and related legislative activities. The report discusses how online pharmacies operate and some of the concerns raised by the sale of drug products in electronic commerce. The report also describes some recent government and private sector actions taken to address these concerns. The report will be updated as needed.

Overview and Issues of Concern

Purchasing prescription drugs over the Internet is a relatively new phenomenon that has arisen with the explosive growth in the public use of the Internet and electronic commerce. Unlike the sale of many goods, the sale of prescription drugs through traditional retail channels is highly regulated. Prescription drugs can be obtained only with a physician's consent and only from licensed pharmacies. Both the physician and the pharmacist dispensing the medication must be licensed. Furthermore, the product sold, as well as the methods by which it was produced and marketed, must be approved by the U.S. Food and Drug Administration (FDA). Thus, the sale of prescription drugs (a regulated product in traditional settings) over the relatively unregulated Internet has become a concern for policymakers, regulators, and medical practitioners. Distinctions are often made between "legitimate" online pharmacies and those that engage in unethical or illegal dispensing practices.[1] The concerns associated with online pharmacies tend to be directed more towards the practices that are unethical or illegal and less towards those of legitimate online pharmacies.

Legitimate online pharmacies operate much the same way as mail-order pharmacies. However, rather than placing the order via telephone or mail, patients order their medications via the Internet. Medications purchased online are either sent directly to patients or, in some instances, picked up by them later at a local affiliated pharmacy. To verify that the prescription ordered online is accurate, patients mail or fax their new prescriptions to the online pharmacy. Alternatively, they can ask their physicians to phone the online pharmacy and provide the new prescription information directly.[2] Patients can also order refills of prescription drugs previously dispensed by the online pharmacy and transfer existing prescriptions from other pharmacies (both online and traditional). Some online pharmacies require patients to submit a medical profile, which the online pharmacy maintains along with a record of previous prescriptions. This allows the online pharmacy to determine if there are any potential drug interactions or side effects which may have an adverse effect on the patient. Online pharmacies usually have telephone numbers or email addresses so that their customers can contact a pharmacist should they need to discuss their medications or other problems they may encounter.

---

[1] See "Issue Brief: Internet Pharmaceutical Services," National Association of Chain Drug Stores, August 2, 1999. Available at
[http://www.nacds.org/news/releases/nr_080299_brief.html].

[2] This method of transmitting prescription information is also acceptable for prescriptions obtained at traditional retail establishments.

Although getting a prescription filled online can be done relatively easily with just a few clicks, receiving the medication may take several days. One online pharmacy, Drugstore.com [www.drugstore.com], instructs consumers to allow 3-5 days for the pharmacy to receive the prescription and another 1-2 days for the pharmacy to process the prescription. The time it takes to deliver the medication from the online pharmacy to the customer can vary depending on the preferences of the customer. Drugstore.com provides free standard delivery via the U.S. Postal Service Priority mail, which requires another 2-3 days. However, customers can opt for UPS 2-Day Shipping for $5.95 or UPS Overnight Shipping for $11.95. Other online pharmacies that deliver prescriptions operate similarly. Some online pharmacies, such as [www.cvs.com], [www.riteaid.com], and [www.walgreens.com], are online extensions of traditional chain pharmacies. The online version of traditional chain pharmacies generally give customers the option of having the medication delivered or picking it up themselves from a local chain outlet.

There is a spectrum of online pharmacies whose activities fall outside what many would consider ethical and legitimate pharmacy practices. One practice that tends to receive criticism is when both the prescribing and the dispensing of the drug are performed online simultaneously. Several websites allow customers to receive a prescription for medication without a physical examination by a physician. In place of a traditional face-to-face consultation, the customer fills out a medical questionnaire. Reportedly, a licensed physician at the online pharmacy evaluates the questionnaire, then, if the prescription is medically justified, authorizes the online pharmacy to send the medication to the patient. This practice tends to be limited more to "lifestyle" prescription drugs, such as those that alleviate allergies, promote hair growth, treat impotence, or control a person's weight. Nevertheless, it is feasible that controlled prescription drugs could be dispensed via the Internet without a medical examination. The American Medical Association (AMA) is critical of prescribing drugs without a physical examination. Such a practice violates AMA's ethical standards, and, in the association's opinion, raises serious quality-of-care issues.[3]

A second practice, and one that is illegal in many circumstances, is the sale of prescription drugs to American consumers via the Internet by foreign-based companies. With some exceptions, it is illegal to import prescription drugs that are not approved by the FDA. FDA approval involves not only assessing a drug's safety and effectiveness, but also inspecting the facility in which it is manufactured.[4] Unless the importing party can prove that the drugs bought from abroad are FDA-approved, and manufactured in an FDA-approved facility, the agency treats the imported drugs as unapproved products.[5] Despite this policy, there are numerous

---

[3] Melba Newsome, "Physicians Cry Foul Over Web Drug Sales," *Investor's Business Daily*, March 8, 1999, p. A1.

[4] For more information on FDA procedures, see CRS Report 95-422 SPR, "Food and Drug Administration: Selected Funding and Policy Issues for FY2000" by Donna U. Vogt, updated January 31, 2000.

[5] See "Information on Importation of Drugs," prepared by the Division of Import Operations and Policy, U.S. Food and Drug Administration. Available at

(continued...)

foreign-based pharmacies that sell prescription drugs to American consumers. These products may be drugs not approved for use in the U.S. by the FDA, counterfeit copies of FDA-approved drugs, or FDA-approved drugs that have not been manufactured, stored, and handled in an FDA-approved manner. Moreover, many foreign countries do not require patients to obtain prescriptions for some drugs while patients buying the same drugs in the U.S. may be sold only by prescription. This means that foreign-based online pharmacies may be selling prescription drugs to American customers who do not have a physician's consent to use the drug. Consequently, drugs obtained from foreign online pharmacies could pose serious health and legal problems for American consumers.

Although most criticism is focused on foreign-based online pharmacies and American online pharmacies with questionable practices, so-called legitimate pharmacies are not free from controversy. Questions have been raised regarding the quality of care received by patients when they are not able to consult with pharmacists in person. In order to provide patient access to a pharmacist, some online pharmacies allow customers to submit personalized questions to pharmacists via email. Furthermore, some online pharmacies do not disclose to patients the name or credentials of the pharmacist. Thus, some have expressed concern that patients may be consulting with a pharmacist who is not licensed in the patient's state.

There are other concerns associated with legitimate online pharmacies. Yet these concerns are not constrained only to the sale of prescription drugs; rather, they apply to electronic commerce transactions in general. One issue is whether using the Internet is secure enough to offer customers an appropriate degree of privacy. Some online pharmacies require customers to submit credit card, medical, and insurance information over the Internet. This practice raises concerns that such personal information could be accessed by other people as it is transmitted. In an attempt to protect the transmission of personal information, several online pharmacies use secure servers that encrypt customers' personal information so that it cannot be read as it travels over the Internet.

Another issue involves the confidentiality of consumer information once it is received by the pharmacy. Some legislators are concerned because it is not certain whether online pharmacies are adequately protecting consumers' personal information.[6] A spokesperson for the online pharmacy Soma (now part of [www.cvs.com]) claimed that, compared to the corner drugstore, online pharmacies offer more privacy.[7] However, this is not an issue that solely affects online pharmacies. For example, the traditional retail pharmacy operations of Giant Food and CVS reportedly shared detailed information on customers with Elensys, a data

---

[5] (...continued)
[http://www.fda.gov/ora/import/pipinfo.htm].

[6] Letter to General Accounting Office from Reps. John D. Dingell, Ron Klink, Henry A. Waxman, and Sherrod Brown requesting investigation into online pharmacies.

[7] Lesly C. Hallman and Joyce Cutler, "Pharmaceutical Industry Seeks Regulations to Guide Growing Use of Internet," *Daily Report for Executives*, Bureau of National Affairs. March 9, 1999.

management company.[8]   According to this report, Elensys arranged for drug manufacturers to pay the pharmacies for this information so that the manufacturers could send "educational" material to consumers. Although the practice was defended as benefitting consumers, both companies announced that it would be discontinued.[9]

Advantages of Online Pharmacies

Despite the concerns raised by legitimate online pharmacies and the existence of some unethical and illegal online pharmacies, purchasing prescription drugs over the Internet can provide consumers many advantages over traditional retail pharmacies. One major advantage is convenience. Online pharmacies deliver the drugs directly to the customer. While the customer may have to wait several days to receive the drugs, he or she does not have to travel to a local traditional pharmacy to order the drug and wait there for the prescription to be filled. Furthermore, for those with easy access to Internet connections, online pharmacies are available 24 hours a day, 7 days a week.

Some online pharmacies advertise that they provide lower prices to consumers than traditional retail pharmacies. Online pharmacies tend to operate similarly to mail-order pharmacies. Because many online pharmacies do not operate retail outlets, they may have lower operating costs. Online pharmacies can also buy in larger volumes than many small, independent pharmacies (but not necessarily more cheaply than large retail chains), possibly leading to greater cost savings. These lower costs could be passed on to consumers in the form of lower prices. However, although consumers may be paying a lower base price for online prescriptions, shipping and handling charges may reduce their savings, or even result in a higher price than the consumer would pay in a retail pharmacy. This is more likely to occur when a consumer chooses overnight delivery over the free standard delivery by the U.S. Postal Service. On the other hand, for relatively high-priced prescription drugs, shipping costs are less likely to mitigate the savings.

Another advantage, often advertised by many online pharmacies, is easier access to health and medical information. Many online pharmacies provide detailed drug information on their websites, such as the availability of a generic substitute, possible food and drug interactions, and other possible side effects. Some online pharmacies provide information about illnesses, allowing customers to learn more about their medical conditions. Online pharmacies also tend to list their prices for commonly prescribed drugs.[10] This could assist consumers in selecting the lowest priced online pharmacy to have their prescriptions filled. While this kind of information may be available from retail pharmacies, some find that computer access provides a more convenient and accessible source of information.

---

[8] Robert O'Harrow, Jr., "Prescription Sales, Privacy Fears; CVS, Giant Share Customer Records with Drug Marketing Firm," *Washington Post*, February 15, 1998.

[9] Robert O'Harrow, Jr., "CVS Also Cuts Ties to Marketing Service; Like Giant, Firm Cites Privacy on Prescriptions," *Washington Post*, February 19, 1998.

[10] These prices are for cash-paying customers. Online pharmacies usually indicate that the prices listed may vary for consumers with prescription drug insurance.

Recent Government Actions

The emergence of online pharmacies has prompted actions by Congress, the Clinton Administration, FDA, and several state governments. These actions have taken the form of proposed policy changes, heightened government oversight, and greater enforcement of existing consumer protection regulations.

Congressional Actions

Three bills related to online prescription drug sales have been introduced in the 106th Congress. The Medical Information Protection Act of 1999 (S. 881) was introduced on April 27, 1999 by Senator Robert Bennett and referred to the Committee on Health, Education, Labor, and Pensions. This bill seeks to prevent the unauthorized disclosure of consumers' health information while at the same time allowing health care professionals to access patient data to improve health care and research. The bill's privacy provisions target all health care delivery, not just online pharmacies. However, online medicine is one factor that influenced the proposed legislation.[11]

On August 5, 1999, the Internet Pharmacy Consumer Protection Act (H.R. 2763) was introduced by Representative Ron Klink and referred to the House Committee on Commerce. This bill would establish a set of minimum requirements for online pharmacies. The bill would require online pharmacies to have a webpage on their sites that displays (1) the name, address of the principal place of business, and telephone number of the online seller, (2) each state in which the business is authorized to dispense prescription drugs, (3) the name of each of the online pharmacy's pharmacists and the state in which he or she is licensed to practice, and (4) when the online pharmacy provides medical consultations, the name, type of profession, and state of licensure of each individual providing consultation. Each page on the online pharmacy's site would be required to have a clearly visible link to the page providing the information described above. Furthermore, the bill would make the Secretary of Health and Human Services responsible for enforcement of these provisions. However, for states that have regulations on online pharmacies more stringent than those specified in the bill, and have the means to enforce the regulations, the measure gives them primary enforcement responsibility.

A third bill related to the sale of prescription drugs over the Internet was introduced on February 10, 2000. The bill, entitled the Pharmaceutical Freedom Act of 2000 (H.R. 3636) was introduced by Representative Ron Paul and referred to the Committee on Commerce and the Committee on Ways and Means. Among other things, the bill seeks to make it easier to import prescription drugs. The bill would allow authorized importers to bring prescription drugs into the United States if the importer submits an application to the Secretary of Health and Human Services and the Secretary approves the application. H.R. 3636 also contains a section specifying how the bill is to be enforced with respect to online pharmacies. The bill states that the Secretary may not take any action against online drug sales under the Act as long as (1) the online sale was made in compliance with the Act and applicable state laws,

---

[11] See Senator Bennett's website [http://www.senate.gov/~bennett/mipaspeech.html].

and (2) the online pharmacy provides on its website accurate information regarding compliance with the Act and applicable state laws.

On July 30, 1999, the Subcommittee on Oversight and Investigations of the House Commerce Committee held a hearing on the benefits and risks of online pharmacies. Witnesses that testified at the hearing included officials from the FDA, the U.S. Department of Justice, and the Federal Trade Commission. Other witnesses included state officials in charge of enforcing laws pertaining to the practices of online pharmacies as well as the chief executive officers (CEO) of two licensed online pharmacies. Federal enforcement officials testified that they believed no new laws were needed to deal with the practices of online pharmacies. Instead, federal officials stated that what was needed is more assistance for enforcement of existing laws. State officials, on the other hand, favored new legislation. State officials stated that, at a minimum, a law requiring online pharmacies to post information on how to contact the pharmacy operators is needed. State officials also advocated allowing state attorneys general to file suits against illegal online pharmacies in federal courts. This would allow the states to obtain injunctions against the nationwide operations of illegal online pharmacies, as opposed to obtaining injunctions only against operations being conducted within the state filing the lawsuit. The CEOs at the hearing represented the licensed online pharmacies of PlanetRx [www.planetrx.com] and Drugstore.com. These executives advocated enforcement of existing laws for online pharmacies operating illegally and industry self-regulation for those operating within the law.

The Clinton Administration's Proposal

In December 1999, the Clinton Administration introduced a proposal to address problems raised by online pharmacies. The proposal would require online pharmacies to demonstrate to the FDA that their practices comply with state and federal prescription drug laws. Sites operating without demonstrating compliance with agency rules would be subject to sanctions. The Administration proposal would create new civil monetary penalties of $500,000 per violation for the sale of prescription drugs to consumers without valid prescriptions. To facilitate FDA investigations into online pharmacy practices, the Administration's proposal would provide the agency with administrative subpoena authority when investigating potentially illegal drug sales over the Internet. Furthermore, the Administration's proposal would provide $10 million in the FDA's FY 2001 budget for the agency to develop a rapid response team and to upgrade its computer technology so that the agency can more effectively identify, investigate, and prosecute illegal prescription drug sales practices conducted over the Internet. The Administration also announced a new public education campaign, both over the Internet and through traditional media outlets, informing consumers on how to safely purchase prescription drugs online.

FDA Enforcement

In December 1999, the FDA announced the launching of an Internet site aimed at helping consumers choose legitimate and safe online pharmacies. The website, [www.fda.gov/oc/buyonline], provides consumers with tips and precautions for buying prescription drugs over the Internet. The FDA website warns consumers to avoid buying from online pharmacies that do not require a prescription, do not provide access to a pharmacist, or are located in foreign countries. The website also allows consumers to report suspicious online pharmacies to the FDA.

The FDA has also taken action against foreign online pharmacies selling prescription drugs to American consumers. In February 2000, the agency announced that it had sent letters via the Internet ("cyber" letters) to potentially illegal foreign-based pharmacy websites. The "cyber" letters warned the foreign operators that their businesses may be operating illegally and informed the websites of U.S. prescription drug laws and regulations. The "cyber" letters also warned the websites that future shipments of their products into the U.S. may be detained and subject to refusal of entry. Hard copies of the "cyber" letters were sent to the website operator, U.S. Customs officials, and officials in the home country of the website operator. As of February 2, 2000, one targeted website had responded to the FDA and had indicated that it will cease its illegal activities.[12]

Actions at the State Level

Some states have taken their own action against online pharmacies. In June 1999, the State of Kansas filed lawsuits against five online pharmacies. Illinois and Missouri filed separate but similar lawsuits in October 1999. Online pharmacies must be licensed in each state to which the pharmacy sends its products. The state lawsuits are targeting online prescription drug sales by companies and individuals who allegedly are not licensed to practice medicine or dispense prescription drugs in the states to which drugs have been delivered. The parties charged in the lawsuits also allegedly engaged in prescribing medication over the Internet without any physical contact with customers or without verifying the validity of the medical information the customers provided.

Private Sector Actions

The private sector has also taken its own actions to address problems raised by the sale of prescription drugs over the Internet. On February 9, 1999, the National Association of Boards of Pharmacy (NABP) announced the development of an online pharmacy verification program. This program, known as the Verified Internet Pharmacy Practice Sites (VIPPS) program, developed a set of criteria that online pharmacies should meet. An online pharmacy meeting the criteria can display the VIPPS seal of approval which indicates to consumers that the online pharmacy engages in ethical and legitimate practices. NABP also provides a list of online pharmacies meeting the VIPPS criteria on its website.[13] As of March 1, 2000, four online pharmacies (CVS, Drugstore.com, Merck-Medco Managed Care, and PlanetRx.com) were approved under the VIPPS program. The VIPPS criteria cover

---

[12] To view copies of the "cyber" letters, see
[http://www.fda.gov/cder/warn/cyber/cyber2000.htm].

[13] To view a list of VIPPS-approved pharmacies, see
[http://www.nabp.org/vipps/consumer/listall.asp].

licensure by state agencies, compliance with state and federal laws, protection of patient confidentiality, communication with a pharmacist, storage and shipment of medication, and various other issue areas.[14]

Internet Policies and Issues
Volume 2

INTERNET TRANSACTIONS AND THE SALE TAX

Steven Maguire

ABSTRACT

This report describes state sales and use taxes and the potential effect of Internet transactions on the administration and revenue generation of the tax. Topics covered include state and local tax rates, state tax base, efficiency and equity of differential sales taxes, and sales tax revenue data for the 50 states and the District of Columbia. The moratorium on new or discriminatory Internet taxes, part of the Internet Tax Freedom Act of 1998 (ITFA), is discussed briefly as is the proposed extension and expansion of the legislation. The Advisory Commission on Electronic Commerce, formed as a part of ITFA, is a source of additional information on the taxation of electronic commerce. This report will be updated as legislative events merit.

Introduction

This report serves as an introduction to the economics of the sales and use tax and the emergence of electronic commerce. Presently, 45 states (and the District of Columbia) require that retail outlets add a fixed percentage to the sales price of all taxable items (inclusive of federally imposed excise taxes). The sales tax is applied to transactions occurring in the store and is collected and remitted by the vendor. For remote transactions where the vendor and consumer are in different states, the consumer is responsible for remitting the use tax.[1] The use tax is levied on the *use* of a product or service.

In addition to the states, there are numerous localities and special taxing jurisdictions comprising an estimated 6,400 different sales and use tax rates in the United States.[2] For transactions physically taking place at the store or retail outlet, collection of the sales tax is straightforward. The vendor simply applies the appropriate tax rate. However, with the expanding acceptance of the Internet as an alternative to traditional retail transactions, the collection of the sales and use tax has become an issue of significant importance to vendors, sub-national governments, and consumers.

There are currently several bills addressing the taxation of Internet based commerce awaiting congressional action. Three bills would extend the moratorium on multiple or discriminatory taxation of internet sales: S. 2255 (McCain), S. 2028 (Wyden), and H.R. 3709 (Cox). A fourth bill, H.R. 4267 (Hyde), extends the moratorium and incorporates most of the recommendations of the Advisory Commission on Electronic Commerce. Yet another bill, H.R. 3252 (Kasich and Boehner), makes the moratorium permanent. A sixth bill, S. 2401 (Gregg and Kohl), formalizes nexus (physical presence) standards which are currently defined primarily by Supreme Court rulings. S. 2775 (Dorgan) extends the expiring moratorium four years and encourages states to adopt a streamlined sales and use tax system. In return for tax simplification, states are authorized to join a compact that requires remote sellers with more than $5 million in sales to collect and remit sales and use taxes. And one bill, S. 1433 (Hollings), introduces a federal sales tax of 5% on all Internet and mail order sales. The proceeds from this tax would be collected by the federal

---

[1]This is true only if the vendor does not have physical presence, or substantial nexus, in the consumer's state of residence.

[2]Goolsbee, Austan and Jonathan Zittrain, "Evaluating the Costs and Benefits of Internet Transactions," *National Tax Journal*, vol. 52, no. 3 (September, 1999) p. 413-428. In addition, research by *Vertex Inc.*, a private company that collects and sells jurisdiction tax data to vendors, found that over the last six years an average of 639 jurisdictions implemented tax rate changes a year.

government then redistributed to the states by an apportionment formula loosely based on population and poverty rate. For a more in-depth review of all pending internet related legislation, see CRS Report RL30412, *Internet Taxation: Bills in the 106th Congress.*

The first section describes the imposition of the sales and use tax from the tax administrator's point of view. The second section provides an overview of the economic aspects of sales taxes and how Internet transactions, or 'Internet taxes,' have changed the role of the sales tax in state and local government finance. The report concludes with some further observations.

The Imposition of the Sales and Use Tax

State and local governments that impose a general sales tax on transactions typically calculate the tax as a fixed percentage of a retail good's purchase price.[3] In theory, the sales and companion use tax are seen in part as a benefits received taxes on businesses and consumers for state and local expenditures such as fire protection, road maintenance, education, and police protection. Most states require monthly remittance of the sales tax and often offer discounts to businesses that pay early or have total sales exceeding a threshold amount.[4] The use tax is remitted by the consumer.

Sales Tax Pyramiding. However, not all transactions are taxed. Business-to-business transactions are in some cases not subject to the retail sales tax with the understanding that the purchaser is using the good as an input to production. Including business to business transactions leads to 'pyramiding' of the sales tax. For example, if a coffee shop were to pay a retail sales tax on the purchase of wholesale coffee beans, and then impose a retail sales tax on coffee brewed for the final consumer, the total sales tax paid for the cup of coffee would exceed the statutory rate.

In addition to some business purchases, many individuals and organizations are exempt from the sales tax. Entities wishing to claim the sales tax exemption are often issued a certificate indicating their tax-free status and are required to present their certification at the point of transaction. Non-profit organizations, such as those whose mission is religious, charitable, educational, or to promote the public health, are often the beneficiaries of sales tax-exempt status.

Substantial Nexus. The United States Supreme Court has held that a state has no authority to require a vendor to withhold that state's sales and use taxes unless the vendor has a "substantial nexus" with the taxing state.[5] Generally, substantial nexus

---

[3]Some states impose a gross receipts tax which is similar to a general sales tax. A gross receipts tax is levied on businesses receipts and not the consumer expenditure. However, businesses in these states collect the tax on each transaction.

[4]Seventeen of the 45 states with a sales tax do not offer a vendor discount.

[5]There are two decisions that clarified the taxation of out-of-state vendors. In *National Bellas*

(continued...)

means physical presence. Out-of-state businesses without substantial nexus in the taxing state are not required to collect state and local sales use taxes on transactions involving customers in the home taxing state. The residence of the purchaser is not a sufficient nexus. However, the Court has also held that Congress, under its power to regulate interstate commerce, could grant authority to the states to require the vendor to collect use taxes.

Because interstate Internet transactions do not have the sales and use tax added to their price by out-of-state vendors, it is argued that Internet retailers and catalogue retailers have a competitive advantage over traditional 'bricks and mortar' vendors who are required to collect the tax. The equitable treatment of all vendors is the objective of many of the proposed changes to the administration of the sales and use tax.

If the vendor does not have substantial nexus the *consumer* is required to remit the use tax to their state government. All states with a sales tax also impose a use tax though compliance is very low. Thus, contrary to what some observers say, Internet purchases are not "tax free."[6]

The Economics of the Sales and Use Tax

In 1932, Mississippi was the first state to impose a general state sales tax.[7] During the remainder of the 1930, an era characterized by declining revenue from income and corporate taxes, 23 other states followed suit and implemented a general sales tax to compensate for the lost revenue.[8] At the time, the sales tax was relatively easy to administer and could raise a significant amount of revenue with a relatively low rate.[9] Given the relative success of the sales tax, all but five other states added the sales tax to their tax infrastructure by the late 1960. Use taxes are in practice analogous to the sales tax though the tax is on the *use* of the product purchased rather than the transaction. The last of the 45 states to enact a general sales tax (along with a use tax) was Vermont in 1969.

---

[5](...continued)
Hess v. Illinois Department of Revenue (1967) the court established the substantial nexus argument. In *Quill v. North Dakota* (1992) the court upheld the nexus argument and further specified the physical presence standard for substantial nexus.

[6]The much discussed moratorium on Internet taxation applies to any multiple or discriminatory taxes targeted explicitly at Internet retailers. The sales and use tax is not a new tax.

[7]The *use* tax, the companion to the sales tax, was added in 1938. In the early years of the sales tax, states began with general sales then added the use tax to capture revenue from sales made out-of-state. Eventually, states adopting a sales tax included the use tax in the initial legislation.

[8]Fox, William F., ed., *Sales Taxation: Critical Issues in Policy and Administration, Sales Tax Trends and Issues*, by Ebel, Robert and Christopher Zimmerman (Westport, CT: Praeger, 1992), pp. 3-26.

[9]The highest rate in 1934 was 3%. At the time the 3% rate was considered quite high.

The revenue a sales and use tax generates depends upon the chosen rate and the base to which the rate applies. The more narrow the base the higher the rate must be to raise an equivalent amount of revenue. States often have somewhat similar consumption expenditures included in their tax base, but they are far from uniform. Tax rates also vary considerably from state to state depending in part on their reliance on other revenue sources. Following is a brief economic analysis of the sales tax and the challenges electronic commerce pose for the imposition and collection of the tax.

Efficiency. A commonly held view among economists is that a "good" tax (or more precisely, an efficient tax) is one that does not significantly distort behavior. Broadly speaking, individuals should make the same relative choices before and after a tax is imposed. The greater the distortions in behavior, the greater the economic welfare loss.

Products purchased over the Internet that escape taxation (i.e., the consumer does not remit the required use taxes), are cheaper and thus generally preferred to the products offered at traditional retail outlets which are required to collect the tax. However, if the transaction costs associated with the Internet purchase, e.g. shipping and internet access, exceed the sum of the traditional transaction costs (time and transportation) and the applicable sales tax, the consumer will choose the traditional means of transaction. Note that the shipping costs added to Internet purchases are analogous to the transaction costs associated with traditional "main street" shopping, not to the sales taxes imposed.

Equity. The sales tax has often been criticized as a regressive tax, or a tax that disproportionately burdens the poor.[10] Assuming Internet shoppers are relatively better off and do not remit use taxes as prescribed by state law, they can avoid paying tax on a significant portion of their consumption expenditures.[11] Those without Internet access at home or work, on the other hand, are not afforded the same opportunity to "evade" the sales and use tax. In this way, electronic commerce may actually exacerbate the regressiveness of the sales tax, at least in the short run.

Tax Base. In theory, the base of a comprehensive consumption tax should include all income that is not saved.[12] The sales tax, which is often considered a consumption tax, is perhaps better identified as a transaction tax on tangible personal property. Most states only tax tangible goods purchased at the retail level. Services, such as legal and medical, are expenditures often omitted from the sales tax base.[13]

Ideally, the sales tax base should be broad enough to avoid drastic fluctuations in the revenue stream. State budgets must be balanced annually, thus a consistent revenue stream engendered by a broad base sales tax is important for fiscal stability.

---

[10]A regressive tax collects a smaller percentage of personal income as income increases.

[11]Goolsbee and Zittrain (1999) found that the average Internet user had on average two more years of education and $22,000 more in family income than non-Internet users.

[12]A common identity in the economics of income accounting is the following: C=Y-S. Or, consumption (C) equals income (Y) less saving (S).

[13]Only two states tax medical services, Hawaii and New Mexico.

With the apparent shift in the United States from an economy based on transactions of tangible personal property to intangible products and services, the sales and use tax base will continue to narrow.[14] It is then likely that sales tax revenue will also begin to show greater volatility.[15] However, for services, the move from traditional means of transaction to transactions over the Internet does not portend a large loss in state and local sales tax revenue because services are often outside the sales tax base.[16]

It is difficult to determine the base erosion that results from growth in untaxed Internet transactions because reliable estimates of consumption expenditures at the state level are not available. The total potential loss can be estimated with greater precision; the loss in revenue can only be as great as the revenue currently collected from the sales and use tax. For comparative purposes, Table 1 presents a rough estimate of the sales tax base for the fifty states, their localities, and the District of Columbia relative to personal income.[17] The last column (f) of Table 1 is the tax rate on unadjusted personal income (in addition to any existing personal income taxes) that would be necessary to achieve the revenue produced by the current state sales and use tax.

Tax Rate. Sales tax rates low enough to avoid altering consumer behavior create fewer distortions than do high rates. However, state sales tax rates vary considerably as do the local rates piggy-backed onto the state levy. Mississippi and Rhode Island have the highest state sales tax rate of 7%. Oklahoma and Louisiana have the highest potential combined state and local rate of 9.5%. The higher rates in these states create an even larger wedge between those that must collect the sales tax and those that do not. Clearly, residents in the high sales tax jurisdictions gain more from Internet purchases (and tax evasion) than do those in low tax rate states.

Table 2 presents the sales tax rates for the 50 states, their localities, and the District of Columbia. Also reported in Table 2 is the reliance of the states on the general sales (and gross receipts) tax (as measured by CRS). The Bureau of Economic Analysis (BEA) also collects data on excise taxes and selective sales. We do not report these receipts because they are typically collected at the wholesale stage, not at the point of retail transaction. For example, the gasoline excise tax is typically paid by the carrier (tanker truck) at the point of collection (the end of the pipeline), not retail sale. Even though gross receipts taxes have more in common with traditional business taxes, the BEA combines them with general sales taxes. Six states, indicated by italics in Table 2, identify their retail sales tax as gross receipts or general income tax. The base of the gross receipts is sometimes broader than the

---

[14]Bruce, Donald and William Fox, "E-Commerce in the Context of Declining State Sales Tax Bases," (February, 2000). Mimeo, University of Tennessee, Knoxville.

[15]States without groceries in the sales tax base, considered a relatively constant expenditure, are more vulnerable to cyclical shocks to the sales tax base.

[16]According the Boston Consulting Group, sales of financial services were second to sales of computer goods in the first six months of 1998. Goolsbee and Zittrain (1999).

[17]Assuming all states had a uniform base, which they do not.

retail sales tax. Depending on the vendor, revenue generated by Internet transactions with out-of-state purchasers may or may not fall under the gross receipts tax.

Sales Tax Reliance. Based upon our calculations, the states most reliant upon general sales and gross receipts taxes, with over 57% of total revenue derived from the tax, are Tennessee, Washington, and Florida. This result is not surprising: these states do not have a personal income tax. In fact, the top six states in terms of reliance upon the general sales tax do not have a personal income tax.

In Table 1, States without a personal income tax are identified in italics. Alaska is dissimilar from all other states because of the absence of personal income taxes and sales and use taxes. States without a sales and use tax are represented in bold. Ordinal rankings in terms of reliance appear in the last column of Table 2.

A permanent ban on sales and use taxes on Internet sales would affect states proportionately to their reliance on the sales and use tax for revenue. States that rely heavily on the sales tax also have generally higher rates which exacerbate the difference between the after sales tax retail price and the Internet price. Alternatively, states with low rates (and in turn less reliance) would tend to have a smaller 'wedge' between the two modes of transaction. High rate-high reliance states would tend to recognize the greatest revenue loss given the expected change in consumer's behavior resulting from a ban on the taxation of Internet transactions. The economic welfare loss, defined as the degree to which individuals change their behavior in response to tax law, will also be significant.

If sales taxes were eliminated entirely to achieve equity between Internet transactions and traditional retail transactions, states may turn to an additional tax on personal income to help balance their budgets. Assuming this course of action is pursued, i.e total elimination of the sales tax, column (f) in Table 1 offers the minimum personal income tax rate necessary to yield equal revenue. The calculation also assumes that all personal income is included in the income tax base.

The Advisory Commission's Final Report

The Advisory Commission on Electronic Commerce submitted its final report to Congress in early April of 2000. The final report included three recommendations or findings: 1) to close the "digital divide", 2) to explore internet privacy issues, and 3) to support making permanent the moratorium on international tariffs at the earliest possible date. However, the commission did not arrive upon the necessary two-thirds vote for six additional "policy proposals." The six "policy proposals" included a five year extension of the moratorium on multiple and discriminatory taxes and clarification of nexus (physical presence rules).

Conclusion

Ultimately, eliminating the sales and use tax on a select type of transactions and not others will likely lead to distortions in consumer behavior. These distortions would be minimized by taxing all transactions, regardless of mode, at the same rate (perhaps even zero). Whether this can be achieved with the current sales and use tax structure is an open question.

Table 1. Potential Sales and Use Tax Base of the Fifty States

State (*italics* =no personal income tax) (**bold**=no sales tax)	GSGR[a] State Tax Revenue 1998 ($000's)	Clothing in Base (in 2000)	Groceries in Base (in 2000)	State Personal Income 1998 ($000's)	GSGR Tax as Percent of Personal Income 1998
(a)	(b)	(c)	(d)	(e)	(f)
Alabama	1,570,650	Y	Y	93,566,943	1.68%
Alaska	0	n/a	n/a	15,823,391	0.00%
Arizona	3,050,111	Y	N	108,086,511	2.82%
Arkansas	1,513,673	Y	Y	51,762,820	2.92%
California	21,301,860	partial	N	900,899,903	2.36%
Colorado	1,530,832	Y	N	114,449,124	1.34%
Connecticut	3,031,699	partial	N	123,430,960	2.46%
Delaware	0	n/a	n/a	22,257,563	0.00%
District of Columbia[b]	855,000	Y	N[d]	19,525,661	4.38%
Florida	12,923,644	holiday	N	386,654,430	3.34%
Georgia	3,993,493	Y	N	191,864,830	2.08%
Hawaii	1,425,352	Y	Y	31,268,323	4.56%
Idaho	652,843	partial	Y	25,901,148	2.52%
Illinois	5,596,046	Y	Y[e]	349,029,419	1.60%
Indiana	3,166,706	partial	N	143,362,349	2.21%
Iowa	1,528,824	Y	N	68,719,683	2.22%
Kansas	1,619,246	Y	Y	65,854,217	2.46%
Kentucky	1,981,290	Y	N	84,833,878	2.34%
Louisiana	1,981,231	Y	Y[f]	93,429,786	2.12%
Maine	830,758	Y	N[d]	28,619,679	2.90%
Maryland	2,161,233	Y	Y	154,163,998	1.40%
Massachusetts	2,962,535	partial	N	202,252,119	1.46%
Michigan	7,572,789	Y	N	255,038,802	2.97%
Minnesota	3,243,611	partial	N	130,736,634	2.48%
Mississippi	2,034,804	Y	Y	52,283,212	3.89%
Missouri	2,627,839	Y	Y[e]	132,955,487	1.98%
Montana	0	n/a	n/a	17,826,735	0.00%
Nebraska	919,750	Y	N	41,211,643	2.23%
Nevada	1,771,955	Y	N	47,794,729	3.71%

State (italics =no personal income tax) (bold=no sales tax)	GSGR[a] State Tax Revenue 1998 ($000's)	Clothing in Base (in 2000)	Groceries in Base (in 2000)	State Personal Income 1998 ($000's)	GSGR Tax as Percent of Personal Income 1998
New Hampshire[c]	0	n/a	n/a	34,625,867	0.00%
New Jersey	4,766,195	partial	N	275,531,478	1.73%
New Mexico	1,454,913	Y	Y	24,753,112	5.88%
New York	7,615,370	holiday	N	575,767,817	1.32%
North Carolina	3,272,774	Y	Y	182,035,666	1.80%
North Dakota	309,139	Y	N	13,854,813	2.23%
Ohio	5,531,207	Y	N	282,920,265	1.96%
Oklahoma	1,328,295	Y	Y	70,469,389	1.88%
Oregon	0	n/a	n/a	81,309,693	0.00%
Pennsylvania	6,313,056	partial	N	322,705,796	1.96%
Rhode Island	525,672	partial	N	26,614,157	1.98%
South Carolina	2,162,858	Y	Y	82,039,415	2.64%
South Dakota	442,549	Y	Y	16,388,045	2.70%
Tennessee[c]	4,027,787	Y	Y	128,244,293	3.14%
Texas	12,474,161	holiday	N	494,543,763	2.52%
Utah	1,277,126	Y	Y	44,297,177	2.88%
Vermont	194,501	Y	N	14,309,450	1.36%
Virginia	2,225,021	Y	Y	186,685,782	1.19%
Washington	6,909,239	Y	N	159,673,674	4.33%
West Virginia	856,276	Y	Y	35,086,721	2.44%
Wisconsin	3,047,406	partial	N	131,546,684	2.32%
Wyoming	335,383	Y	Y[g]	11,169,256	3.00%

Sources: Columns (b) and (e): Bureau of Economic Analysis. Columns (c) and (d): State Tax Handbook 2000. Column (f): author's calculations.

Notes: [a] General sales and gross receipts tax (GSGR). [b] General sales and gross receipts data are from the annual report of the District of Columbia municipal government which is not directly comparable to the other states. [c] Only capital income is included in the personal income tax. [d] Snack food excluded from exemption. [e] Subject to a reduced rate. [f] Exemption is partially suspended. [g] Some snack foods are taxable.

Table 2. Reliance of State and Local Governments on the
Sales and Use Tax

State (*italics*=gross receipts tax) (**bold**=no local tax)	State Rate 2000	Total Potential State & Local Combined Rate 2000	Total State Tax revenue 1998 ($000's)	GSGR[a] State Tax Revenue 1998 ($000's)	GSGR Tax as Percent of Tax Revenue	Reliance Rank
(a)	(b)	(c)	(d)	(e)	(f)	(g)
Alabama	4	5 to 8	5,734,128	1,570,650	27.39%	37
Alaska	0	0	1,186,235	0	0.00%	47
Arizona	5	5.5 to 6	6,949,270	3,050,111	43.89%	9
Arkansas	4.625	6.125 to 8.125	4,056,582	1,513,673	37.31%	13
California	6	7.25 to 8.25	67,713,433	21,301,860	31.46%	27
Colorado	3	4 to 6.75	5,898,349	1,530,832	25.95%	39
Connecticut	6	6	9,393,604	3,031,699	32.27%	23
Delaware	0	0	1,981,473	0	0.00%	48
District of Columbia[b]	5.75	5.75	2,444,800	855,000	34.97%	16
Florida	6	6 to 7.5	22,513,115	12,923,644	57.41%	3
Georgia	4	5 to 7	11,589,495	3,993,493	34.46%	20
Hawaii	4	4	3,176,246	1,425,352	44.88%	8
Idaho	5	5 to 7	2,057,378	652,843	31.73%	26
Illinois	6.25	7 to 8.75	19,771,284	5,596,046	28.30%	34
Indiana	5	5	9,747,426	3,166,706	32.49%	22
Iowa	5	6	4,802,531	1,528,824	31.83%	25
Kansas	4.9	5.9 to 7.4	4,647,921	1,619,246	34.84%	19
Kentucky	6	6	7,115,149	1,981,290	27.85%	36
Louisiana	4	7 to 9.5	6,082,026	1,981,231	32.58%	21
Maine	5*	5	2,369,820	830,758	35.06%	15
Maryland	5	5	9,190,482	2,161,233	23.52%	42
Massachusetts	5	5	14,488,496	2,962,535	20.45%	45
Michigan	6	6	21,692,742	7,572,789	34.91%	18
Minnesota	6.5	6.5 to 7.5	11,503,928	3,243,611	28.20%	35
Mississippi	7	7	4,343,435	2,034,804	46.85%	7
Missouri	4.225	4.725 to 7.475	8,222,326	2,627,839	31.96%	24
Montana	0	0	1,331,895	0	0.00%	49
Nebraska	5	5 to 6.5	2,633,216	919,750	34.93%	17
Nevada	6.5	6.5 to 7	3,228,206	1,771,955	54.89%	4

State (*italics*=gross receipts tax) (**bold**=no local tax)	State Rate 2000	Total Potential State & Local Combined Rate 2000	Total State Tax revenue 1998 ($000's)	GSGR[a] State Tax Revenue 1998 ($000's)	GSGR Tax as Percent of Tax Revenue	Reliance Rank
New Hampshire	0	0	1,008,518	0	0.00%	50
New Jersey	6	6	15,604,971	4,766,195	30.54%	30
New Mexico	5	5.125 to 6.9375	3,574,537	1,454,913	40.70%	10
New York	4	7 to 8	36,154,533	7,615,370	21.06%	44
North Carolina	4	6	13,869,426	3,272,774	23.60%	41
North Dakota	5	6 to 7	1,078,375	309,139	28.67%	32
Ohio	5	5.5 to 7	17,642,836	5,531,207	31.35%	28
Oklahoma	4.5	5 to 9.5	5,300,829	1,328,295	25.06%	40
Oregon	0	0	4,999,091	0	0.00%	51
Pennsylvania	6	6 to 7	20,629,483	6,313,056	30.60%	29
Rhode Island	7	7	1,783,913	525,672	29.47%	31
South Carolina	5	5 to 6	5,683,148	2,162,858	38.06%	12
South Dakota	4	5 to 8	833,662	442,549	53.08%	5
Tennessee	6	7 to 8.75	6,996,120	4,027,787	57.57%	2
Texas	6.25	6.75 to 8.25	24,629,000	12,474,161	50.65%	6
Utah	4.75	5.75 to 7.5	3,457,679	1,277,126	36.94%	14
Vermont	5	5	957,656	194,501	20.31%	46
Virginia	3.5	4.5	10,542,966	2,225,021	21.10%	43
Washington	6.5	7 to 8.6	11,806,170	6,909,239	58.52%	1
West Virginia	6	6	3,011,990	856,276	28.43%	33
Wisconsin	5	5 to 5.5	11,149,754	3,047,406	27.33%	38
Wyoming	4	4 to 6	855,716	335,383	39.19%	11

Sources: Columns (b) and (c): Federation of Tax Administrators. Columns (d) and (e): Bureau of Economic Analysis. Column (f) and (g): author's calculations.

Note: [a] General sales and gross receipts tax (GSGR). [b] General sales and gross receipts data are from the annual report of the District of Columbia municipal government which is not directly comparable to the other states.

INTERNET TAXATION

Nonna A. Noto

ABSTRACT

This report reviews the bills introduced in the 106th Congress involving taxation of the Internet. It is organized in three sections, according to whether the bills address (1) state and local taxation; (2) federal taxes, charges, and fees; or (3) foreign taxes and tariffs on the Internet. It briefly explains the main issues differentiating the bills on state and local taxation of the Internet. It describes the legislative evolution of H.R. 3709, which passed the House on May 10, 2000, and summarizes several bills introduced in response to the final report of the Advisory Commission on Electronic Commerce, submitted to Congress in April 2000. This report will be updated to reflect further action on Internet tax bills in the second session of the 106th Congress.

This report describes the bills introduced in the 106th Congress addressing taxation of the Internet. As background, the first section of the report provides a brief description of the main provisions of the Internet Tax Freedom Act. The second section provides an overview of the bills introduced thus far in the 106th Congress. It is organized according to whether the bills primarily involve (1) state and local taxation; (2) federal taxes, charges, and fees; or (3) foreign taxes and tariffs. The third section lists congressional hearings on Internet taxation. The final section provides references, including several Websites that are following the Internet tax issue.

This report does not attempt to discuss the policy arguments for and against these legislative proposals. Rather, it points out the major component issues differentiating the bills. The report will be updated to reflect further legislative action on Internet tax bills in the second session of the 106th Congress.

Background: The Internet Tax Freedom Act

The Internet Tax Freedom Act (ITFA) was enacted on October 21, 1998, as part of the Omnibus Consolidated and Emergency Supplemental Appropriations Act, 1999.[1,2] The Act imposed a 3-year moratorium on the ability of state or local governments to impose new taxes on "Internet access services" or to impose any "multiple or discriminatory taxes on electronic commerce." The moratorium is scheduled to expire on October 21, 2001. The Act expressed Congress's opposition to imposing new federal taxes on the Internet and to international taxes, tariffs, and regulation of the Internet and telecommunications.

The Act also created the Advisory Commission on Electronic Commerce (ACEC) to study a variety of issues related to the taxation of electronic commerce and telecommunications. The Commission presented its final report to Congress on April 12, 2000.[3] Only a few of the proposals before the Commission received the two-thirds vote needed to qualify as a formal recommendation of the Commission. However, Virginia Governor James Gilmore, chairman of the Advisory Commission,

---

[1]The Internet Tax Freedom Act comprises Titles XI and XII of Division C of the Omnibus Consolidated and Emergency Supplemental Appropriations Act, 1999 (H.R. 4328, P.L. 105-277, 112 Stat. 2681).

[2]For an account of the legislative evolution of the Internet Tax Freedom Act, see CRS Report 98-509 E, *Internet Tax Bills in the 105th Congress*, by Nonna A. Noto, final version, December 31, 1998.

[3]The text of the *Report to Congress* is available on the website of the Advisory Commission on Electronic Commerce [http://www.ecommercecommission.org].

ruled that any proposal receiving votes from a simple majority of the 19 Commission members could be included in the final report, but it would be labeled as a "majority proposal" rather than a "recommendation."

Under the Act's definition of discriminatory taxes, sales transacted through electronic commerce are to be treated the same way as catalog or mail order sales. Under current law, for interstate sales that means a seller in another state can only be required to collect the sales and use tax and remit it to the buyer's home state government if the seller has a substantial nexus, defined as physical presence, in the buyer's state.[4] The legal obligation to pay a "use tax" to one's home state nonetheless remains with the consumer. In practice, few individuals voluntarily remit use taxes to their home state.[5]

Bills in the 106th Congress

This section offers an overview of the bills introduced thus far in the 106th Congress regarding taxation of the Internet. It is organized according to whether the bills primarily address issues of (1) state and local, (2) federal, or (3) international taxation of the Internet. Each part begins with a summary discussion of all the bills in the group. This is followed by a separate entry for each piece of legislation which gives details on the bill's content and congressional action to date.

A few bills have already been approved in one or both Houses. In May 2000, the House approved two bills. H.R. 3709 extends for five years the current moratorium on state and local taxation of the Internet. H.R. 1291 prohibits FCC (Federal Communications Commission) access charges on providers of Internet data services. During 1999, Congress approved two provisions opposing international taxation of the Internet: a restriction in the FY2000 appropriation for the Department of State and H.Con.Res. 190. All of the other bills listed have been introduced, but not yet voted upon.

State and Local Taxes

Four basic issues differentiate the bills addressing state and local taxation of the Internet. These issues will be explained briefly in these introductory paragraphs. Next, H.R. 3709, which passed the House on May 10, 2000, is summarized as a benchmark for the discussion which follows. The issues are then discussed in more detail, with references to specific bill numbers and comparison to H.R. 3709. Finally, individual bills are described, in numerical order.

---

[4]For further explanation of current law, see CRS Report RS20577, *State Sales Taxation of Internet Transactions*, by John R. Luckey.

[5]For an introduction to the economics of state and local sales and use taxes and related electronic commerce issues, see CRS Report RL30431, *Internet Transactions and the Sales Tax*, by Steve Maguire.

The first issue differentiating the Internet tax bills is the position taken on the *extension of the current 3-year moratorium*. Like H.R. 3709 which passed the House May 10, 2000, several other bills would extend the current moratorium on state and local taxation of the Internet by five years. Others would extend the moratorium by two or four years. Still other bills would convert the temporary moratorium into a permanent ban. Some bills would make the ban on Internet access taxes permanent, but would temporarily extend the moratorium against multiple and discriminatory taxes on electronic commerce.

A second issue is whether or not to continue the *grandfathering protection* provided by the Internet Tax Freedom Act for state and local taxes on Internet access that were already in place at the time of enactment. Some bills would continue the grandfathering. Others would remove this grandfathering protection, thereby banning all state and local taxes on Internet access.

A third issue is whether the *scope of the moratorium* will be extended to explicitly protect electronic commerce from sales and use taxation. A distinction is sometimes made between the tax treatment of digitized goods that are both sold and delivered over the Internet, and more traditional goods and services that are sold over the Internet but delivered otherwise, in tangible physical form.

A fourth issue is whether to move toward or away from *applying sales and use taxes to transactions arranged over the Internet*. Several bills have been introduced in response to the final report of the Advisory Commission on Electronic Commerce (ACEC), presented to Congress in April 2000. Some bills represent the so-called "majority proposals" drafted by the Business Caucus of the Advisory Commission and included in the Commission's final report. These bills would help protect many sales over the Internet from taxation by defining what would *not* be considered "physical presence" for purposes of determining nexus for interstate e-commerce.

Other bills represent the so-called ACEC "minority proposals." These proposals were not included in the final report of the Advisory Commission, but have been presented separately as part of the Streamlined Sales Tax Project, represented by Utah Governor Mike Leavitt, a member of the ACEC. All of these bills propose guidelines for the simplification of state and local sales taxes. However, some bills pursue simplification as a means to encourage a system of voluntary compliance by remote sellers. Other bills provide a formal mechanism whereby the Congress would grant states the authority to require out-of-state sellers to collect and remit use taxes if the states complied with certain criteria for sales tax simplification.

These issues will now be discussed in more detail. Specific bill numbers are mentioned under each topic. Some of the bills addressing state and local taxation of the Internet contain multiple provisions and therefore may be mentioned under more than one subheading that follows.

H.R. 3709 passed the House. On May 10, 2000, the House approved an amended version of H.R. 3709[6] which would extend the current moratorium on state

---

[6]The version of H.R. 3709 passed by the House differed from the version originally introduced

(continued...)

and local taxation of the Internet for five additional years, until October 21, 2006. H.R. 3709 would eliminate the current law's "grandfather" provision that permits states to continue to levy taxes on Internet access that were already in place at the time the Internet Tax Freedom Act was enacted.

H.R. 3709 expresses the sense of Congress that, to avoid being characterized as multiple or discriminatory (and consequently subject to the moratorium) a state tax relating to electronic commerce should include 14 listed features.[7] These features relate to achieving simplification and interstate standardization of state and local sales taxes. While this sense of Congress provision has no enforcement authority, it acknowledges the issue of state and local sales tax simplification. (The legislative evolution of H.R. 3709 is discussed below in the Legislation section.)

Temporarily extend moratorium. Like H.R. 3709 which passed the House, four other bills also propose to extend the current moratorium by five years. S. 2255 (McCain) would solely extend the current moratorium by five years. H.R. 4202 (Ehrlich) would extend the current moratorium by five years, in addition to addressing the levying of FCC charges and regulatory fees on the Internet (described in the section below on Federal Taxes, Charges, and Fees). H.R. 4267 (Hyde and Conyers, ACEC majority) would provide a 5-year extension to the current moratorium on state and local, multiple and discriminatory taxes on electronic commerce, but would make the ban on Internet access taxes permanent; it would also expand the scope of the moratorium for five years (discussed below). H.R. 4462 (Bachus) would extend the moratorium for five years, and S. 2775 (Dorgan) for four years, both while pursuing sales tax simplification and congressional authorization for states to require collection.

H.R. 4460 (Hyde and Conyers, ACEC minority) would extend the moratorium on taxes on Internet access by five years and the moratorium on multiple and discriminatory taxes by two years. H.R. 4267 (Hyde and Conyers, ACEC majority) would extend the moratorium on multiple or discriminatory taxes for five years and impose a new 5-year moratorium on taxation of digitized goods and products and their nondigitized counterparts, but would make the ban on Internet access taxes permanent.

Make moratorium permanent. Three bills would solely make permanent the current 3-year federal moratorium on state and local taxes on the Internet enacted in 1998: S. 328 (Smith, B.), S. 2028 (Wyden), and S. 2036(Smith, B.). Two bills would both make the moratorium permanent and expand the scope of the moratorium to ban any sales and use taxes on electronic commerce: S. 1611 (McCain) and H.R. 3252 (Kasich and Boehner). H.R. 4267 (Hyde and Conyers, ACEC majority) would make the ban on Internet access taxes permanent, but would extend the moratorium on multiple or discriminatory taxes for five years, and impose a new 5-year moratorium on taxation of digitized goods and products and their nondigitized counterparts.

---

[6](...continued)
by Representative Cox, which solely would have made the moratorium permanent.

[7]The features are listed below in a footnote to the section on "Simplification of state and local use taxes."

Grandfathering protection for access taxes. Like H.R. 3709 which passed the House, H.R. 3252 (Kasich and Boehner) and H.R. 4267 (Hyde) would remove the grandfathering protection provided in the Internet Tax Freedom Act for taxes on Internet access that were in place prior to October 1, 1998.[8] In contrast, any bill that simply extends the current moratorium or makes the moratorium permanent would extend the grandfathering protection. H.R. 4460 (Hyde and Conyers, ACEC minority) and S. 1611 (McCain) would explicitly continue to grandfather existing taxes on Internet access.

Expand scope of moratorium. H.R. 4267 (Hyde and Conyers, ACEC majority) would expand the scope of the moratorium to include taxes on sales of digitized goods and products – and their non-digitized counterparts. This approach would approach the goal of a "level playing field," or nondiscriminatory tax treatment, not by extending the sales tax to e-commerce, but rather by removing from the sales tax base non-digitized counterparts that are currently subject to tax in most states, such as books, videos, and music CDs.

S. 1611 (McCain) and H.R. 3252 (Kasich and Boehner) would expand the moratorium to ban any sales and use taxes on electronic commerce. This would pre-empt existing state authority to have sales taxes collected by e-commerce vendors on within-state sales to individuals and businesses; to have businesses pay use taxes on their e-commerce purchases from out-of-state; and for states to make efforts to collect use taxes from resident individuals on their out-of-state purchases over the Internet.

Codify e-commerce nexus guidelines. Two bills offer new physical presence nexus guidelines to help protect interstate e-commerce from state sales and use taxation, as well as from business activity or income taxes. The guidelines also would apply to other interstate commerce, not just activity conducted over the Internet. These guidelines are one of several components of H.R. 4267 (Hyde and Conyers, ACEC majority), which includes other majority proposals from the Commission's

---

[8]According to the Federation of Tax Administrators (FTA) as of May 10, 2000, there were 10 states with taxes of various types on Internet access that are protected by the grandfathering provision of the ITFA. Connecticut, Hawaii, New Mexico, North Dakota, Ohio, South Dakota, Tennessee, Texas, and Wisconsin levy their regular retail sales tax on Internet access. (The Connecticut tax is scheduled for repeal effective July 1, 2001.) New Hampshire applies a telecommunications services tax to two-way communications provided by certain types of entities, including Internet access provided by cable TV companies. Washington state has a business and occupations tax, which is a gross receipts tax levied on all entities doing business in the state, including firms offering Internet access. The FTA estimates a combined revenue loss of $75 million for these 10 states for the fiscal year beginning July 1, 2000. In addition, Montana is currently prevented by the moratorium from applying to Internet access charges its retail telecommunications excise tax which is levied on two-way voice, video and data communications, regardless of the medium.

report.[9] It is the main purpose of S. 2401 (Gregg and Kohl), which defines a new term, "substantial physical presence."

Voluntary system or authorize states to require collection by sellers. A major issue differentiating the bills is whether the bill would simply endorse sales tax simplification as a means of encouraging voluntary cooperation by sellers, or whether the bill would have Congress grant a state the authority to require out-of-state sellers to collect and remit use taxes to the buyer's home state if that state meets certain criteria for simplifying its sales and use tax system. H.R. 4460 (Hyde and Conyers, ACEC minority), H.R. 4462 (Bachus), and S. 2775 (Dorgan) provide a mechanism in the form of a multistate compact through which Congress would grant a participating state the authority to require collection if the state conformed with certain simplification requirements including a single, uniform state-wide use-tax rate for remote sellers. H.R. 3709 which passed and H.R. 4267 (Hyde and Conyers, ACEC majority) endorse simplification of state and local sales and use taxes, but do not offer the states authority to require collection.

Simplification of state and local use taxes. There is widespread agreement that states need to simplify their systems of state and local sales and use taxes and make them more uniform across the states if they hope to improve collection of use taxes on interstate sales. The need for simplification applies regardless of whether this is to occur through voluntary collection by remote sellers or through authorization from the Congress for states to require collection by sellers. Reflecting the general consensus for simplification, a large number of bills include, with some small variations, the same list of 14 criteria for simplification and uniformity included in H.R. 3709 which passed the House.[10] These are H.R. 4267 (Hyde and Conyers,

---

[9]The factors included in H.R. 4267 that are not to be considered as evidence of physical presence are (in the language of the Report of the Advisory Commission on Electronic Commerce):
(1) a seller's use of an Internet service provider (ISP) that has a physical presence in a state;
(2) the placement of a seller's digital data on a server located in that particular state;
(3) a seller's use of telecommunications services provided by a telecommunications provider that has physical presence in that state;
(4) a seller's ownership of intangible property that is used or is present in that state;
(5) the presence of a seller's customers in a state;
(6) a seller's affiliation with another taxpayer that has physical presence in that state;
(7) the performance of repair or warranty services with respect to property sold by a seller that does not otherwise have physical presence in that state;
(8) a contractual relationship between a seller and another party located within that state that permits goods or products purchased through the seller's Web site or catalogue to be returned to the other party's physical location within that state; and
(9) the advertisement of a seller's business location, telephone number, and Web site address.

[10]The 14 sales and use tax simplification criteria listed in H.R. 3709 are:
(1) a centralized, one-stop, multi-state registration system for sellers;
(2) uniform definitions for goods or services that might be included in the tax base;
(3) uniform and simple rules for attributing transactions to particular taxing jurisdictions;
(4) uniform rules for the designation and identification of purchasers exempt from the non-multiple and non-discriminatory tax system, including a database of all exempt entities and

(continued...)

ACEC majority), H.R. 4460 (Hyde and Conyers, ACEC minority), H.R. 4462 (Bachus), and S. 2775 (Dorgan).

Work through NCCUSL or Streamlined Sales Tax System Project. The bills supporting sales tax simplification may differ in terms of which of two organizations they endorse to oversee the simplification effort – the National Conference of Commissioners on Uniform State Laws (NCCUSL) or the Streamlined Sales Tax Project (SSTP).

The National Conference of Commissioners on Uniform State Laws (NCCUSL) is a long-standing non-profit association, founded in 1892. Through NCCUSL, the commissioners of uniform state laws from each state join together to promote uniformity in laws among the states. They study existing laws and then draft and propose specific model statutes or uniform legal codes in areas of the law where uniformity seems desirable. The NCCUSL is perhaps best known for developing the Uniform Commercial Code (UCC). For a uniform code proposed by NCCUSL to take effect, it must be approved by individual state legislatures. It may be adopted either exactly as written or adapted to the particular preferences of a state. Drafting and enacting a uniform act is typically a lengthy process. For example, it took ten years for the NCCUSL to draft the Uniform Commercial Code and another 14 years before it was enacted by states across the country.[11] H.R. 4267 (Hyde and Conyers, ACEC majority), H.R. 4460 (Hyde and Conyers, ACEC minority), and S. 2775 (Dorgan) call upon the involvement of NCCUSL in the simplification of the sales tax system.

---

[10](...continued)
a rule ensuring that reliance on such database shall immunize sellers from liability;
(5) uniform procedures for the certification of software that sellers rely on to determine non-multiple and non-discriminatory taxes and taxability;
(6) uniform bad debt rules;
(7) uniform tax returns and remittance forms; .
(8) consistent electronic filing and remittance methods;
(9) state administration of all non-multiple and non-discriminatory taxes;
(10) uniform audit procedures;
(11) reasonable compensation for tax collection that reflects the complexity of an individual state's tax structure, including the structure of its local taxes;
(12) exemption from use tax collection requirements for remote sellers falling below a specified de minimis threshold;
(13) appropriate protections for consumer privacy; and
(14) such other features that the member states deem warranted to remote [sic, instead of promote] simplicity, uniformity, neutrality, efficiency, and fairness.

These features reflect considerations raised in the Advisory Commission on Electronic Commerce's *Report to Congress* as well as efforts currently underway under the Streamlined Sales Tax Project sponsored by the National Governors' Association and other state and local umbrella groups.

[11]More information about The National Conference of Commissioners on Uniform State Laws is available on their Web site [http://www.nccusl.org].

The Streamlined Sales Tax Project (SSTP) is an ad hoc effort that began in September 1999 as an outgrowth of the proposals of the "minority" on the Advisory Commission on Electronic Commerce, who primarily represented state and local governments. The SSTP is a voluntary, cooperative effort among state governments. The project has two main components. One is to simplify state and local sales and use taxes and standardize their administration among the states. The other is to identify both the computer software and a financial transmission system that could be used to implement the collection of use taxes on out-of-state sales at a reasonable cost, for which vendors could be compensated by the states. The Streamlined Sales Tax Project's motivating purpose was to reduce the complexity of the sales tax system sufficiently that remote sellers would be willing to voluntarily collect and remit use taxes on out-of-state sales, or that Congress would eventually be willing to authorize states to require use tax collection by remote sellers. The SSTP has been holding monthly meetings and is aiming to formulate model legislation in time to present to state legislatures in 2001. The SSTP is also planning to conduct a pilot project, scheduled to begin in October 2000, to test the capabilities of existing tax collection software under current sales tax law.[12] H.R. 4462 (Bachus) encourages the states to work voluntarily through the Streamlined Sales Tax System Project.

Uniform state-wide rate or local-option rate. One of the commonly listed guidelines for sales tax simplification is that each state have a single, uniform, statewide use tax rate applicable to all remote sales (purchases made from out-of-state). An average local sales tax rate could be added to the state rate. But remote (out-of-state) sellers could only be expected to apply one combined tax rate to a purchase by a customer from any locality in a given state. That is, remote sellers could not be expected to administer varying local-option taxes. The findings section of H.R. 4460 (Hyde and Conyers, ACEC minority) would have the state administer all taxes and distribute revenues to subdivisions of the state "according to precedent and applicable State law." None of the other bills addresses how states would distribute the local portion of the use tax collections among their local governments.

Some local government representatives want to leave open the possibility of having remote sellers collect the actual local tax levy. They argue that computer software is, or will soon be, available to make that feasible at a reasonable administrative cost. S. 2775 (Dorgan) provides that a remote seller has the annual option of collecting the actual applicable state and local use taxes throughout a state, as an alternative to collecting a single, uniform, state-wide use-tax rate.

Legislation

H.R. 3252 (Kasich and Boehner). The *Internet Tax Elimination Act* was introduced November 8, 1999, and referred to the Committee on the Judiciary and the Committee on Ways and Means. It would expand the scope of the moratorium and make it permanent.

---

[12]More information about the Streamlined Sales Tax Project is available on their Web site [http://www.streamlinedsalestax.org] or [http:www.geocities.com/streamlined2000].

Like S. 1611, H.R. 3252 would broaden the scope of the moratorium to explicitly ban "any sales or use tax on domestic or foreign goods or services acquired through electronic commerce." H.R. 3252 would remove the grandfathering protection provided under the Internet Tax Freedom Act for state and local taxes on Internet access that were imposed and enforced prior to October 1, 1998.

H.R. 3252 contains a sense-of-Congress section which includes the detailed international tax recommendations made in H.Con.Res. 190 (approved, see below), as well as the broader international statement found in S. 1611(McCain).[13] It expresses opposition to "bit" taxes in addition to the multiple and discriminatory taxation and tariffs enumerated in the original Internet Tax Freedom Act. H.R. 3252 makes specific separate reference to electronic commerce, the Internet, and electronic transmissions.

H.R. 3709 (Cox). The *Internet Nondiscrimination Act of 2000* was introduced February 29, 2000, and referred to the Committee on the Judiciary, Subcommittee on Commercial and Administrative Law. The original bill was a companion to S. 2028 (Wyden). The original version of the bill would have made the current moratorium permanent and made no other changes to the Internet Tax Freedom Act. However, on May 4, 2000, the House Judiciary Committee approved, by a vote of 29-8, an amendment proposed by Representative Goodlatte. H.R. 3709, as amended and approved by the Judiciary Committee, would extend the current moratorium by an additional five years, until October 21, 2006. It would eliminate the "grandfathering" provision under current law which protects the state and local taxes on Internet access that were already in place when the Internet Tax Freedom Act was enacted in October 1998.

On May 10, 2000, the House approved H.R. 3709 by a vote of 352 to 75. The full House added to the Judiciary Committee substitute amendment an amendment by Rep. Istook which became section 4 of the bill. Section 4 expresses the sense of Congress that, to avoid being characterized as multiple or discriminatory, a state tax relating to electronic commerce should include 14 listed features which relate to

---

[13] Specifically, H.R. 3252, like H.Con.Res. 190 (approved), would have the President:

1) seek a global consensus supporting a permanent international ban on tariffs on electronic commerce and an international ban on bit, multiple, and discriminatory taxation of electronic commerce and the Internet;
2) seek to make permanent and binding the moratorium on tariffs on electronic transmissions adopted by the World Trade Organization (WTO) in May 1998;
3) seek adoption by the Organization for Economic Cooperation and Development (OECD), and implementation by its 29 member countries, of an international ban on bit, multiple, and discriminatory taxation of electronic commerce and the Internet; and
4) oppose any proposal to establish a "bit tax" on electronic transmissions--by any country, the United Nations, or any multilateral organization.

H.R. 3252 also includes the provision found in S. 1611 instructing U.S. trade representatives to advocate the firm position of the United States that "...electronic commerce conducted via the Internet should not be burdened by national or local regulation, taxation, or the imposition of tariffs...."

achieving simplification of the sales and use tax and uniformity across state and local governments.[14]

Also on May 10, the House rejected an amendment (by Rep. Delahunt) which would have extended the moratorium for two years and one (by Rep. Chabot) that would have extended the moratorium for 99 years. It also rejected a motion (by Rep. Conyers) to recommit the bill to the Judiciary Committee with instructions to report it back with a two-year extension of the moratorium.

No hearings were held on the bill. H.R. 3709 was considered under a rule that waived clause 4(a) of rule XIII that requires a three-day layover of the committee report, which was introduced the night of May 8. A point of order was raised, but ignored, that the bill is an unfunded intergovernmental mandate as defined in the Unfunded Mandates Reform Act (UMRA), according to the judgment of the Congressional Budget Office. That is, the bill would cost state and local governments lost revenues in excess of the statutory threshold of $55 million per year, at some point over the next five years. CBO points out that the removal of the grandfathering protection for Internet access taxes currently in place, in itself, is estimated to cause revenue losses above the threshold, based on estimates of actual revenue collections. Added to this would be revenue losses attributable to the other part of the moratorium, against multiple and discriminatory taxes on Internet commerce. These prospective revenue losses – for taxes which do not currently exist – cannot be observed, but only estimated.

U.S. Congress. House. Committee on the Judiciary. *Internet Nondiscrimination Act of 2000.* Report together with Minority Views to accompany H.R. 3709. 106th Cong., 2d Sess., H. Rept. No. 106-609, May 8, 2000.

U.S. Congressional Budget Office. H.R. 3709: Internet Nondiscrimination Act of 2000. Mandates Statement, as ordered reported by the House Committee on the Judiciary on May 4, 2000. Washington, May 8, 2000. Available through the CBO Home Page at [http://www.cbo.gov].

H.R. 4202 (Ehrlich). The *Internet Services Promotion Act of 2000* was introduced April 6, 2000, and referred to the Committee on Commerce, Subcommittee on Telecommunications, Trade, and Consumer Protection, and to the Committee on the Judiciary, Subcommittee on Commercial and Administrative Law. It would extend the current moratorium imposed by the Internet Tax Freedom Act by an additional five years, until October 21, 2006.

In addition, H.R. 4202 would prohibit the Federal Communications Commission from imposing on the provision of Internet access services any interstate access charges (for the support of universal service or other access charges) that are based on a measure of the time the telecommunications services are used. It would also prohibit imposing other FCC regulatory fees on providers of Internet access services. A hearing was held by the Commerce Committee's Telecommunications

---

[14]The 14 features are listed above in a footnote to the section on "Simplification of state and local use taxes."

Subcommittee on May 3, 2000. See the discussion of H.R. 4202 and H.R. 1291 (which passed the House) in the section below on Federal Taxes, Charges, and Fees.

H.R. 4267 (Hyde and Conyers, ACEC majority).[15] The *Internet Tax Reform and Reduction Act of 2000* was introduced April 13, 2000, and referred to the Committee on the Judiciary. It puts into legislative language many of the "majority proposals" included in the final report of the Advisory Commission on Electronic Commerce, submitted to Congress on April 12, 2000.

H.R. 4267 would make permanent the current moratorium on state and local taxes on Internet access. It would extend for five years the current moratorium on multiple and discriminatory taxes on electronic commerce. It would impose a new five-year moratorium on the taxation of sales of digitized goods and products, and their nondigitized counterparts. It would encourage states to adopt both a uniform sales and use tax and a uniform telecommunications state and local excise tax act.

State and local governments would be encouraged (through a sense of the Congress resolution) to work with the National Conference of Commissioners on Uniform State Laws (NCCUSL) to develop and draft a Uniform Sales and Use Tax Act by October 21, 2004. This would be a major simplification and standardization of the existing state and local sales and use tax system. The bill lists 10 simplification criteria, comparable to those found in other bills.[16] One of the important goals of H.R. 4267 is parity of tax collection costs (net of vendor discounts) between in-state sellers and remote sellers not physically present in the state. A new advisory commission would be created to monitor the work of the NCCUSL and present a report to Congress with a recommendation as to whether any state that enacted the uniform act should be permitted by Congress to collect sales and use taxes from out of state sellers selling goods to purchasers in the state. The bill repeats legislative language used in the Internet Tax Freedom Act to create the Advisory Commission on Electronic Commerce.

State and local governments would also be encouraged to work with the NCCUSL to develop and draft a Uniform Telecommunications State and Local Excise Tax Act. Different criteria for the simplified telecommunications tax are listed,

---

[15]H.R. 4460 and H.R. 4267 were both introduced in the Judiciary Committee by Representatives Hyde and Conyers, Gekas and Nadler, the Chairmen and Ranking Members, respectively of, first, the full Judiciary Committee and, second, the Subcommittee on Commercial and Administrative Law. H.R. 4267 reflects the position of the so-called majority on the Advisory Commission on Electronic Commerce, including the "Business Caucus" and represented by Commission chairman and Virginia Governor James Gilmore. (Only a few of the proposals before the Commission received the two-thirds vote needed to qualify as a formal recommendation of the Commission. Chairman Gilmore ruled that any proposal receiving votes from a simple majority of the 19 Commission members could be included in the final report, but it would be labeled as a "majority proposal" rather than a "recommendation.") H.R. 4460 reflects the position of the so-called minority on the Advisory Commission on Electronic Commerce, including most of the representatives of state and local governments and represented by Utah Governor Mike Leavitt.

[16]See the list of 14 criteria in the footnote to the section above on "Simplification of state and local use taxes."

depending upon whether a local tax is permitted. Furthermore, the sense of Congress is expressed that state and local governments should eliminate excessive and discriminatory taxes on the telecommunications industry, that the states should establish a deadline for enacting the uniform telecommunications act and removing excess and multiple taxation, and that federal penalties should apply to any state that fails to adopt the uniform telecommunications act before October 21, 2004.

In addition, H.R. 4267 would codify new nexus guidelines enumerating factors that would *not* be considered as evidence of physical presence for businesses involved in electronic commerce, and hence not incur tax obligations to a state.[17] These guidelines would apply for purposes of determining a business's nexus not only for state use tax collection responsibilities, but also for paying state business activity and income taxes. Furthermore, a business's registration with a state relating to sales or use taxes, or the collection or remittance of use taxes for a state, would not be sufficient evidence to require a business to report and pay business activity and income taxes to that state.

H.R. 4460 (Hyde and Conyers, ACEC minority).[18] The *Internet Tax Simplification Act of 2000* was introduced May 16, 2000, and referred to the Committee on the Judiciary. H.R. 4460 would extend the moratorium on taxes on Internet access by nearly five years, until October 1, 2006, and the moratorium on multiple and discriminatory taxes by two and a quarter years, until December 31, 2003. It would preserve the grandfathering protection for Internet access taxes already in place as of October 1, 1998.

H.R. 4460 expresses the sense of Congress that the states and local governments should work cooperatively with the National Conference of Commissioners on Uniform State Laws (NCCUSL) to develop and draft a Streamlined Uniform Sales and Use Tax Act by January 1, 2004. The bill lists 13 criteria to be included in such an act. This is similar to the list included in H.R. 3709 (which passed the House), H.R. 4462 (Bachus), and S. 2775 (Dorgan).[19] H.R. 4460 provides for the Secretary of the Treasury to report to Congress in a timely fashion about whether the streamlined sales and use tax system prescribed by the compact meets the simplification criteria set forth in the bill.

The bill would give Congress's consent for the states to enter into an Interstate Sales and Use Tax Compact that requires the member states to adopt the streamlined tax system. In exchange, a state that has adopted the streamlined system prescribed by the compact would be authorized to begin collecting use taxes on remote sales. A state that did not join the compact initially could still qualify for authority in a later year by adopting the streamlined uniform system.

---

[17]These are enumerated in a footnote to the section above on "Codify e-commerce nexus guidelines."

[18]See the footnote to the subheading for H.R. 4267 above.

[19]See the list of 14 criteria in the footnote to the section above on "Simplification of state and local use taxes."

A state would be authorized to administer a single uniform statewide use tax rate on all remote sales. H.R. 4460 provides that a state may use a blended tax rate that reflects the weighted average of state and local taxes across the state. The level of the statewide rate in a current year is restricted by a revenue-neutral limit such that if that rate had been assessed two calendar years before on all sales on which a sales tax was assessed by the state or its local jurisdictions, the total taxes that would be assessed on sales would not have exceeded the total taxes actually assessed on such sales. In its findings section, H.R. 4460 refers to the state administering all state and local use taxes on remote sellers, with distribution of revenues to political subdivisions of the state "according to precedent and applicable State law." The bill would have no effect on a seller's nexus with any state for purposes of the sales tax, or franchise taxes, income taxes, or licensing requirements.

H.R. 4460 also expresses the sense of Congress that state and local governments should continue to work with the telecommunications industry and other relevant groups to make the taxation of the telecommunications industry simpler, more uniform, and less discriminatory.

H.R. 4462 (Bachus). The *Fair and Equitable Interstate Tax Compact Simplification Act of 2000* was introduced May 16, 2000, and referred to the Committee on the Judiciary and the Committee on Rules. The measure was originally offered on the House floor on May 10, 2000, as an amendment to H.R. 3709, but was withdrawn because of concerns of germaneness.

H.R. 4462 would extend the current moratorium (on Internet access taxes and on new, multiple, and discriminatory taxes on electronic commerce) for five years, until October 21, 2006. During that time states and localities would be encouraged to work together voluntarily to develop a streamlined sales and use tax system through the Streamlined Sales Tax System Project. The bill provides a framework, in the form of a multi-state compact, under which the Congress would grant states the authority to require remote sellers to collect use taxes on interstate sales from the customer and remit them to the buyer's home state – if the states in the compact met certain simplifying conditions for their use tax. The 14 criteria listed in H.R. 4462 for a streamlined sales and use tax system are similar to those contained in H.R. 3709 which passed the House and other bills.[20]

The streamlined tax system prescribed by the compact must be submitted to the President by January 31, 2004, with the approval of at least 20 member states, or the authorization will expire. The President must submit a report to Congress certifying that the compact satisfies the 14 simplification criteria. (No time limit is specified for the President to act.) Congress then has 90 days to enact a joint resolution disapproving the system, under a procedure set forth in the bill. If Congress does not act to disapprove, the states participating in the compact will automatically be authorized to require all remote sellers not qualifying for the de minimis exception to collect and remit use taxes on sales into their state. (The de minimis amount is not specified in dollar terms.)

---

[20]See the list of 14 criteria in the footnote to the section above on "Simplification of state and local use taxes."

H.R. 4462 authorizes any state levying a sales tax to administer a single uniform statewide use tax rate on all remote sales on which it assesses a use tax. It does not explicitly mention the local component of the sales and use tax. However, it limits the level of the statewide rate in a current year in a revenue-neutral way such that if that rate had been assessed two calendar years before on all sales on which a sales tax was assessed *by the state or its local jurisdictions* [emphasis added], the total taxes that would be assessed on sales would not have exceeded the total taxes actually assessed on such sales. (The bill makes no provision for distributing the local component of the revenues back to local governments in a state.) In its findings section, the bill explicitly notes that reasonable compensation for sellers for tax collection obligations should reflect the complexity of an individual state's tax structure, including the structure of its local taxes.

In its findings section, H.R. 4462 expresses the objective that similar sales transactions be treated equally–without regard to the manner in which the sales are transacted, whether in person, through the mails, over the telephone, on the Internet, or by other means. The authority granted in this bill does not affect a seller's nexus with a state for any tax purpose, or permit a state to license or regulate any person, to require them to qualify to transact intrastate business, or to tax them other than on sales of tangible personal property.

S. 328 (Smith, B.). S. 328 was introduced January 28,1999, and referred to the Committee on Commerce, Science, and Transportation. It would make the current moratorium permanent but make no other changes to the Internet Tax Freedom Act.

S. 1611 (McCain). S. 1611 was introduced September 22, 1999, and referred to the Committee on Commerce, Science, and Transportation. It would broaden the scope of the Internet Tax Freedom Act to ban sales and use taxes on electronic commerce and would make the moratorium permanent. It would encourage establishment of the Internet as a worldwide tax-free zone.

Unlike H.R. 3252, S. 1611 would continue to grandfather taxes on Internet access that existed before October 1, 1998. Like H.R. 3252, S. 1611 would broaden the scope of the moratorium to explicitly ban "...sales or use taxes for domestic or foreign goods or services acquired through electronic commerce." S. 1611 includes a brief sense of the Senate resolution encouraging U.S. trade representatives to multilateral organizations to advocate that the Internet not be burdened by national or local regulation, taxation, or tariffs.

S. 2028 (Wyden). The *Internet Non-discrimination Act* was introduced on February 3, 2000, and referred to the Committee on Commerce, Science, and Transportation. It was the companion bill to the original H.R. 3709 (Cox). It would make the current moratorium permanent but make no other changes to the Internet Tax Freedom Act.

S. 2036 (Smith, B.). S. 2036 was introduced February 7, 2000. It was read the second time and placed on the calendar February 8, 2000. It is identical in language to S. 328. By being placed on the calendar, S. 2036 would be available for floor consideration if S. 328 was not reported from committee. Both S. 2036 and S. 328

would make the current moratorium permanent but make no other changes to the Internet Tax Freedom Act.

S. 2255 (McCain). S. 2255 was introduced March 21, 2000, and referred to the Committee on Commerce, Science, and Transportation. It would extend the current moratorium by five years, until December 31, 2006. A hearing was held on April 12. The markup scheduled for April 13 was postponed, reportedly in response to objections by retailers.

S. 2401 (Gregg and Kohl). The *New Economy Tax Simplification Act (NETSA)* was introduced April 11, 2000, and referred to the Committee on Finance. It would amend the provisions of P.L. 86-272[21] enacted in 1959 (establishing federal standards for the power of states to impose net income taxes on income derived from interstate commerce) to apply to business activity taxes as well as sales and use taxes. It introduces a new term, "substantial physical presence," and enumerates conditions that would not establish substantial physical presence. None of the conditions listed in the bill would obligate a business to pay a business activity tax or to collect and remit a sales or use tax to a state.[22]

Some examples of conditions that would not establish substantial physical presence are: the presence or use of intangible personal property in the state (including money, deposits, loans, electronic or digital signals, and web pages); the use of the Internet to create or maintain a World Wide Web site accessible by persons in the state; the use of an Internet service provider to take and process orders via a web page or site on a computer located in the state; the use of any service provider for transmission of communications; and the use of an unaffiliated representative or independent contractor to perform warranty or repair services with respect to property sold by a person outside the state. There is emphasis, not found in other bills, on conditions surrounding the solicitation of orders or contracts and whether a business's affiliated person in another state is considered an agent. In addition, the bill would exempt a business from nexus in another state if its sales in that state were made by independent contractors whose only relationship to the business is making those sales.

S. 2775 (Dorgan). The *Internet Tax Moratorium and Equity Act* was introduced on June 22, 2000, and referred to the Committee on Finance. The bill would extend the current moratorium for just over four years, until December 31, 2005. It encourages states and localities to work together to develop a streamlined sales and use tax system, with advice from the National Conference of Commissioners on Uniform State Laws. The bill provides a mechanism under which Congress would grant a state authority to require remote sellers to collect and remit sales and use taxes to the buyer's home state. This takes the form of a multi-state sales and use tax compact. Once 20 states signed the compact, they could submit it to Congress for approval. Unless the Congress disapproved the compact within 120 days, states

---

[21] 15 U.S.C. 381 et seq.

[22] For a lengthy critical discussion of S. 2401 and related nexus issues, see Sheppard, Lee A. Business Taxpayers Resist State Tax Nexus, in Courts and Congress. *Tax Notes*, vol. 87, no. 6, May 8, 2000. p. 740-47.

belonging to the compact would have the authority to require remote sellers to collect their use tax. States not adopting the uniform, streamlined sales and use tax system could not require collection. A seller's obligation to collect use tax under this compact would not affect the seller's nexus for any other tax purpose. The compact must be formed by January 1, 2006, or the authorization will expire.

A state may impose only a single, uniform statewide use tax rate on remote sellers. This uniform rate would apply to all out-of-state sellers, whether Internet, mail order, telephone, or other. A local component may be included in the statewide rate. A state's tax rate for the current year may not be greater than the combined state-local weighted-average sales tax rate actually imposed by the state and its local jurisdictions two calendar years before. The revenue-neutrality test is that if the current year combined rate had been applied to taxable sales two calendar years prior, it would not have yielded a greater total assessment of state and local taxes than the taxes actually assessed on sales in that year.

The bill makes no provision for distributing the local component of the revenues from a uniform statewide rate back to local governments in a state. However, S. 2775 offers sellers the option to collect the actual state and local sales tax rate that applies in the buyer's home jurisdiction. (Potentially, the local component could then be forwarded to the correct local jurisdiction.) In the criteria for the streamlined system, the bill includes a specific de minimis threshold of $5 million in gross annual sales, under which remote sellers would be exempt from use tax collection requirements. It also provides sellers the option to be subject to no more than a single audit per year using the uniform audit procedures. The authority granted in this bill does not affect a seller's nexus with a state for any other tax purpose, or permit a state to license or regulate any person, to require any person to qualify to transact intrastate business, or to tax them other than on sales of goods and services.

Federal Taxes, Charges, and Fees

Impose a federal tax on interstate sales. In contrast to the other bills listed which would restrict taxation of the Internet in some way, S. 1433 (Hollings), the *Sales Tax Safety Net and Teacher Funding Act*. S. 1433 would impose a new 5% federal retail sales tax on the interstate sales of goods arranged over the Internet or by mail order, for which state and local taxes are not otherwise collected. The revenues collected would be placed in a federal trust fund and then distributed back to the states, on a formula basis, to help supplement teacher salaries.[23]

Prohibit FCC access fees. In another area, bills have been introduced to prohibit the Federal Communications Commission (FCC) from levying charges and

---

[23]Not discussed in this report are bills like H.R. 2525 (Linder and Peterson) which would impose a broad-based national retail sales tax. Such a national sales tax could apply to electronic commerce and mail order sales as well as traditional brick-and-mortar sales, and to interstate as well as intrastate sales.

regulatory fees on Internet service providers (ISPs).[24] H.R. 1291 (Upton), which passed the House on May 16, 2000, prohibits the FCC from imposing per-minute-of-use access charges on providers of Internet data services.[25] However, the bill clarifies that it does not preclude the FCC from imposing access charges on providers of Internet telephone services. H.R. 4202 (Ehrlich) contains a similar provision prohibiting minute-of-use-charges on ISPs but would also prohibit the FCC from imposing regulatory fees on ISPs. In addition, H.R. 4202 would extend the current tax moratorium imposed by the Internet Tax Freedom Act by another five years.

Legislation

H.R. 1291 (Upton). The *Internet Access Charge Prohibition Act of 1999* was introduced March 25, 1999, and referred to the Committee on Commerce, Subcommittee on Telecommunications, Trade, and Consumer Protection. It prohibits the FCC from imposing on any provider of Internet access service any universal service support contribution based on minutes-of-use. The measure also clarifies that it does not preclude the FCC from imposing access charges on Internet telephony providers.

A hearing was held by the Telecommunications Subcommittee on May 3, 2000. The bill was approved by the House Commerce Committee by voice vote on May 10. The bill was approved by the House by voice vote, under a suspension of the rules, on May 16, 2000.

H.R. 4202 (Ehrlich). The *Internet Services Promotion Act of 2000* was introduced April 6, 2000, and referred to the Committee on Commerce, Subcommittee on Telecommunications, Trade, and Consumer Protection, and the Committee on the Judiciary, Subcommittee on Commercial and Administrative Law. It would prohibit the FCC from imposing on ISPs any contribution for the support of universal service or any access charge or successor regulation that is based on a measure of time the telecommunications service is used. It would also prohibit the FCC from imposing regulatory fees on ISPs. In addition, H.R. 4202 would extend the current moratorium imposed by the Internet Tax Freedom Act by an additional five years, until October 2006. A hearing was held by the Telecommunications Subcommittee on May 3, 2000.

S. 1433 (Hollings). The *Sales Tax Safety Net and Teacher Funding Act* was introduced July 26, 1999, and referred to the Committee on Finance. It would impose a 5% federal retail excise tax on merchandise sold over the Internet, through catalogs, or other than through local merchants. It would earmark the revenues to supplement [state and local] funding for salaries and benefits for elementary and secondary school teachers. The tax revenues would be deposited in a newly created federal trust fund and distributed to the states by formula.

---

[24]For a more detailed discussion, see CRS Report RS20579, *Internet Service and Access Charges*, by Angele A. Gilroy.

[25]No such fee currently exists or has been proposed by the FCC.

The proposed federal tax is intended to apply to sales transactions that escape the sales taxes otherwise collected by local merchants. This is likely to include all interstate transactions and possibly also intrastate transactions conducted by Internet or mail order. The tax would be collected by sellers. A credit would be allowed against the federal tax for state and local sales taxes actually paid by the buyer, so that the buyer would not be double-taxed. Taxpayers traditionally exempt from the state sales tax (like non-profit organizations) would continue to receive an exemption under the federal tax. The tax would be levied on merchandise, that is, tangible goods and not services or digitized information.

Foreign Taxes and Tariffs

In 1999, during the first session of the 106th Congress, Congress passed two measures opposing international taxation of the Internet: a restriction in the FY2000 appropriation for the Department of State (S. Amdt. 1317 to S. 1217, included in P.L. 106-113, Title IV, Section 406) and H.Con.Res. 190.

Congressional opposition to the U.N. proposal for a global bit tax.[26] The United Nations Development Program (UNDP) issued its 1999 report on human development on July 12.[27] The report suggested a global "bit tax" as one possible way to raise funds to help bridge the "digital divide" between the world's economic "haves and have-nots," by working to ensure that the Internet communications revolution is truly global.[28]

The report described the "bit tax" as "a very small tax on the amount of data transmitted over the Internet."[29] The UNDP proposal has been described in popular parlance as a tax levied at a rate of 1 cent per 100 emails.[30] The report estimated that globally, such a tax would have raised about $70 billion in 1996.

---

[26]For a fuller explanation, see CRS Report RS20288, *United Nations and Global Taxation: An Update of Proposals in 1999*, by Marjorie Ann Browne.

[27]*Human Development Report 1999.* Published for the United Nations Development Programme by Oxford University Press, New York, 1999. p. 66. Available on the Internet at [http://www.undp.org/hdro]. The *Human Development Report* is written and published for the UNDP in conjunction with a group of outside experts. The report is issued annually. Immediately following the foreword to the 1999 report is a disclaimer stating that "The analysis and policy recommendations of the Report do not necessarily reflect the views of the United Nations Development Programme, its Executive Board or its Member States."

[28]For a brief summary of the report, see: "Reducing the Gap between the Knows and the Know-nots." Press release on *Human Development Report 1999*. United Nations Development Programme, New York, July 12, 1999. [http://www.undp.org/hdro/E3.html].

[29]A "bit" tax refers to a tax on "binary digits." The Internet Tax Freedom Act (Sec. 1104(1)) defined a bit tax as "...any tax on electronic commerce expressly imposed on or measured by the volume of digital information transmitted electronically, or the volume of digital information per unit of time transmitted electronically, but does not include taxes imposed on the provision of telecommunications services."

[30]Specifically, the UNDP report estimated that a user "...sending 100 emails [electronic messages] a day, each containing a 10-kilobyte document (a very long one) would raise a tax of just 1 [US] cent." *Human Development Report 1999*, p. 66.

In reaction, concurrent resolutions were introduced in both Houses of Congress in early August 1999 urging the Administration to aggressively oppose the global "bit tax" proposed in the U.N. Development Programme's report (H.Con.Res. 172, S.Con.Res. 52). In his remarks to the Congress when introducing S.Con.Res. 52 on August 5, 1999, Senator Ashcroft characterized a tax imposed by the U.N. (or any other international organization) as a violation of American sovereignty.[31]

Prior to the introduction of these resolutions, on July 14, 1999, soon after the Human Development Report was issued, the UNDP Administrator issued a statement clarifying that the "...UNDP, as a matter of policy, neither advocates nor supports any so-called global tax, nor any other form of international levy, as a means of funding development aid. UNDP is not engaged now, nor does it plan to engage in the future, in any activity to implement or impose such taxation schemes on any person or group. Neither the United Nations nor UNDP has the mandate or power to create or administer any system of global taxation." On July 21, 1999, the State Department described U.S. policy as being "...opposed to any form of global taxation imposed by the UN or any other international organization."[32]

No votes were taken on either H.Con.Res. 172 or S.Con.Res. 52. However, a provision was included in the FY2000 appropriation for the Department of State stating that "None of the funds appropriated or otherwise made available in this Act for the United Nations may be used by the United Nations for the promulgation or enforcement of any treaty, resolution, or regulation authorizing the United Nations, or any of its specialized agencies or affiliated organiza *Sales Tax Safety Net and Teacher Funding Act.* tions, to tax any aspect of the Internet." (P.L. 106-113, Title IV, Sec. 406; originally S.Amdt. 1317 to S. 1217.)

In addition, the U.N. bit tax proposal was opposed in H.Con.Res. 190 (approved, discussed below) as a threat to the U.S. policy position against special, multiple, and discriminatory taxation of the Internet. Opposition to the U.N. bit tax proposal is also mentioned among the international provisions included in H.R. 3252(Kasich).

Congressional opposition to foreign taxes and tariffs. In anticipation of multilateral trade talks scheduled for the World Trade Organization (WTO) in Seattle in November 1999 and the Organization for Economic Cooperation and Development (OECD) in Israel in October 1999, H.Con.Res. 190, a non-binding sense-of-Congress resolution, was introduced and approved in both Houses of Congress during the first session of the 106th Congress.[33] The resolution specifically urged the President to ask

---

[31]Mr. Ashcroft. S.Con.Res. 52. *Congressional Record* (Daily ed.), Vol. 145, No. 114-Part II, August 5, 1999. p. S10497.

[32]For the State Department release, the July 16 letter from C. David Welch, the Assistant Secretary of International Organization Affairs to the UNDP Administrator Mark Malloch Brown, and the Administrator's July 16 response, see "UN's 1999 Human Development Report Raises International Tax Proposal" on the State Department Website [http://www.state.gov/www/issues/un_internettax_9907.html].

[33]H.Con.Res. 190(Cox) was approved by both Houses. S.Con.Res. 58(Wyden) was the

(continued...)

the U.S. delegate to the WTO ministerial meeting to seek to make permanent and binding the one-year moratorium on tariffs on electronic transmissions that had been adopted by the WTO in May 1998. The resolution also urged the President to have the OECD adopt, and its 29 member countries implement, an international ban on bit, multiple, and discriminatory taxation of electronic commerce and the Internet.[34]

More generally, H.Con.Res. 190 encouraged the President to seek a global consensus supporting a permanent international ban on tariffs on electronic commerce and an international ban on bit, multiple, and discriminatory taxation of electronic commerce and the Internet. It also urged opposition to the U.N. bit tax proposal.

H.Con.Res. 190 restates the international policy position expressed in the Internet Tax Freedom Act.[35] The sponsors viewed this resolution as the international extension of the policy that the Internet Tax Freedom Act imposed on state and local governments in the United States.[36]

H.R. 3252(Kasich) contains a sense-of-Congress section which includes the specific international tax recommendations made in H.Con.Res. 190 as well as the broader statement found in S. 1611(McCain) of the U.S. policy position that electronic commerce conducted via the Internet should not be burdened by national or local regulation, taxation, or tariffs.

Legislation

Congressional opposition to the U. N. proposal for a global bit tax

H.Con.Res. 172 (Sessions). Companion to S.Con.Res. 52. Introduced August 4, 1999. Referred to the House Committee on International Relations. A concurrent resolution expressing the sense of Congress in opposition to a "bit tax" on data

---

[33](...continued)
companion bill introduced in the Senate.

[34]See the first part of footnote 3 for the items contained in the resolution.

[35]The Internet Tax Freedom Act (P.L. 105-277) stated: "Sec. 1203. Declaration that the Internet should be free of foreign tariffs, trade barriers, and other restrictions. (a) In General.–It is the sense of Congress that the President should seek bilateral, regional, and multilateral agreements to remove barriers to global electronic commerce through the World Trade Organization, the Organization for Economic Cooperation and Development, the Trans-Atlantic Economic Partnership, the Asia Pacific Economic Cooperation forum, the Free Trade Area of the America [sic], the North American Free Trade Agreement, and other appropriate venues.
(B) Negotiating Objectives.–The negotiating objectives of the United States shall be--
    (1) to assure that electronic commerce is free from--
        (A) tariff and nontariff barriers;
        (B) burdensome and discriminatory regulation and standards; and
        (C) discriminatory taxation;...."

[36]Whiskeyman, Dolores. Permanent Tariff Ban Sought by Cox, Wyden on International Electronic Commerce. *Daily Tax Report.* Washington, Bureau of National Affairs. No. 190, October 1, 1999. p. G-2 to G-3.

transmitted over the Internet proposed in the Human Development Report 1999 published by the United Nations Development Programme.

S.Con.Res. 52 (Ashcroft).   Companion to H.Con.Res. 172. Introduced August 5, 1999. Referred to the Committee on Foreign Relations. A concurrent resolution expressing the sense of Congress in opposition to a "bit tax" on data transmitted over the Internet proposed in the Human Development Report 1999 published by the United Nations Development Programme.

S.Amdt.1317 to S.1217 (Gregg). Approved by the Senate, July 22, 1999. Included in the Consolidated Appropriations Act, 2000 (P.L. 106-113, Title IV, Section 406).[37] To provide that none of the funds appropriated or otherwise made available in this [appropriations] Act may be used by the United Nations for the promulgation or enforcement of any treaty, resolution, or regulation authorizing the United Nations, or any of its specialized agencies or affiliated organizations, to tax any aspect of the Internet.

Congressional opposition to foreign taxes and tariffs on the Internet

H.Con.Res. 190 (Cox). Companion to S.Con.Res. 58 (Wyden). Introduced September 30, 1999. Referred to the Committee on Ways and Means. Passed House October 26, 1999, 423 to 1; passed Senate November 19, 1999, by unanimous consent. Urges the United States to seek a global consensus supporting a moratorium on tariffs and on special, multiple, and discriminatory taxation of electronic commerce.

S.Con.Res. 58 (Wyden). Companion to H. Con. Res. 190, which passed (see above). Introduced September 30, 1999. Referred to the Committee on Finance. A concurrent resolution urging the United States to seek a global consensus supporting a moratorium on tariffs and on special, multiple, and discriminatory taxation of electronic commerce.

---

[37]S. 1217 was the original Senate FY2000 appropriations bill for the Departments of Commerce, Justice, and State, the Judiciary, and Related Agencies. The text of S.Amdt. 1317 was included in the Consolidated Appropriations Act, 2000 (H.R. 3194, P.L. 106-113), Division B, Section 1000(a)(1), under the cross-reference to H.R. 3421, Appropriations for the Departments of Commerce, Justice, State, the Judiciary, and Related Agencies for the fiscal year ending September 30, 2000. Title IV (General Provisions, Department of State and Related Agency), Section 406.

    U.S. Congress. House of Representatives. *Conference Report on the Consolidated Appropriations Act for FY2000.* 106th Cong., 1st Sess., H.Rpt. 106-479, Nov. 17, 1999. Reprinted in: *Congressional Record* (Daily ed.), Vol. 145, No. 163–Part II, November 17, 1999. Text of bill, p. H12273. Explanatory statement, p. H12307.

Hearings

U.S. House. Committee on Commerce. Subcommittee on Telecommunications, Trade, and Consumer Protection. Hearing on H.R. 4202 and H.R. 1291, bills to prohibit the imposition of (federal FCC) access charges on the provision of Internet services. H.R. 4202 would also extend for five additional years the current moratorium on taxation of the Internet. May 3, 2000.

U.S. House. Committee on the Judiciary. Subcommittee on Commercial and Administrative Law. H.R. 4267 (Hyde), *Internet Tax Reform and Reduction Act of 2000*; H.R. 4460 (Hyde and Conyers), *Internet Tax Simplification Act of 2000*. (These bills are based, respectively, on the majority and minority reports of the Advisory Commission on Electronic Commerce.) May 17, 2000.

___. Hearing on legislation dealing with taxation of the Internet: H.R. 4267 (Hyde and Conyers, ACEC majority); H.R. 4460 (Hyde and Conyers, ACEC minority); and H.R. 4462 (Bachus). June 29, 2000.

U.S. House. Committee on Ways and Means. Subcommittee on Oversight. Matters within the jurisdiction of the Committee on Ways and Mean included in the Report to Congress of the Advisory Commission on Electronic Commerce. Internet taxation and federal telephone excise tax. May 16, 2000.

U.S. Senate. Committee on the Budget. *Internet Taxation in the New Millennium.* February 2, 2000.

U.S. Senate. Committee on Commerce, Science, and Transportation. Hearing on S. 2255, A bill to amend the Internet Tax Freedom Act to extend the moratorium through calendar year 2006. April 12, 2000.

For Additional Information

Advisory Commission on Electronic Commerce. Internet Home Page. [http://www.ecommercecommission.org]

CRS Report RL30431. *Internet Transactions and the Sales Tax*, by Steven Maguire.

CRS Report RS20577. *State Sales Taxation of Internet Transactions*, by John R. Luckey.

For coverage of arguments generally against applying current sales and use taxes to sales made over the Internet, see:

e-Freedom Coalition. Internet Home Page. [http://www.e-freedom.org]

Representative Christopher Cox's Office. Internet Tax Freedom Act Home Page. [http://www.house.gov/cox/nettax]

For coverage of arguments generally in support of applying current sales and use taxes to sales made over the Internet, see:

National Conference of State Legislatures (NCSL).   Internet Home Page.
    [http://www.ncsl.org]. Within the Website, press "E-Commerce."

National Governors' Association (NGA). Internet Home Page.
    [http://www.nga.org/internet/equality.asp].

Internet Policies and Issues
Volume 2

INTERNET PRIVACY—PROTECTING PERSONAL INFORMATION: OVERVIEW AND PENDING LEGISLATION

Marcia S. Smith

Summary

The privacy of information collected by operators of World Wide Web sites and of personal information stored in computers is a growing issue of concern. Congress and the Administration prefer to rely on industry self regulation to protect consumer privacy, but frustration at industry's slow pace led to passage of the Children's Online Privacy Protection Act in 1998 (P.L. 105-277, Title XIII, Division C). The 106th Congress continues to debate Internet privacy issues and many bills have been introduced and hearings held. This report will be updated. (This report does not address privacy of financial or medical records. See CRS Report RS20185 or CRS Issue Brief IB98002, respectively, for those issues.)

Consumer Identity Theft

The widespread use of computers for storing and transmitting information is thought to be contributing to consumer identity theft, in which one individual assumes the identity of another using personal information such as credit card and Social Security numbers. That belief is based primarily on anecdotal information, however. Some attribute the rise in reports of identity theft instead to carelessness by businesses in handling personally identifiable information, and by credit issuers that grant credit without proper checks. The Federal Trade Commission (FTC) has a toll free number (877-ID-THEFT) to help victims of identity theft.

A 1997 study by the Federal Reserve Board, *Report to the Congress Concerning the Availability of Consumer Identifying Information and Financial Fraud*, assessed the public availability of sensitive identifying information, whether such information could be used to commit financial fraud, and the risk to insured depository institutions, concluding there were insufficient data to draw conclusions. A May 1998 General Accounting Office report (GAO/GGD-98-100BR) also found that few statistics are available on identity fraud, but that many of the individuals it interviewed believed the Internet increases opportunities for identity theft and fraud.[1]

The Identity Theft and Assumption Deterrence Act (P.L. 105-318) sets penalties for persons who knowingly, and with the intent to commit unlawful activities, possess, transfer, or use one or more means of identification not legally issued for use to that person. Subsequent hearings (April 22, 1999, House Commerce; March 7 and July 12, 2000, Senate Judiciary) have discussed ongoing issues and new legislation has been introduced. H.R. 4311 (Hooley)/S.2328 (Feinstein) would impose requirements on credit card issuers, consumer reporting agencies, and individual reference services to reduce the likelihood of identity theft. H.R. 4611 (Markey)/S. 2699 (Feinstein) would regulate the sale and use of Social Security numbers (SSNs); the bills were introduced at the request of Vice President Gore. H.R. 4857 (Shaw)/S. 2876 (Bunning) prohibit the sale of and otherwise protects SSNs. H.R. 4857 has been marked up by a House Ways and Means subcommittee. Separately, a Senate Governmental Affairs subcommittee held a hearing May 19, 2000 on how the Web makes it easier to produce false identification documents.

Individual Reference or "Look-Up" Services

The FTC held a public workshop in June 1997 on the collection of information about consumers by "individual reference services" or "look-up services" that operate computerized databases of personal information: *Individual Reference Services: A Report to Congress* [http://www/ftc/gov/opa/9712/inrefser.htm]. Just prior to the workshop, several of those companies announced voluntary principles they would follow in the future to protect consumer privacy. Among the principles are that individual reference services will not distribute to the general public non-public information such as Social Security numbers, birth dates, mother's maiden names, credit histories, financial histories, medical records, or any information about children. Look-up services may not allow the general public to run searches using a Social Security number as a search term or make available information gathered from marketing transactions. Also, consumers may obtain access to the non-public information maintained about them and to "opt-out" of that non-public information. The principles led to voluntary guidelines that went into effect January 1, 1999. As noted above, H.R. 4311 and S. 2328 would place restrictions on what information can be disseminated by these services.

Online Privacy: Collection of Data by Web Site Operators

The Internet ("online") privacy debate focuses on whether industry self regulation or legislation is the best route to assure consumer privacy protection. Repeated media stories about privacy violations by Web site operators have kept the issue in the forefront of

---

[1]Other types of Internet fraud also are of concern. Although the types of fraud and scams that have been identified on the Internet are not new, perpetrators have easy access to a wide audience via the Internet. Computer fraud is addressed by 18 U.S.C. 1030. The Federal Trade Commission, Securities and Exchange Commission, and Justice Department are all involved in fighting Internet fraud. The Justice Department has set up a Web site for reporting suspected Internet fraud [http://www.ifccfbi.gov]. Four hearings have been held: Senate Governmental Affairs Committee, February 10, 1998 and March 22 and 23, 1999; and House Commerce Committee, June 25, 1998. Three bills are pending: H.R. 612 (Weygand)and S. 699(Wyden) focus on protecting senior citizens; S. 1015 (Schumer) seeks to protect online investors.

public debate about the Internet. Although Congress and the Clinton Administration both prefer self regulation, the 105th Congress passed legislation to protect the privacy of children under 13 as they use the Internet. Many bills are pending in the 106th Congress dealing with online privacy for all consumers (see table). Several hearings have been held: House Commerce subcommittee, July 13, 1999; House Government Reform subcommittee, May 15-16, 2000; House Judiciary subcommittee, May 27, 1999; Senate Commerce Committee, July 27, 1999, May 25, 2000, and June 13, 2000; and Senate Judiciary Committee, April 21, 1999 and May 25, 2000.

Children's Online Privacy Protection Act (COPPA), P.L. 105-277. Congress, the Clinton Administration, and the FTC initially focused their attention on protecting the privacy of children under 13 as they use the Internet. Not only are there concerns about information children might divulge about themselves, but also about their parents. Congress passed and the President signed into law the Children's Online Privacy Protection Act (COPPA) as Title XIII of Division C of the FY1999 Omnibus Consolidated and Emergency Supplemental Appropriations Act (P.L. 105-277). The law requires operators of World Wide Web sites to obtain verifiable parental consent before collecting, using, or disseminating information about children under 13, and allowing parents to "opt out" of dissemination of information already collected about that child.

The FTC's final rule [http://www.ftc.gov/privacy/index.html] implementing the law became effective April 21, 2000. Under the rule, commercial Web sites and online services directed to children under 13 or that knowingly collect information from them must inform parents of their information practices and obtain verifiable parental consent before collecting, using, or disclosing personal information from children [http://www.ftc.gov/opa/1999/9910/childfinal.htm]. Verifiable parental consent is defined as "any reasonable effort (taking into consideration available technology) ... to ensure that a parent of a child ... authorizes the collection, use, and disclosure" of a child's personal information." For two years, Web site operators can use different methods to obtain consent depending on how they plan to use the information. If the information will be used internally by the operator, consent via email is permitted. If it will be disclosed to third parties, however, "a more reliable method"—print/send via postal mail or fax, use of a credit card or toll-free telephone number, digital signature, or e-mail accompanied by a PIN or password—is required. After two years, the FTC will require more reliable methods unless "more secure electronic methods of consent are not widely available."

Administration Position on Online Privacy. In its July 1997 report, *A Framework for Global Electronic Commerce,* the Clinton Administration endorsed industry self regulation for protecting consumer Internet privacy, but stressed that if industry did not self regulate effectively the government might have to step in, particularly regarding children. On May 14, 1998, Vice President Gore called for an "electronic bill of rights" to protect consumers' privacy. He encouraged Congress to pass medical records privacy legislation (see CRS Issue Brief IB98002), and announced the establishment of an "opt-out" Web site [http://www.consumer.gov] by the FTC to allow individuals to indicate they do not wish personal information passed on to others. In July 1998, Vice President Gore reiterated his call for Congress to pass legislation protecting medical records, hailed passage of the identity theft bill, and asked Congress to pass legislation requiring parental consent before information is collected about children under 13. The Vice President renewed the Administration's emphasis on industry self regulation, but noted the test of success would be the degree of industry participation. According to press reports, the

White House disagrees with the FTC's May 2000 decision to seek Internet privacy legislation (see next section).

In May 1998, President Clinton directed federal agencies to ensure that their information collection practices adhered to the Privacy Act of 1974. In June 1999, the Office of Management and Budget (OMB) directed agencies to post privacy policies on their Web sites and stated that agencies must protect an individual's right to privacy when collecting personal information. In June 2000, the White House announced that it had just learned that contractors for the Office of National Drug Control Policy (ONDCP) had been using "cookies" (small text files placed on users' computers when they access a particular Web site) to collect information about those using the site during an anti-drug campaign. That campaign placed anti-drug ads on various Web sites. Users clicking on ads were taken to an ONDCP site. Cookies then were placed on users' computers to count the number of users, what ads they clicked on, and what pages they viewed on the ONDCP site. The White House directed ONDCP to cease using cookies, and OMB issued another memorandum reminding agencies to post and comply with privacy policies and detailing the limited circumstances under which agencies should collect personal information. GAO is conducting a study of whether government Web sites conform to administration privacy guidelines. The House adopted an Inslee amendment to the FY2001 Treasury-Postal Appropriations bill (H.R. 4871) requiring Inspectors General of agencies funded by the bill to report to Congress on any activity taken to monitor individuals who access any Internet site of their agencies, and a Frelinghuysen amendment prohibiting any funding in the bill to be used to collect information on individuals using a federal Internet site.

FTC Activities. The FTC has been active in online privacy issues since 1995. It has conducted or sponsored several Web site surveys to determine the extent to which Web site operators abide by four fair information practices: providing *notice* to users of their information practices before collecting personal information, allowing users *choice* as to whether and how personal information is used, allowing users *access* to data collected and the ability to contest its accuracy, and ensuring *security* of the information from unauthorized use.

The first FTC survey, in December 1997, found 86% of the 126 children's Web sites surveyed collected information from children but fewer than 30% posted a privacy policy statement and only 4% required parental notification. A broader survey was conducted in June 1998. In its subsequent report, *Privacy Online: A Report to Congress,* the FTC noted that of the 212 children's sites surveyed, 89% collected personally identifiable information but only 54% disclosed their information collection practices and fewer than 10% provided any form of parental control. The survey also included 674 commercial Web sites of which 92% collected personal information. Only 14% provided any notice of their information collection practices and only 2% provided a comprehensive privacy policy. Frustrated at the survey results, the FTC announced on June 4, 1998 that it would seek legislation protecting children's privacy on the Internet by requiring parental permission before a Web site could request information about a child. COPPA was enacted four months later.

A year later, the FTC released another report, *Self Regulation and Online Privacy: A Report To Congress,* that concluded that additional legislation was not needed at that point. The conclusion was based on indications of progress by industry, including creation of "seal" programs (see below), and by two surveys conducted by Georgetown University that looked at 361 ".com" Web sites and reported that 66% posted either a privacy policy or an information practice statement, but only 36% posted both. Of the top 100 Web sites, 93% posted at least one of those disclosures, while 59% posted both. Of the 93%, only 20% provided the four elements of fair information practices (notice, choice, access, and security). The statistics thus provided ammunition to both sides in the debate.

The FTC changed its position in May 2000, voting (3-2) to release its latest survey, *Privacy Online: Fair Information Practices in the Electronic Marketplace* [http://www/ftc/gov/opa/2000/05/privacy2k.htm], and seek legislation requiring Web sites to adhere to the four fair information practices. The FTC survey found that only 20% of randomly visited Web sites with at least 39,000 unique monthly visitors, and 42% of the 100 most popular Web sites, had implemented all four fair information practices.

Industry Activities and "Seals". In 1998, members of the online industry formed the Online Privacy Alliance (OPA) to encourage industry self regulation. OPA developed a set of privacy guidelines and its members are required to adopt and implement posted privacy policies. The Better Business Bureau (BBB), TRUSTe, and WebTrust, among others, have established "seals" for Web sites. To display a seal from one of those organizations, a Web site operator must agree to abide by certain privacy principles (some of which are based on the OPA guidelines), a complaint resolution process, and to being monitored for compliance. Advocates of self regulation argue that these seal programs demonstrate industry's ability to police itself. Advocates of legislation argue that while the seal programs are useful, they do not carry the weight of law, limiting remedies for consumers whose privacy is violated. They also point out that while a site may disclose its privacy policy, that does not necessarily equate to having a policy that protects privacy.

Concerns of Public Interest and Other Groups. Representatives of consumer, privacy rights and other interest groups, such as the Center for Democracy and Technology (CDT) and the Electronic Privacy Information Center (EPIC), continue to express concern that self regulation is insufficient. CDT and EPIC both have released reports [http://www.cdt.org/privacy/990727privacy.pdf] and [http://www.epic.org/reports/surfer-beware3.html] questioning whether privacy policies actually ensure privacy. A particular concern is online profiling where companies collect data about what Web sites are visited by a particular user and develop profiles of that user's preferences and interests for targeted advertising. The FTC held a one-day workshop on online profiling on November 8, 1999. The Senate Commerce Committee's June 13, 2000 hearing focused on this topic.

European Data Directive. A European Union (EU) policy, the "European data directive," went into force in October 1998 requiring member countries to pass laws prohibiting the transfer of personal data to countries that are not members of the EU ("third countries") unless the third countries ensure an "adequate level of protection" for personal data. Since the United States does not have such laws, the U.S. Department of Commerce (DOC) negotiated with the EU that it would accept "safe harbor" certifications whereby U.S. companies can satisfy the intent of the EU data directive through adhering to certain self regulatory principles. The European Commission (EC, the "executive arm" of the EU) approved the agreement in May 2000, but on July 5, the European Parliament (composed of individuals elected by EU member states) rejected it. The EC is considering what to do next. The principles are available at the following Web site: [http://www.ita.doc.gov/td/ecom/RedlinedPrinciples31600.htm].

Table 1. 106th Congress Internet Privacy Legislation

Bill	Summary
H.R. 313 (Vento)	**Consumer Internet Privacy Protection Act.** Regulates the use by interactive computer services of personally identifiable information provided by subscribers. (Commerce Committee)
H.R. 367 (Franks)	**Social Security On-line Privacy Protection Act.** Regulates the use by interactive computer services of Social Security numbers and related personally identifiable information. (Commerce)
H.R. 369 (Franks)	**Children's Privacy Protection and Parental Empowerment Act.** Prohibits the sale by list brokers of personal information about children without their parents' consent. (Judiciary)
H.R. 1685 (Boucher)	**Internet Growth and Development Act.** Broadly based Internet bill that includes requiring commercial Web site operators to provide notice of their collection, use, and disclosure policies regarding personally identifiable information. (Commerce and Judiciary)
H.R. 2882 (Vento)	**Internet Consumer Information Protection Act.** Places restrictions on interactive computer service providers regarding disclosure of certain personal information. (Commerce)
H.R. 3321 (Markey)	**Electronic Privacy Bill of Rights.** Requires Web site operators to post privacy policies with opt-in/opt-opt options and allow consumers access to information; state and local governments may not impose liabilities inconsistent with the Act; states may file civil actions but FTC must be notified and may intervene; persons or entities may file actions if permitted by state laws. (Agriculture, Banking, Commerce, Transportation & Infrastructure)
H.R. 4049 (Hutchinson)	**Privacy Commission Act.** Creates 18-month commission to study privacy issues, including those associated with the Internet. (Government Reform; ordered reported 6/29)
H.R. 4311 (Hooley)/**S. 2328** (Feinstein)	**Identity Theft Prevention Act.** Imposes requirements on credit card issuers, consumer reporting agencies, and individual reference services to reduce the likelihood of identity theft. (House and Senate Banking)
H.R. 4611 (Markey)/**S. 2699** (Feinstein)	**Social Security Number Protection Act.** Regulates sale and purchase of Social Security numbers. (House Commerce and Ways & Means; Senate Finance)
H.R. 4857 (Shaw)/ **S. 2876** (Bunning)	**Privacy and Identity Protection Act.** *Inter alia*, prohibits the sale of Social Security numbers (SSNs) by the private sector, federal, state, and local government agencies and provides other means for protecting SSNs. (House Ways & Means, Judiciary, Banking, and Commerce; Senate Finance). House Ways and Means subcommittee marked up bill July 20, 2000.
H.R. 4871 (Kolbe)	**FY2001 Treasury-Postal Service Appropriations.** House-passed version contains language requiring Inspectors General of agencies funded in the bill to report to Congress on whether those agencies collect information about persons visiting Web sites of their agencies, and prohibiting funds in the bill from being used to collect information about an individual using a federal Web site.
S. 809 (Burns)/ **H.R. 3560** (Frelinghuysen)	**Online Privacy Protection Act.** Requires FTC to prescribe regulations protecting the privacy of personal information collected from and about individuals not covered by COPPA. (House and Senate Commerce)
S. 854 (Leahy)	**Electronic Rights for the 21st Century.** Broadly based electronic privacy bill, including the Internet, particularly government access to information. (Judiciary)
S. 2063 (Torricelli)/ **H.R. 3770** (Jackson)	**Secure Online Communications Enforcement Act.** Restricts Web site operators re the disclosure of records and other information relating to the use of such sites. (House and Senate Judiciary)
S. 2448 (Hatch)	**Internet Integrity and Critical Infrastructure Protection Act.** Restricts collection, use, disclosure of, and establishes penalties for fraudulently obtaining or releasing, personally identifiable information by or from interactive computer services; permits Justice Department to conduct national media campaign to raise awareness of Internet privacy rights, laws, and regulations. (Judiciary)
S. 2554 (Gregg)	**Amy Boyer's Law.** Restricts use of Social Security numbers. (Finance)
S. 2606 (Hollings)	**Consumer Privacy Protection Act.** Broadly based privacy bill that *inter alia* requires Web site operators to provide notice, consent, access, and security to their users re personally identifiable information. (Commerce)
S. 2857 (Leahy)	**Privacy Policy Enforcement in Bankruptcy Act.** Prohibits the sale of personally identifiable information by a failed business if sale or disclosure violates a privacy policy in effect when the information was collected. (Judiciary)
S. 2871 (Shelby)	**Social Security Number Privacy Act.** Amends the Gramm-Leach-Bliley Act to prohibit financial institutions from selling or purchasing Social Security numbers in violation of regulations required to be promulgated by federal financial regulators under this Act. (Banking)

Internet Policies and Issues
Volume 2

INTERNET—PROTECTING CHILDREN FROM UNSUITABLE MATERIAL AND SEXUAL PREDATORS: OVERVIEW AND PENDING LEGISLATION

Marcia S. Smith

Summary

Protecting children from unsuitable material and sexual predators on the Internet is a major concern for Congress and the Administration. The 105th Congress passed the Child Online Protection Act (Title XIV, Division C, P.L. 105-277), which is currently under review in the courts (see CRS Report 98-670); and the Protection of Children from Sexual Predators Act (P.L. 105-314). Several bills have been introduced in the 106th Congress. Attention is now focused on amendments added by the House and Senate to the FY2001 Labor-HHS appropriations bill (H.R. 4577), which are quite different. This report will be updated.

Overview

Concern is growing about what children are encountering on the Internet, particularly in terms of indecent or otherwise unsuitable material or contacts with strangers who intend to do them harm. The private sector has responded by developing filtering and tracking technologies to allow parents either to prevent their children from visiting certain Web sites or to provide a record of what sites their children have visited.

Congress passed the Communications Decency Act (CDA) as part of the 1996 Telecommunications Act (P.L. 104-104). Among other things, CDA would have made it illegal to send indecent material to children via the Internet. In June 1997, the Supreme Court overturned the portions of the CDA dealing with indecency and the Internet. (Existing law permits criminal prosecutions for transmitting obscenity or child pornography over the Internet.) Congress passed a replacement law, the Child Online Protection Act, in 1998 (see next section) and other legislation to protect children as they use the Internet. Debate continues in the 106th Congress.

Legislation Passed by the 105th Congress

The Child Online Protection Act (P.L. 105-277): Prohibiting Access by Children to Material That is "Harmful to Minors". The 105th Congress passed the Child Online Protection Act (COPA) as part of the Omnibus Appropriations Act (P.L. 105-277, Title XIV of Division C). The language was based on S. 1482 (Coats) and H.R. 3783 (Oxley). The law prohibits commercial distribution of material over the Web to children under 17 that is "harmful to minors." Web site operators are required to ask for a means of age verification such as a credit card number before displaying such material. It replaces provisions of the 1996 Communications Decency Act that were overturned by the Supreme Court. By limiting the language to commercial activities and using the court-tested "harmful to minors" language instead of "indecent" as was used in the 1996 Act, the sponsors hoped they had drafted a law that would survive court challenges.

The American Civil Liberties Union (ACLU) and others filed suit against the part of COPA dealing with commercial distribution of material harmful to minors over the Internet in the U.S. District Court for the Eastern District of Pennsylvania on October 22, 1998, the day after President Clinton signed it into law. Judge Lowell A. Reed, Jr. issued a preliminary injunction against enforcement of that part of the Act on February 1, 1999. The Justice Department appealed the ruling. The U.S. Court of Appeals for the Third Circuit let stand the injunction on June 22, 2000. (See also CRS Report 98-670, *Obscenity, Child Pornography, and Indecency: Recent Developments and Pending Issues*.)

COPA established a Commission on Online Child Protection to conduct a study of technologies and methods to help reduce access by children to material on the Web that is harmful to minors. (This part of the Act is not affected by the injunction.) The Commission is composed of 16 industry members appointed by the Republican and Democratic congressional leaders plus one ex officio representative each from the Federal Trade Commission (FTC) and Departments of Commerce and Justice. The final members were appointed on October 19, 1999. Originally, the Commission was given one year to complete its task, but since naming the members took longer than expected Congress extended the Commission's life for another year in the FY2000 Consolidated Appropriations Act (P.L. 106-113). Congress did not allocate any funding for the Commission's operations, however, and although the original law established it under the auspices of the National Telecommunications and Information Administration (NTIA, part of the Department of Commerce) that section was eliminated when the Commission's lifetime was extended. The Commission now operates independently [http://www.copacommission.org]. The Commission met on March 7, April 28, and June 8-9, 2000. Separately, P.L. 105-314 (see next section) requires the Attorney General to contract with the National Research Council (NRC) to conduct a two-year study on the capabilities of computer-based technologies and other approaches to the problem of the availability of pornographic material to children on the Internet. NRC anticipates that the study will be completed in late 2001.

Sexual Predators on the Internet (P.L. 105-314 and P.L. 105-277). The 105th Congress also was concerned about sexual predators using the Internet to approach children. Because conversations can take place anonymously on the Internet, a child may not know that (s)he is talking with an adult. The adult may persuade the child to agree to a meeting, with tragic results. Congress passed H.R. 3494 (P.L. 105-314), the Protection of Children from Sexual Predators Act, to address those and other non computer-related issues related to protecting children from sexual predators. The law: prohibits using the mail or any facility or means of interstate or foreign commerce (a) to initiate the transmission of the name, address, telephone number, social security number, or electronic mail address of an individual under 16 with the intent to entice, encourage, offer, or solicit any person to engage in any sexual activity for which any person can be charged with a criminal offense, or (b) to persuade, induce, entice, or coerce any individual under 18 to engage in prostitution or any sexual activity for which any person can be charged with a criminal offense; makes it a crime to transfer obscene matter by mail or any facility or means of interstate or foreign commerce to anyone under 16; calls for the U.S. Sentencing Commission to recommend appropriate changes to Federal Sentencing Guidelines if a defendant used a computer with the intent to persuade, induce, entice, coerce, or facilitate the transport of a child to engage in any prohibited sexual activity; requires electronic communication or remote computing services that have knowledge of violations of child pornography laws to report it to law enforcement officials; prohibits federal prisoners from having unsupervised access to the Internet and recommends that states do the same with their prisoners; and requires a study of technologies to control the electronic transmission of pornography (discussed earlier).

Filtering Technology: Debate in the 105th and 106th Congresses

Software to block access to Web sites or e-mail addresses has existed for many years. Commercial products include Cyber Patrol, Cyber Sitter, Net Nanny, Net Shepherd, and SurfWatch. Links to information about many of these and other products and other tools for protecting children on the Web are available at [http://www.GetNetWise.org]. Other products (such as Net Snitch) do not prohibit access to sites, but maintain a record that a parent can review to know what sites a child has visited. Some filtering products screen sites based on keywords, while others use ratings systems based on ratings either by the software vendor or the Web site itself.

Existing filtering software products have received mixed reviews because they cannot effectively screen out all objectionable sites on the ever-changing Web, or because they inadvertently screen out useful material. The Electronic Privacy Information Center (EPIC) released a report on filtering software in November 1997 entitled *Faulty Filters: How Content Filters Block Access to Kid-Friendly Information on the Internet* [http://www2.epic.org/reports/filter-report.html]. EPIC tested a filtering program called Net Shepard, searching the Web for sites it expected to be useful to and suitable for children. For example, EPIC searched for Web sites about the "American Red Cross" (entered into the search engine in quotes to ensure that only items with that exact set of words in that order would be returned) with and without Net Shepard activated. EPIC reported that Net Shepard prevented access to 99.8% of the sites. From this and other examples, EPIC concluded that in the effort to protect children from a small amount of unsuitable material, they were being denied access to a large amount of suitable information.

Congress and the Administration have been debating whether to require schools and libraries to use filtering technology when children are using computers with Internet access, or to require Internet Service Providers (ISPs) to offer such technology to subscribers in general. Action in the 105th and 106th Congress legislation in this regard is discussed below.

On May 5, 1999, Vice President Gore held a press conference with representatives of the Internet industry to announce that by July 1999 a "Parents' Protection Page" would appear automatically on most Web sites to help parents identify tools already available for them to guide their children in using the Internet, including filtering software. The Vice President stated: "The best protection is an involved parent, taking time to pass on the right values to children. But government and industry do have a responsibility to make it easier and simpler for parents to do so." (White House press release 1999-05-05, *Remarks by the Vice President on the Internet*).   The GetNetWise Web site mentioned above, sponsored by the Internet industry and public interest groups, debuted in August 1999 providing "one click" tools for parents to guide their children when using the Internet and to report trouble. Many ISPs already were providing parents with tools and information. They had created another Web site [http://www.americalinksup.org] following a December 1997 "Kids Online Summit" to offer filtering software to parents and implement an outreach campaign to increase its use.

Despite these efforts at industry-sponsored solutions, debate continues over whether schools and libraries should be required by law to use filtering technology on computers that have Internet access when children are using them.   Policies adopted by local communities reflect the spectrum of attitudes on this topic. Some allow children to use computers at local libraries only with parental permission, some use filtering software, and others impose no restrictions.   Quality Education Data reported in October 1999 (*Communications Daily*, October 25, 1999, p. 2-3) that 58.3% of schools use filtering software and 90.5% have "acceptable use" policies where adults and children have an agreement regarding how the children should behave when using the Internet.

Supporters of attempts to pass a law requiring schools and libraries to use filtering technology argue that children must be protected from inappropriate material, particularly when their parents are not present to supervise them. Critics assert that it is censorship, prevents access to appropriate sites, and that such decisions should be left to the local community. Some believe "acceptable use" policies are preferable. The American Library Association, the National Education Association, and the Center for Democracy and Technology are among the groups opposing filtering legislation.

105th Congress Action. The 105th Congress included a section in the Child Online Protection Act (P.L. 105-277, discussed earlier) requiring interactive computer services to advise customers that parental control protections (hardware, software, or filtering services) are commercially available.

The 105th Congress also considered, but did not pass, legislation to require most schools and libraries to use filtering technology to screen out unsuitable Web sites. Senator McCain and Representative Franks introduced bills to require schools receiving federally-provided "E-rate" subsidies through the universal service fund to use filtering software on computers that have access to the Internet to block sites that might contain material unsuitable for children. (For information on universal service and the E-rate, see CRS Issue Brief IB98040, *Telecommunications Discounts for Schools and Libraries: the "E-Rate" Program and Controversies)*. The bills would have required libraries with computers that have access to the Internet and receive E-rate funds to equip one or more computers with filtering software. The determination of what was inappropriate was left to local officials. The Senate adopted the McCain bill (S. 1619) as an amendment to the FY1999 Commerce-Justice-State appropriations bill (S. 2260) on July 21. The House Appropriations Committee adopted an Istook amendment to the FY1999 Labor-HHS appropriations bill (H.R. 4274) requiring schools and libraries to install filtering software if they received funds under any federal agency program or activity to acquire or operate any computer that is accessible to minors and has access to the Internet. Neither was included in the final version of those appropriations bills, however..

106th Congress Legislation: The FY2001 Labor-HHS Appropriations Bill (H.R. 4577). The debate on filtering has continued in the 106th Congress. Many bills are pending, but attention is currently focused on language in the House- and Senate-passed versions of the FY2001 Labor-HHS appropriations bill, H.R. 4577. The language is quite different in the House and Senate versions, and the three amendments adopted by the Senate differ among each other.

In the version of H.R. 4577 that passed the House on June 14, 2000, schools receiving funds under title III of the Elementary and Secondary Education Act (ESEA) for purchasing computers used to access the Internet or paying direct costs associated with accessing the Internet must install filters on any computer to which minors have access. The filter must block material that is obscene, child pornography, and material harmful to minors. Local educational agencies or schools specifically are not prohibited from filtering other materials. The filters may be disabled if the computer is being used by an adult for bona fide research or other lawful purposes.[1] The House language does not address libraries.

By contrast, the Senate adopted language during floor debate on June 27, 2000, placing various requirements on schools and libraries receiving E-rate funding (described earlier) and on Internet Service Providers (ISPs). First, the Senate adopted (95-3) a McCain amendment,[2] as amended by a Hatch/Leahy amendment.[3] The McCain amendment requires schools and libraries receiving E-rate funding to certify to the Federal Communications Commission (FCC) that they have selected a technology for computers that have Internet access to filter or block material that is obscene and child pornography, and are enforcing a policy ensuring its operation when the computers are being used by minors. Local school officials also are *permitted* to use the technology to filter or block access to other materials they determine to be "inappropriate for minors," while libraries are *required* to do so. Libraries also must block child pornography during any use of the computer, not only when a computer is being used by minors. Determination of what material is to be filtered or blocked would be made by local officials. The FCC has 120 days to prescribe regulations for administering the legislation. Schools and libraries then must comply within 30 days unless state or local procurement rules or regulations or competitive bidding requirements prevent it, in which case they must notify the FCC. If the school or library does not comply, it must repay the E-rate funds it received. The school or library may resume receipt of E-rates funds once it does comply. E-rate funds may be

---

[1] The provision is the same as language in H.R. 4141, the "Education OPTIONS," bill as reported by the House Education and the Workforce Committee (H. Rept. 106-608). The House Appropriations Committee adopted the language as an Istook amendment to the Labor-HHS bill during full committee markup.

[2] The McCain amendment to H.R. 4577 is similar, but not identical, to Senator McCain's S. 97 as reported from the Senate Commerce Committee (S.Rept. 106-141) in August 1999.

[3] This language originally was adopted (100-0) as an amendment to the juvenile justice bill, H.R. 1501 (Section 1504), during Senate floor debate in July 1999. There has been no further action on that bill.

used to purchase or acquire the filtering or blocking products needed to comply with the legislation.

The Hatch/Leahy amendment to the McCain amendment requires ISPs with more than 50,000 subscribers to provide filtering software or blocking systems to all residential customers at the time they sign up for service. The software or system must be provided for free or at a cost no higher than what the ISP paid for it. The provision's effective date is tied to determinations required to be made by the Department of Justice and the FTC as to whether ISPs are providing such software or systems voluntarily. The provision becomes effective one year after enactment if those agencies determine that less than 75% of residential subscribers are provided such software or systems by their ISPs; after two years if that number is less than 85%; or after three years if the number is less than 100%.

The Senate then adopted (75-24) a Santorum amendment (based on S. 1545) that would permit schools and libraries to choose between using filtering technology or having "acceptable use" policies, called "Internet use" policies in the amendment. The Santorum amendment requires schools and libraries applying for E-rate funding to certify either that they have selected and installed filtering systems on computers dedicated to student use or that they have adopted and implemented Internet use policies. Filtering systems must filter or block access to matter considered to be inappropriate for minors as determined by the school board or library or other authority, but not an agency or instrumentality of the U.S. government. Internet use policies must address specific matters identified in the bill and reasonable public notice of the policy must be provided and at least one public hearing or meeting conducted. The National Telecommunications and Information Administration must initiate a notice and comment proceeding to evaluate whether filtering software adequately addresses the needs of educational institutions, make recommendations on fostering the development of products to meet such needs, and evaluate the development and effectiveness of local Internet use policies currently in operation after community input. The FCC has 100 days after enactment to adopt rules implementing this provision.

Senator McCain argued that voting in favor of the Santorum amendment would "basically negate the amendment we just adopted [the McCain amendment]," but Senator Santorum insisted that those voting for his amendment would "see a much more comprehensive policy put in place" (*Congressional Record*, June 27, 2000, p. 5869). Senator Santorum cited the American Association of School Administrators, National Rural Education Association, American Library Association, National Education Association, and the Catholic Conference and several other groups as supporting his amendment. Senator McCain cited the American Family Association, Family Research Council, National Law Center for Children and Families, Morality in Media, Family Friendly Libraries, and several other groups as opposing the Santorum amendment. The Senate completed action on H.R. 4577 on June 30; Senate conferees have been named.

106th Congress Legislation: Other Bills..   Apart from the amendments adopted to H.R. 4577 and their predecessor bills, other pending bills are: H.R. 368 (Franks); H.R. 543 (Franks); H.R. 896 (Franks); a Franks amendment to the House version of H.R. 1501 (the "juvenile justice" bill); and H.R. 4600 (Pickering). All require schools and libraries to use filtering technologies if they receive e-rate funding, although the specifics in the bills are different. Also, as noted above, different filtering language in H.R. 4141 (Goodling), the Education OPTIONS Act, was added to the House-passed version of the FY2001 Labor-HHS appropriations bill (H.R. 4577).

INTERNET GAMBLING: A SKETCH OF LEGISLATIVE PROPOSALS

Charles Doyle

Summary

S. 692 as passed by the Senate and H.R. 3125 as brought to the House floor on a suspension motion (each styled the Internet Gambling Prohibition Act) outlaw commercial use of the Internet to gamble or facilitate gambling with fairly broad exceptions for certain forms of legalized gambling. Individual bettors are not covered and there are exemptions for parimutuel betting on horse racing and dog racing, and for state lotteries, among others. Violations are subject to criminal penalties and court injunctions. Service providers who cooperate with authorities in good faith enforcement of the Act are immunized for their cooperation and for violations occurring through use of their facilities. Although similar in most respects, S. 692 and H.R. 3125 have some differences. For instance, they describe the exemptions certain gambling and gambling-related activities conducted under the Indian Gaming Regulatory Act somewhat differently.

H.R. 4419, as reported out of the House Committee on Banking and Financial Services (H.Rept. 106-771), prohibits gambling businesses from accepting bettors' credit cards, electronic fund transfers, or checks, in connection with illegal internet gambling, and establishes criminal, civil and regulatory mechanism for enforcement of its proscriptions.

S. 692 and H.R. 3125

Subject to various exceptions, S. 692 and H.R. 3125 prohibit anyone, engaged in the gambling business, from using the Internet (a) to place or receive a bet or wager or (b) to send, receive, or invite information assisting in the placement of a bet or wager, proposed 18 U.S.C. 1085(b). The proscriptions are reenforced by criminal penalties, injunctive relief, and provisions designed to enlist service provider cooperation in enforcement.

By focusing on those in the "gambling business," the bills intentionally exclude the casual bettor who patronizes such businesses, S.Rept. 106-121 at 23; H.Rept. 106-655.

The bills use special definitions and exclusions to carve out other exceptions to their prohibitions. For instance, the definition of:

- "bets or wagers" do not include
    + bona fide securities transactions,
    + commodities transactions,
    + indemnity contracts,
    + various kinds of insurance, or
    + certain simulated sports games (only in H.R. 3125), proposed 18 U.S.C. 1085(a)(1);

- "gambling business" does not include any small or intermittent gambling business unless it generates more than $2000 during any given 24 hour period or operates substantially continuously for more than 10 days, proposed 18 U.S.C. 1085(a)(4);

- "information assisting in the placing of a bet or wager" does not include
    + certain kinds of parimutuel information,
    + information exchanged among state-licensed gambling facilities,
    + news reporting including odds and schedules, or
    + education information on to make a bet or wager, proposed 18 U.S.C. 1085(a)(5)(B).

The prohibitions are made specifically inapplicable under some circumstances to:

- state lotteries,
- legalized off-track betting on horse races, dog races, or in the case of H.R. 3125, jai alai,
- legalized subscription Internet gambling, and
- gambling conducted under the Indian Gaming Regulatory Act, proposed 18 U.S.C. 1085(f).

Internet gambling offenses are punishable by imprisonment for not more than 4 years and/or a fine of the greater $20,000 or the amount wagered, proposed 18 U.S.C. 1085(b)(2). Federal and state officials, and under S. 692 various sports organizations, may invoke the jurisdiction of the federal courts to enjoin violations, proposed 18 U.S.C. 1085(c),(d).

The bills grant immunity to cooperative Internet service providers for their enforcement assistance. The immunity grant extends to any federal or state gambling violation. To qualify, when notified by state or federal law enforcement of an offending site, providers must remove or bar access to Internet gambling material on sites that they control and help authorities identify the source of offending sites they do not control, proposed 18 U.S.C. 1085(d).

Differences Between S. 692 and H.R. 3125

Although the difference have been reduced, a few remain. For example, H.R. 3125's definition of bets or wages excludes participation in simulated sports and education games, proposed 18 U.S.C. 1085(a)(1); the definition in S. 692 does not.

S. 692 allows various sports leagues to sue to enjoin Internet gambling violations involving the use of their contests; H.R. 3125 limits access to civil enforcement to federal and state authorities, proposed 18 U.S.C. 1085(c)(2).

H.R. 3125 includes jai alai in the exceptions granted horse racing and dog racing; S. 692 does not, proposed 18 U.S.C. 1085(a)(2), (f)(1), (f)(2).

H.R. 4419 (as reported)

Using the same definitions of gambling business and gambling (bets or wagers) as the House Internet Gambling Prohibition bill (H.R. 3125), the funding prohibition bill (H.R. 4419) outlaws a gambling business' acceptance of a bettor's credit cards, electronic fund transfers, checks, or the like in connection with illegal internet gambling business. Offenders are punishable by imprisonment for more than 5 years and/or a fine of not more than $250,000 (not more than $500,000 if the offender is an organization) and may be enjoined from ever gambling again.

The United States Attorney General, state attorney generals, or (in the case of violations occurring on Indian lands) Indian Gaming Regulatory Act compact enforcement authorities may enforce the bill's proscriptions by bringing a civil action federal court. Unwitting, financial intermediaries are exempt from liability under the bill, but federal bank regulatory agencies are empowered to order federally insured banks to discontinue various financial services to gambling business that violate the bill's prohibitions.

In order to combat offshore internet gambling operations, the bill indicates that the United States should:

- encourage foreign government and international entities to cooperate in identifying internet gambling operations being used for money laundering, corruption, or other crimes;

- promote enforcement of the Act by sharing information with foreign governments; and

- encourage inclusion in the Financial Action Task Force on Money Laundering's annual report of the extent to which internet gambling is being used for money laundering.

Background

The Internet Gambling Funding Prohibition Act (H.R. 4419) was introduced by Representative Leach for himself and Representatives LaFalce, Roukema and Baker on May 10, 2000. June 20, the House Banking and Financial Services Committee held hearings at which representatives from the Department of Justice, the Department of the Treasury and the Wisconsin Department of Justice testified (prepared statements available at [www.house.gov/banking]). The Committee approved an amended version of H.R. 4419 the following week (H.Rept. 106-771). The amendments limit the bill to financial transactions associated with *illegal* internet gambling and encourage international cooperation to identify any criminal activity associated with internet gambling.

The Internet Gambling Prohibition Act of 1999 (S. 692), was introduced by Senators Kyl and Bryan, favorably reported by the Senate Judiciary Committee (S.Rept. 106-121) and passed the Senate on November 19, 1999, 145 *Cong.Rec.* S 14870. H.R. 3125, a similar bill with the same name was introduced by Representative Goodlatte for himself and Representatives LoBiondo, Wolf, Boucher, Gibbons and Good. It was favorably reported by the House Judiciary Committee (H.Rept. 106-655). It was then brought to the floor with a manager's amendment (which sought to make clear that the bill would not legalize any activity that is illegal now) under a motion for suspension of the rules which failed to secure the necessary two-third vote, 145 *Cong.Rec.* H 6057 (daily ed. July 17, 2000).

Both Houses have held hearings on the subject in each of the last two Congress,[1] and the Senate passed an earlier version as part of the Commerce-Justice-State appropriations bill at the end of the 105th Congress, 144 *Cong.Rec.* S8801-803 (daily ed. July 23, 1998)(text). The Internet gambling provision was stricken from the appropriations measure in conference, and the 105th Congress adjourned before the House could take up the measure separately.

The Department of Justice had suggested that Congress await the report of the National Gambling Impact Study Commission before enacting legislation. The Commission released its report recommending an Internet gambling ban on June 18, 1999, FINAL REPORT, *Rec. 5.1*, 5-12.

The legality and regulation of gambling is first and foremost a matter of state law that varies considerably from state to state. The role of federal law in large measure has been to guard against unwelcome intrusions of interstate or international gambling into states where the activity in question has been outlawed.

---

[1]   *Internet Crimes Affecting Consumers: Hearing Before the Subcomm. on Technology, Terrorism, and Government Information of the Senate Comm. on the Judiciary (Senate Hearing)*, 105th Cong., 1st Sess. (1997); *The Internet Gambling Act of 1997: Hearing Before the Subcomm. on Technology, Terrorism, and Government Information of the Senate Comm. on the Judiciary (Senate Hearing II)*, 105th Cong., 1st Sess. (1997); *Internet Gambling Prohibition Act of 1997: Hearings Before the Subcomm. on Crime of the House Comm. on the Judiciary (House Hearing I)*, 105th Cong., 2d Sess. (1998); *Internet Gambling: Hearing Before the Subcomm. on Technology, Terrorism, and Government Information of the Senate Comm. on the Judiciary (Senate Hearing III)*, 106th Cong., 1st Sess. (1999); *Internet Gambling: Hearing Before the Senate Comm. on Indian Affairs (Senate Hearing IV)*, 106th Cong., 1st Sess. (1999). Witness statements from the hearings before the Crime Subcommittee of the House Committee on the Judiciary during the 106th Congress (*House Hearing II*) and the Telecommunications, Trade & Consumer Protection Subcommittee of the House Committee on Commerce are available as of this writing on the Committees' home pages at [www.house.gov/judiciary] and [www.house.gov/cchear], respectively.

For background information on existing law see, *Internet Gambling: Overview of Federal Criminal Law*, CRS Report 97-619 A (Feb. 2, 1998).

The Commission's report and witnesses during Congressional hearings argued that unregulated Internet gambling threatens the effectiveness of this approach.[2] Some contend that it fosters consumer fraud,[3] gambling addiction,[4] corruption of our young,[5] and affords a possible avenue for money laundering.[6] They urge that Internet service providers be used as an avenue of regulatory enforcement,[7] that the Department of Justice be encouraged to prosecute more vigorously,[8] and/or that every effort be made to secure international cooperation for enforcement.[9]

S. 692, and in some cases H.R. 3125, address some of the objections raised by proposals in the 105th Congress. The Department of Justice, for example, advised against coverage of mere bettors. Some of the bills would have punished bettors as well as those engaged in a gambling business;[10] both S. 692 and H.R. 3125 penalize only "a person engaged in a gambling business," proposed 18 U.S.C. 1085(b).[11]

The Gambling Commission recommended that the Internet gambling ban not create any new exceptions to any existing gambling proscriptions. Some of the original proposals were crafted as amendments to the Wire Act, 18 U.S.C. 1084, and thus adjustments made to accommodate exceptions to an Internet gambling ban might have had a more sweeping impact. S. 692 and H.R. 3125 place their Internet gambling prohibitions within a new section, 18 U.S.C. 1085, so that their exemptions and exceptions apply only to the ban in

---

[2] *Senate Hearing II* at 1 (opening statement of Sen. Kyl); 8 (Wis.Att'y Gen. James E. Doyle); *House Hearing* (jt. statement of Reps. Goodlatte & LoBiondo).

[3] *House Hearing* (jt. statement of Reps. Goodlatte & LoBiondo); (testimony of Frank J. Fahrenkopf, Jr., American Gaming Association).

[4] *Senate Hearing II*, at 18-9 (prepared statement of Ann Geer, National Coalition Against Gambling Expansion); FINAL REPORT, 5-5.

[5] *Senate Hearing II*, at 14 (statement of Jeff Pash, Executive Vice President, National Football League); FINAL REPORT, 5-4 to 5-5.

[6] *Senate Hearing I*, at 24 (prepared statement of Dep. Att'y Gen. Robert S. Litt); *Senate Hearing II*, at 5 (statement of Sen. Bryan); FINAL REPORT, 5-6.

[7] *House Hearing* (testimony of Bill Saum, National Collegiate Athletic Association).

[8] *House Hearing* (testimony of Bernard P. Horn, National Coalition Against Gambling Expansion); FINAL REPORT, *Rec. 5.1*, 5-12 (Department of Justice should develop enforcement strategies).

[9] FINAL REPORT, *Rec. 5.4*, 5-12; *Senate Hearing II*, at 24 (statement of Anthony Cabot, Esq.).

[10] The bill that passed the Senate in the 105th Congress as part of the Commerce-Justice-State appropriation, for instance, subjected Internet bettors to 3 months imprisonment and/or a fine, proposed 18 U.S.C. 1085(b)(1),(2), Amend. 3266, *reprinted at*, 144 *Cong.Rec.* S8802 (daily ed. July 23, 1998). Although tracking the amendment in several other respects, neither S. 692 nor H.R. 3125 have any such provision.

[11] *See also*, S.Rept. 106-121, at 23 ("the prohibitions of section 1085(b) apply only to persons engaged in a gambling business and not to 'casual bettors'").
The Justice Department also proposed that any legislation should (1) treat gambling on and off the Internet the same; (2) be technology neutral; and (3) avoid "stifling the growth of the Internet or chilling its use a medium of communication and commerce," *House Hearing II*,(statement of Dep.Ass't Attorney General Kevin V. DiGregory).

section 1085 and, with the exception of the service provider immunity provisions, have not effect on liability under other gambling laws.

Some hearing witnesses expressed concerns that a ban on the use of the Internet for gambling and gambling information purposes would deny the advantages of technological development to the horse racing industry and to other gambling industries that are lawful and regulated in the states in which they are located.[12] Both bills contain exceptions to permit the use of technology in various legalized gambling businesses.

Internet Policies and Issues
Volume 2

FINANCIAL REFORM LEGISLATION IN THE 106TH CONGRESS: EARLY ACTIVITY

F. Jean Wells

Summary

Financial reform refers to proposals to modernize the financial services industry. Legislative proposals would update laws addressing the structure and regulation of financial services firms, thus affecting how financial services are delivered to individual, business, and governmental users. The Chairmen of the Senate and the House Banking Committees initiated early legislative action, following up on consideration of the issue in the 105th Congress. The House and the Senate are considering separate bills: H.R. 10, the Financial Services Act of 1999, and S. 900, the Financial Services Modernization Act of 1999. H.R. 10 originated in the House Banking Committee which approved an amended version, by a vote of 51-8, March 11, 1999. The bill was then referred to the House Commerce Committee. The Senate passed S. 900 amended, 54-44, May 6, 1999. The two bills address affiliations of banking, securities, and insurance firms, but specific provisions differ.

This report explains how the bills evolved in the first months of the 106th Congress. It will not be further updated. For overall tracking of financial services modernization legislation in the 106th Congress, see CRS Issue Brief IB10035.

Reasons for the Legislation

Congressional interest in legislation addressing financial institution diversification and regulation reflects changes occurring in the marketplace, including the "megabank" mergers of 1998. A bellwether change was the merger of Citicorp and Travelers Group into Citigroup, Inc. That combines insurance, securities, and banking activities despite some legal limitations.[1] Numerous other financial innovations, court decisions, and regulatory interpretations are contributing to the breakdown in distinctions among banking, securities and insurance firms that formerly offered distinctive financial services.

---

[1] In approving the merger, the Federal Reserve permitted retention of certain activities that must be divested after five years at the latest should there be no change in current law. For additional background on changes in financial markets leading to interest in financial modernization legislation, see CRS Report 98-550 E, *Financial Modernization/Glass-Steagall Act Issues and the Financial Services Act of 1998, H.R. 10 as Passed in the House*, by William Jackson.

Yet such changes are occurring in piecemeal ways. These developments have led to interest in financial reform proposals to update existing statutes. They are intended to reflect marketplace realities while addressing concerns of safety and soundness attached to banking organizations. .

The Legislative Setting

Proposals to permit affiliations among banking, securities, and insurance firms have been under continuing consideration since the 104th Congress. H.R. 10, the Financial Services Act of 1998, passed the House by one vote in the 105th Congress and was reported amended by the Senate Banking Committee. It then stalled on the Senate floor near the end of the Congress. In the 106th Congress, the Chairmen of the House and Senate Banking Committees both initiated early legislative action in order to build on activity from the 105th Congress.

Proposals addressing diversification in the financial services industry would amend laws limiting activities of banking organizations. The Glass-Steagall Act separates banking and the securities business; the Bank Holding Company Act regulates companies controlling banks. Such laws have the reciprocal effect of preventing other forms of enterprises from owning banking organizations or offering banking services. These proposals involve questions of structure, which in turn raise contentious questions about regulatory jurisdiction. Consumer protections and the application of the Community Reinvestment Act (CRA) to financial conglomerates also figure importantly in the debate.

Comprehensive proposals address questions of how securities and insurance activities should be regulated when performed in banks, as contrasted with traditional securities and insurance firms. Differences of view result, partly because affected industries bring their individual perspectives to various proposed approaches. An issue that has assumed increased prominence in the 106th Congress is the extent to which, and how, affiliations should be permitted between depository institutions (banks and thrifts) and commercial firms. Reform of the Federal Home Loan Bank System has also been incorporated in some legislative proposals.

Specific Legislative Developments

The Senate passed S. 900 amended, May 6, 1999, following markup by the Senate Banking Committee (S.Rept. 106-44). On April 28, the House Commerce Finance and Hazardous Materials Subcommittee began hearings on H.R. 10, reported out earlier by the House Banking Committee (H.Rept. 106-74, Part 1).

The Senate bill and the House Banking Committee's bill both would use a holding company structure to permit affiliations of banking, insurance, and securities companies. However, H.R. 10 amended would give many more banks the option of providing specified nonfinancial services in operating subsidiaries rather than requiring that nonbanking activities be conducted primarily in holding company affiliates. The bills' provisions on unitary thrift holding companies (UTHCs) differ. [2]   They both would

---

[2] A unitary thrift holding company (UTHC) is a holding company that owns a single thrift
(continued...)

grandfather existing UTHCs. However, the Senate bill would not allow the transfer of UTHCs to commercial firms after May 4, 1999, unlike the House bill. Provisions addressing insurance and securities activities of banks have become more alike as the bills have progressed, although differences remain.[3] The bills have similar provisions making changes in the Federal Home Loan Bank System; neither provides for a comprehensive overhaul which others have proposed.

Community Reinvestment Act provisions differ. H.R. 10 amended would require that banks in a financial holding company would have to have a satisfactory CRA rating both as a condition of affiliation and subsequently. It also specifies the instances in which the Federal Reserve would have to hold hearings on proposed mergers. That is the time when community groups have the best opportunity to make their views heard on banks' community reinvestment efforts. The Senate bill, on the other hand, would establish that banks with a history of "satisfactory" or better ratings on CRA exams would be deemed in compliance until their next regularly scheduled examinations unless successfully challenged.

H.R. 10 and the Senate bill both include consumer protection provisions, and address ATM (automated teller machine) fees and privacy issues.[4] Following is information about how H.R. 10 and S. 900 evolved in the early months of the 106th Congress.

House Banking Committee Activity. Legislation approved by the House Banking Committee, The Financial Services Act of 1999 (H.R. 10 amended), developed in several stages. The Chairman and the Ranking Member of the House Banking Committee first introduced H.R. 10 and H.R. 665 respectively. Following hearings, they announced that they would work together to produce legislative language for markup. That language was released March 1, 1999 in a Committee Print to H.R. 10. A markup was held March 4, 10, and 11, 1999, at the end of which H.R. 10 amended was approved by a vote of 51 to 8 (H. Rept. 106-74, Part 1). These developments are described chronologically below.

Initial Legislation: H.R. 10 as introduced and H.R. 665. The Chairman of the House Banking Committee introduced H.R. 10, the Financial Services Act of 1999, the first day of the 106th Congress. H.R. 10 as introduced is similar to a version of H.R. 10 that was circulating when the 105th Congress ended. It allows banking, insurance, and securities affiliations in a financial holding company (FHC). The Federal Reserve would be the primary regulator for the new FHCs. Banking and commercial combinations would be limited, including unitary thrift holding companies. The bill as introduced also includes provisions covering regulation of securities and insurance activities of banks and Federal

---

[2] (...continued)

institution. It is distinguished from other thrift holding companies in that it may be involved in any lines of business, whereas the others are restricted to certain activities primarily financial in nature. Definitions of terms in financial modernization legislation are available in CRS Report RL30039, *Financial Institution Reform and Diversification: A Legislative Glossary of Often Used Terms,* by F. Jean Wells and William Jackson.

[3] Insurance provisions are further examined in CRS Report RS20098, *Insurance Provisions of Financial Services Modernization Bills in the 106th Congress,* by M. Maureen Murphy.

[4] For an overview of privacy issues, see CRS Report RS20185, *Privacy Protection for Customer Financial Information,* by M. Maureen Murphy.

Home Loan Bank System reform. An important difference from H.R. 10 in the 105th Congress affects Community Reinvestment Act applications. Under H.R. 10 as introduced, a conglomerate that owns a bank found not to be in compliance with CRA would no longer be expected to divest the bank. That provision was changed again in the Committee Print to H.R. 10.

The Ranking Minority Member of the House Banking Committee introduced alternative legislation, H.R. 665, the Financial Services Modernization Act, February 10, 1999. Its affiliation and other important provisions differ from H.R. 10 (as introduced) in several ways. Some of the alternative proposals were later incorporated in the Committee Print to H.R. 10. For example, H.R. 665 authorizes subsidiaries of banks to engage in financial activities, except real estate investment and insurance underwriting. An "operating subsidiary" option was carried over to the Committee Print to H.R. 10. The Administration has not proposed separate legislation; rather at the time H.R. 665 was introduced, the Secretary of the Treasury issued a statement indicating support for many of its provisions including the "operating subsidiary" arrangements.

Subsequent Legislative Language: Committee Print to H.R. 10. In mid-February 1999, the Committee held hearings on financial modernization (H.R. 10). Subsequently, a Committee Print to H.R. 10 was released, reflecting changes to H.R. 10 as introduced agreed to by the Committee's Chairman and Ranking Member. An accompanying fact sheet highlights major changes from the original bill. Subsidiaries of national banks would be permitted to engage in any financial activity authorized for financial holding companies, except insurance underwriting and real estate development. With regard to CRA, banks in a financial holding company would first be required to have a satisfactory CRA rating as a condition of affiliation and then would have to continue to have a satisfactory CRA rating in order to continue to engage in new financial activities, subject to appropriate enforcement authority. The statement accompanying the Committee Print also identifies matters on which views differ, including Community Reinvestment Act and unitary thrift holding company provisions.

Committee Markup. During the Committee markup, March 4, 10, and 11, many amendments were considered. However, the basic structure of H.R. 10 as modified in the Committee Print, is retained. Banking, insurance, and securities affiliations would be permitted in a financial holding company (FHC) structure. Subsidiaries of national banks would also be permitted to engage in financial activities authorized for FHCs, except insurance underwriting, real estate development and title insurance. The Federal Reserve and the U.S. Department of the Treasury both have roles in approving new activities whether performed in bank subsidiaries or holding company affiliates. Proposed restrictions on unitary thrift holding companies are relaxed to permit the sale of existing unitary thrifts to commercial firms. Provisions addressing regulation of securities and insurance activities conducted by banks are not much changed. Community Reinvestment Act provisions contained in the Committee Print are retained. New consumer protection measures are added, stipulating that banks and thrifts must clearly disclose ATM fees, and addressing institutions' privacy policies on consumer information. Proposed Federal Home Loan Bank System provisions are amended.

Senate Activity. The development of legislation in the Senate progressed through several stages. On February 16, 1999, the Chairman of the Senate Banking Committee released for comment a staff draft of a basic bill to be known as the Financial Services

Modernization Act of 1999. Hearings followed. The Committee then released a Committee Print containing language for markup. The Committee approved the language in the Committee Print, with amendments, March 4, 1999. The bill was introduced April 28, 1999 as S. 900 (S.Rept. 106-44). The Senate passed S. 900 amended, May 6, 1999.

Staff draft of legislative language. The staff draft of a basic bill titled the Financial Services Modernization Act of 1999 was released February 16, 1999. It had two parts. As described in a press release accompanying the materials, the first part was an effort to embody in legislative language the principles outlined in talks among Republican members of the Banking Committee. The second part contained draft legislative language for provisions then still under discussion.

As specified in the "Executive Summary," among provisions in the first part of the draft were those that would:

- allow financial affiliations, generally through a holding company framework. However, national banks with total assets of $1 billion or less could conduct financial activities through operating subsidiaries, and national banks of any size could engage in financial activities on an agency basis through operating subsidiaries. Municipal revenue bond underwriting would be specifically authorized as a permissible banking activity.

- provide for functional regulation (by nature of the activity) of holding company components. The Federal Reserve would be the umbrella regulator, using information to the extent possible supplied by the functional regulators.

- provide for customer protection rules and procedures for bank sales of insurance, including preemption of state laws and rules where federal law is considered more protective, unless within three years a state "opts out" of such coverage,

- establish a dispute resolution process between federal banking regulators and state insurance regulators on insurance issues through the court system, and

- change compliance standards for insured depository institutions under the Community Reinvestment Act.

Among undecided proposals in the second part were those that would:

- permit bank holding companies (bhc) to engage in commercial activities, or acquire companies engaged in such activities, limited to specified formulas based on a bhc's consolidated annual net revenues and total assets ("a commercial basket"),

- permit commercial companies to own a single national bank through a new form of bank holding company: a unitary bank holding company, subject to revenue and assets limitations ("a reverse basket"),

- reform the Federal Home Loan Bank System, and

- establish criminal penalties for improper influence regarding the Community Reinvestment Act.

Committee Print for Markup. On March 1, 1999, a Committee Print was released for markup in the form of an unnumbered bill. It consists of the earlier "decided" proposals and Federal Home Loan Bank System reform, formerly "undecided." It also refines language from the first part of the earlier draft. For example, with regard to insurance, there is a distinct difference in the standard for review for conflicts between state and federal regulators involving insurance matters. This version accords equal deference to the federal and state regulators. New titles address functional regulation of brokers and dealers and would prohibit new unitary thrift holding companies.

Other earlier "undecided proposals" were omitted, including the "basket" provisions allowing the mixing of banking and commerce (the "commercial basket" and "reverse basket"), and provisions establishing criminal penalties for improper influence regarding the Community Reinvestment Act.

Committee Markup. The Committee approved the Committee Print language, with amendments, by a vote of 11 to 9, March 4, 1999. Among the adopted amendments to the Committee Print are those (1) exempting banks in non-metropolitan areas with less than $100 million in assets from the requirements of the Community Reinvestment Act and (2) permitting state insurance regulators to establish safeguards for the sale of insurance by banks. As approved by the Committee, the proposed Financial Services Modernization Act of 1999 consists of seven titles addressing affiliations among banks, securities firms, and insurance companies; insurance sales regulation; regulatory improvements; Federal Home Loan Bank System modernization; securities regulation; unitary thrift holding companies; and ATM (automated teller machine) fee reform. The bill was introduced as S. 900, April 28, 1999.

Senate Floor Action. The Senate completed debate and passed S. 900 amended, 54-44, May 6, 1999. The substance of S. 753, offered as a substitute to S. 900, was rejected. Also rejected were amendments to permit expanded financial activities in bank subsidiaries and to change Community Reinvestment Act provisions in the bill, except to add some CRA disclosure and reporting requirements. An amendment was approved to limit transfers of unitary thrift holding companies to financial firms. The Senate also adopted ATM (automated teller machine) fee and privacy provisions. "Managers Amendments" addressed a number of other financial issues.

For Further Information

The home pages for the Senate and House Banking Committees and the House Commerce Committee contain information on legislative developments in the 106th Congress, including hearings testimony from industry and consumer groups and federal and state regulators. CRS Issue Brief IB10035 provides general background and lists other CRS reports that examine marketplace developments and specific issues that have figured importantly in deliberations on financial reform legislation.

Internet Policies and Issues
Volume 2

INTERNET VOTING: ISSUES AND LEGISLATION

Kevin Coleman

Richard M. Nunno

Summary

Among the many issues in the ongoing, national discussion about the Internet is its use in the voting process. Since voting determines who runs the government and entails two absolute requirements—the secret ballot and security from fraud—the stakes are higher than for many other transactions routinely conducted via the internet. While public confidence about Internet security is increasing, many feel that voting on the Internet requires a degree of security from fraud beyond the current standard for everyday internet use.

Aside from voting process issues, observers often refer to a "digital divide" that exists between those who have access to computers and the Internet (and the skills to use it) and those who do not. Although Internet access is increasing, estimates show that those with higher incomes and education levels are more likely to have Internet access, and that access for blacks and Hispanics lags behind that for whites. Also part of the debate are issues concerning the ensuing change to our political tradition, public confidence in Internet voting, and equal access to the ballot. In the meantime, a number of limited experiments with Internet voting in public elections have taken place already this election year and more are likely in the future as the technology for protecting the voting process online evolves. This report will be updated to reflect new developments.

Overview

As computer ownership increased in the early 1990s, the Internet introduced the concept of electronic democracy to a wide audience. By 1996, the national parties and scores of candidates maintained websites to disseminate information, attract donors and volunteers, and communicate directly with supporters. As an ever larger segment of the population uses the Internet to conduct business, find news, pursue leisure activities, and so on, the potential to use it for more than campaign purposes—to conduct elections—has become part of the discussion of applying technology to the democratic process. Electing officeholders via the Internet requires a level of security from fraud beyond what exists with current online use, according to many observers.[1] For example, credit card fraud on the Internet, "is recognized at the level of 10% of all transactions," according to one estimate.[2] Such a level of potential fraud in an election would undermine its legitimacy, which depends on a fair and accurate count of the ballots cast. An Internet voting system, even one used on a limited basis in conjunction with traditional voting methods, needs to be at least as secure as current voting methods in its ability to safeguard a voter's identity and provide an accurate vote count.

Internet voting has been widely reported on in the press, and policy makers at the federal and state levels are studying its implications. In Congress, Representative Jesse Jackson Jr. introduced H.R.3232 on Nov. 5, 1999, which directs the President to appoint a commission to study Internet voting and make recommendations about its possible use in the future. In December 1999, the President directed the National Science Foundation to conduct a one-year study of Internet voting. On January 18, 2000 an Internet Task Force organized by California's Secretary of State issued its report. The Task Force report said "At this time, it would not be legally, practically or fiscally feasible to develop a comprehensive remote Internet voting system that would completely replace the current paper process." The Task Force recommended phasing in Internet voting, with remote voting as the last phase.[3] In Arizona and Alaska, some voters cast ballots on the Internet during the 2000 presidential primary season and several other voting trials are scheduled for the November general election.

Types of Internet Voting

Two types of Internet voting are possible, and both were used in voting trials in 2000. One method, the more basic from a technical standpoint, is Internet voting at a traditional polling site, with computer voting machines connected to the Internet and where election officials authenticate voters before ballots are cast. The other method, more technically advanced, is to cast ballots over the Internet from remote locations using electronic authentication and computer security technologies. The Arizona Democratic primary, for example, used both methods; voters could cast their ballots from remote locations or at

---

[1] For example, the Love Bug virus of May 4, 2000, affected an estimated one million computers, including those at many federal agencies, and caused an estimated $1 to $10 billion in damage. As with many other viruses, the Love Bug virus destroyed computer files once an email to which it was attached was opened and spread to other computers using email addresses in the computer that was attacked. Such large-scale "hacking" is only part of the problem, and attempts to breech public and private systems occur regularly. The Pentagon estimates that its networks are hacked 250,000 times a year, of which an estimated 500 are serious attempts to access classified systems. Scott Nance, "'I Love You' Doesn't Sway CERT," *New Technology Week*, May 8, 2000, p. 5, and Gregory Vistica, "Inside the Secret Cyberwar," *Newsweek*, Feb. 21, 2000, p 48.

[2] Ed Gerck, "From Voting to Internet Voting," *The Bell*, vol. 1, May 2000, p. 5. Another estimate noted that "about 5 percent to 6 percent of a typical Net retailer's transactions are fraudulent, compared to less than half of one percent for brick-and-mortar retailers. Fraudulent transactions account for about 10 percent of Net retailer's total sales." Craig Bickenell, "Credit Card Fraud Bedevils Web," *WiredNews*, [http://www.wired.com/news/business/0,1367,18904,00.html], visited Apr. 3, 1999.

[3] California Internet Voting Task Force, *A Report on the Feasibility of Internet Voting*, Jan., 2000, p. 1.

any polling place. Some observers believe that remote Internet voting should not be attempted until voters become comfortable with polling site Internet voting and when procedures are well established to ensure accurate voter authentication, ballot secrecy, and security. Others, however, argue that polling site Internet voting will have little value to voters, who want the convenience of remote Internet voting.

Technologies Behind Internet Voting

Internet voting systems use several technologies to ensure authentication, secrecy, and security. These include encryption (the scrambling of information in data transmissions to provide confidentiality), and electronic signatures (methods that use such techniques as passwords, personal identification numbers (PINs), smart cards, biometrics, and digital signatures) to verify the identity of the voter and provide data integrity (i.e., assurance that the data is not altered during transmission). Other computer security technologies, such as firewalls, antivirus programs, and intrusion detection systems, are also used to prevent unauthorized hacker access to computer systems used in the election process.[4]

Different types of elections require different standards for voter verification, data integrity for ballots, and assurance against tampering. For example, private sector elections (conducted and funded by private organizations and regulated by the sponsoring organization) typically have lower standards for these factors than public sector elections (conducted, funded, and regulated by government). Private sector elections have been conducted using the Internet to a far greater extent than public sector elections.

The Current Debate: Issues and Challenges

While the computer security technologies mentioned above are well established in theory, they have not yet been used on a wide scale. Some government agencies, large companies, and financial institutions use encryption, electronic signatures, and other computer security techniques in conducting business transactions with established suppliers and customers. Some analysts predict that computer security technologies will proliferate at an accelerated rate in the next few years. Few businesses, however, have implemented these technologies for use with the general public today. Some argue that the public needs to become more familiar and comfortable with the Internet in other aspects of life, such as by engaging in Internet commerce, before governments should adopt Internet voting systems. Internet voting systems could be phased in over time, from the use of Internet-connected computers at state and local government-controlled polling sites, to remote Internet voting from users' home PCs. The new voting systems must also be user-friendly enough that many voters will prefer to use the Internet method over the traditional method of voting. Many current security components to computer systems are thought to be cumbersome for users. The following areas are the principal concerns with Internet voting at present:

Security issues. Protecting the voting process from electronic attacks is a fundamental challenge both for vendors who design online voting systems and election administrators who run elections. As with current voting systems, any vulnerability that

---

[4] For a background on these technologies, see CRS Report 98-67, *Internet: An Overview of Key Technology Policy Issues Affecting its Use and Growth.*

could allow for voting more than once, changing a voted ballot or the election tally, or otherwise compromising the integrity of the process, raises the potential for fraud. In addition, Internet voting systems could be vulnerable to "denial-of-service" attacks in which the system is flooded with e-mail messages, causing it to shut down. Internet voting, like absentee voting, entails casting a vote from remote location and raises a possibility of bribery or vote tampering that does not exist with in-person voting. Safeguards can be provided through the establishment of computer security procedures that prevent unauthorized individuals from seeing the contents of a ballot. Establishing public trust in the security features of Internet voting systems may take time and perhaps the use of an independent oversight or auditing organization. Negative public perceptions of Internet voting security could be significant in the early stages of a transition to online voting, although acceptance might increase along with advances in technology and the successful online voting trials. According to a July 1999 public opinion poll, 62 % believed that it will be many years before Internet voting can be made secure from fraud; 24 % thought it could be made secure soon; and 7 % believed it will never happen.[5]

Ballot secrecy. Ballot secrecy must be ensured in any election in order to prevent vote-buying and other kinds of fraud. Traditional voting at a polling place entails two separate steps for confirming a voter's identity and casting a ballot. The voter signs in at the precinct poll and then proceeds to the voting booth to cast a ballot. With Internet voting, the two steps are combined. An individual's identity must be confirmed and then the ballot is provided to the voter, increasing the possibility that the voted ballot, while in transit over the Internet, could be observed, changed, or recorded along with the voter's identity. While encryption and electronic signatures can provide privacy for voters, there seems to be no technical means of preventing these activities under remote Internet voting systems.

Access. While remote Internet voting from home or the workplace will not likely occur on a large scale for some time, it will probably raise questions concerning equal access to the ballot. Before providing Internet voting for its 2000 Presidential primary, the Arizona Democratic Party sought and received clearance from the Justice Department concerning Voting Rights Act restrictions on instituting changes to the electoral process. In addition, a non-profit group, the Voting Integrity Project, filed a federal lawsuit that alleged the Internet voting plan diluted minority participation (see discussion in the section on internet voting in the 2000 elections). Issues regarding access to computers and the Internet—the digital divide—are likely to continue because of disparities between certain groups in the electorate.

Social and political implications. Some observers are critical of Internet voting on the basis of tradition, arguing that it will erode and eventually replace the most basic form of citizen participation in the democratic process. Some have voiced concerns about the loss of a civic ritual in which democracy, in its simplest form, is based on citizens going to the polls. They say that "Reducing a vote to a mere key stroke of a personal computer may diminish, not heighten, the significance of the act. At a minimum, voters who bother to actually go to the polls tend to be people who are motivated enough to learn about

---

[5] ABC News Poll, July 21, 1999 (based on interviews with 1,018 adults nationally between July 17 and 18).

issues.... The solution to a lack of commitment of voters is not to reduce the necessary commitment needed to vote."[6]

Internet Voting in Elections of 2000

During the 2000 election cycle, a number of limited Internet voting trials are being held in both primary and general elections. Arizona's Democratic party launched what it called "the first-ever, legally-binding public election over the Internet" from March 7-March 11. The election was conducted by Election.com, a New York-based company. Voters cast ballots from their homes or offices between March 7th and 10th, or at polling locations on March 11.[7] The party mailed a personal identification number (PIN) to all 843,000 eligible voters, who could subsequently vote their ballot via the Internet by logging on to the party's website, entering their PIN, and providing two kinds of personal identification. Voters who used the polls could also cast their vote by paper ballot or computer at the polls. According to the Arizona Democratic Party, about 41% of the 86,907 ballots cast in the election were sent via the Internet from remote locations.[8]

The Arizona trial election created problems for some Internet voters, however, and resulted in confusion in some locations because of the new procedures. Some voters with Macintosh computers were unable to cast ballots because their software was incompatible with the security system used for the election. The party added phone lines in the last few days of voting to handle calls from Macintosh users and from voters who lost their PIN and could not vote via the Internet without it. In response to a federal lawsuit, the Party also increased the number of polling places in the month before the primary. The Voting Integrity Project, a nonprofit organization, filed the lawsuit in U.S. District Court in Arizona charging that the process violated the Voting Rights Act. The suit alleged that Internet voting created a disparity between voters with computers and those who did not have computer access, resulting in a dilution of minority votes. The Democratic Party increased the number of polling places in the month preceding the election in response to the suit, but had difficulty finding locations with dedicated phone lines to allow for Internet connections (although paper ballots were available at all polling locations).[9] U.S. District Court Judge Paul G. Rosenblatt permitted the election to proceed, and while the Voting Integrity Project did not appeal the decision, it is continuing to pursue its lawsuit in district court.

---

[6] Jonathan Turley, "The Mouse That Roared ... and Voted, " [http://www.latimes.com/news/comment/ 20000117/t000005269.html],visited Jan. 19, 2000.

[7] Press release, Arizona Democratic Party Announces Internet Voting Registration Procedures for World's First Legally-Binding Public Election, [http://www.election.com/press/pr2000/0113.html], visited Feb. 18, 2000. Federal District Court Judge Paul G. Rosenblatt allowed the election to take place despite a lawsuit that asserted that Internet voting would discriminate against minorities; the court could set aside the election if minorities were under-represented among voters.

[8] Arizona Democrats, "Paper Ballots vs. Internet Votes," [http://www.azdem.org/breakdown.html], visited June 8, 2000.

[9] "Internet Voting Off to Rocky Start in Arizona Democratic Party-Run Primary," *Election Administration Reports*, vol. 30, Mar. 20, 2000, p. 4.

Also during the Presidential primary season, voters in three election districts in Alaska cast ballots via the Internet in the Republican Party's Presidential straw poll on January 24, 2000. The project was conducted by VoteHere.net, an Internet voting company located in Bellevue, Washington, and provided 3,500 voters in remote areas the opportunity to cast ballots in the straw poll. In the past, it was difficult for voters in these areas to participate in the straw poll.

In the November general election, some members of the military and citizens living abroad may be eligible to vote via the Internet on November 7. Voters who are covered by the Uniformed and Overseas Citizens Absentee Voting Act (42 U.S. Code 1973ff) and whose legal residence is one of fourteen counties participating in the project in Florida, South Carolina, Texas and Utah are eligible to participate.[10] The project will be limited to a total of 350 voters who will request and vote an absentee ballot via the Internet.

Legislation in the 106th Congress

Representative Jesse Jackson, Jr. introduced H.R. 3232 on November 5, 1999; it was referred to the Committee on House Administration. The bill directs the President to conduct a study of issues of Internet voting in consultation with an advisory group and to report its findings within six months of approval of the measure. The advisory group would include one member from a list of nominees provided by the Federal Election Commission, the National Association of Secretaries of State, and the International Association of Clerks, Recorders, Election Officials, and Treasurers; an expert on election administration and Internet systems; four members from a list provided by the Speaker and minority leader of the House; and four members from a list provided by the majority and minority leaders of the Senate. The report would include recommendations to address issues raised in the report, including legislative measures.

---

[10] The jurisdictions include Orange County, FL; Dallas County, TX; Weber County, UT; and in South Carolina, Beaufort, Greenville, Greenwood, Horry, Lancaster, Laurens, Lexington, McCormick, Orangeburg, Pickens, and York counties.

INDEX